My Blue Kitchen

Esther Rafaeli

URIM PUBLICATIONS
Jerusalem ✦ New York

My Blue Kitchen
by Esther Refaeli

First Edition. Printed in Israel.
ISBN: 978-965-524-048-1

Designed by Ariel Walden
Cover: Varda and Karni, Purim 1992; photo by E. Rafaeli

Urim Publications, PO Box 52287, Jerusalem 91521 Israel

Lambda Publishers Inc.
3709 13th Avenue Brooklyn, New York 11218 USA
Tel: 718-972-5449 Fax: 718-972-6307 urim_pub@netvision.net.il

www.UrimPublications.com

FOR MY CHILDREN

Asi, Aylon (Lonny), Varda and Karni
and their children

Without them there would have been no stories

Contents

Foreword   7

Shabbat Dinner Address, Hovevei Zion Synagogue, Jerusalem   9
The Window   14
The Apartment in Talbieh   17
Jerusalem Then...   24
The Solitary Streetlight   30
We Took Them With – to the Rome Olympics   32
On Alex's 50th Birthday   74
Rome: Our Olympic Adventure   76
A Poem for Varda, Aged 3+   86
When I Consider...   87
Questionings   88
No Unknown Soldiers   92
Wars...   95
Death in the Family   107
To My Father Alex, on His 70th Birthday   115
Forty Years On   119
Our Trip to China   125
The Modest Genius, Reb Aisel Harif   180
...and Weddings   185
The Turkish Bath – the Hamam   197
Melbourne Revisited 1987 Part I   200
Trip to the North – Ayers Rock Part II   215

Melbourne Revisited with Karni, 1989 Part III   226
Our Trip to Riga and Moscow   228
Maastricht – Fifty Years Later   262
Maria Therese: The Story of an Unusual Friendship   270
That Morning in February   289
Harvard   297
Packing Up   302
Alex Rafaeli: A Eulogy   308

Appendix: Hello, Earth! by Alex Rafaeli   317

Foreword

THESE STORIES WERE NOT ORIGINALLY WRITTEN WITH THE IDEA of creating a book. The reader can see that they were written over a long period of time, and at various stages of my life. I have always had a natural tendency to put important incidents and experiences down on paper, partly because of a strong desire to "catch the moment" and keep it alive; and partly because I have always had a strong sense of the passing of time and the need to remember. I also think the dreadful events of World War II, when people and cultures were so wantonly swept away, convinced me of the importance of saving something of the past with which future generations could connect and strengthen their identities.

It was only after I had decided to close up our home, five years after the death of my husband, that I saw in my stories a record of events which had happened to the family, in the apartment in which we had lived for fifty years, the major part of our lives. Besides the family story, I found that it encapsulated a historical record of how it was then, in the early years of the State of Israel.

One evening, I sat with my friend Miriam Chaiken, who was visiting from New York, and mentioned my idea of putting my stories into a book for the children to have. "Good idea," she said, "and you can call it *The Blue Kitchen*! It seems to be the centre of your lives." We laughed at her idea, but it caught on and I began to consider it seriously. The stories would have to be put into some context, and I began to think of it as a family scrapbook, or memoir, based on this particular half-century, the most important years of our lives. That meant that other stories not fitting into this category had to be put aside but not discarded. Perhaps they will make up a separate collection about my own life, before and after.

So, my thanks to Miriam, herself a writer and poet, for giving me the title for the book, and to David Brauner for his excellent editing, to Jody Blum for practical help, and to our Jerusalem writing group for their encouragement.

Esther Rafaeli

Jerusalem 2010

Shabbat Dinner Address, Hovevei Zion Synagogue, Jerusalem

February 9, 2007

GOOD EVENING AND SHABBAT SHALOM TO ALL.

I don't know who had the idea for this evening's event, but according to the number of participants it is a very good idea, and in keeping with our Jewish tradition of hospitality and togetherness. The theme of hospitality and of communal meals, religious or otherwise, is one of the threads woven into the Bible narrative. In the opening verses of this week's *parasha*, we read of the visit of Yithro, Priest of Midian, to his son-in-law Moses after the Exodus, and how the elders gathered to honor him and participate in a sacrificial meal together. That Moses doesn't bother to greet his wife and sons after a long separation is of course a different matter, but we can't help remembering how Yithro scolded his daughters for not inviting the helpful stranger (Moses) to come and eat with them after he had defended them against the other shepherds.

Parashat Yithro is a special one for Tunisian Jews. Every year on the Thursday evening before the *parasha* is read in synagogue, Tunisian families sit down to a special meal – *Seudat Yithro*. At the meal miniature cakes and sweets are eaten on small dishes with miniature utensils. The main course is meat – once pigeon, today chicken. It is supposed to commemorate a time when many children died from a plague, which ceased on *Parashat Yithro*, as well as marking the giving of the Ten Commandments and the festive meal that Yithro ate with Moses when the Midianite is believed to have become a Hebrew. Whatever the real reason, it is a custom still observed today.

I was asked to speak tonight to bring a personal, informal touch to the program so I thought I would share with you the story of my journey to Eretz Israel.

Our family moved into this area in 1955. This building didn't yet exist and services were held in the Metivta around the corner, on the second floor. It was not very comfortable as the building was as yet unfinished, and eventually the committee of that time, led by Professor Hillel Blondheim, decided to build a new and separate Beit Knesset. (I hope I have this right and am not offending anyone.) It took a long time for the plans to come to fruition, and in the meantime the late Dr. Frankel, *z"l*, had approached my husband for a contribution. Alex decided to sponsor the *bimah*, which he gave in memory of his mother and brother, who perished in Riga in 1941. His father had died a natural death in June 1940, before the Germans arrived. Alex had been a keen Zionist since he first heard Jabotinsky speak in Riga in 1924. He came to Jerusalem in 1933 after graduating from Heidelberg University, and was soon recruited to the Etzel, to which he devoted some fifteen years of his life, including serving in the U.S. Army in Europe.

In spite of his traditional background, he was not a regular *shul*-goer and we did not get caught up in the daily running of the *shul*. I attended services more often and have come to feel that this synagogue is my spiritual shelter. I would like to mention that Rabbi Burstein officiated at the wedding of my older son Asi about twenty years ago, and his two sons celebrated their *bar mitzvot* here. On the *yamim noraim* I look for the white Torah mantle, which I donated in memory of my parents, Fruma and Ze'ev Shapiro, and seeing that gives me a warm and comfortable feeling.

My parents came from Poland, my mother from Łódź, and my father from a nearby town called Lenchitz (Leczyca). Mother's family were Gerer

Hasidim, but Father's family were Misnagdim, and his forebears came from a village near Kovno, that part of Lithuania which was sometimes under Polish rule and sometimes under Russian. His great-grandfather was Rabbi Aisel Harif, officially R. Yehoshua Aisek Shapira, who was rabbi of Slonim from 1853 to 1873, and whose works are still studied in *yeshivot* today.

This family had decided Zionist leanings, and founded the local Zionist group in 1917. My father and his brothers spoke Hebrew and read Hebrew literature and newspapers, a fact that did not endear them to the more Orthodox members of the community, even though their father Yehiel ben Issachar was a popular *ba'al tefilla*.

My father made *aliyah* in 1921, leaving Poland illegally because he had not served in the army. My mother and brother joined him the following year and they settled in Herzliya, where my mother ran a workers' lunch canteen. My father was a *halutz* (pioneer), transporting *ziv-ziv* (sand) by camel to building sites in Tel Aviv. I was born about four years later, in the Hadassah Hospital in Tel Aviv, reportedly the first girl to increase the Herzliya population. Soon after, the family moved to Jerusalem, where my father worked on the building of the Bikur Holim Hospital, during which time we experienced the earthquake of 1927. You can imagine my feelings when I gave birth to my two daughters in this very hospital.

Life was hard, with my father being sometimes unemployed, and eventually my parents decided to join the throng of emigrants leaving the country at that time. I don't know why they didn't go to America, where my father had a cousin whom he had known still in Poland. Instead, they preferred to go with their friends to Australia, and so they took ship, a young couple without money, without the English language, without a profession, without any supporting family and with two small children. Again, life was very difficult, with the depression years coming close on their heels, but Zionists they remained. Zionism was the lodestar of our lives. We spoke Yiddish at home and outside there was the rich, active social life of a Zion-focused community. Many of this group came from Palestine, from places such as Safed, Rosh Pina and Yesod ha-Ma'aleh, and spoke Hebrew: it was they, in fact, who strengthened and enriched the life of the community. One of my earliest memories is of standing on a stage with a large doll in my arms, and singing in Hebrew – "*Yesh li bubah ve-hi yafah,*" etc.

We maintained contact with Palestine, with one of my mother's brothers who had made *aliyah* in the 1920s and was a farmer near Herzliya. In 1936 he was one of the founding members of Moshav Rishpon, where his descendants still live. There were also two nieces of my father's who made *aliyah* in the early 1930s, and we renewed contact with these relatives when we made an unsuccessful attempt at *aliyah* in 1936.

My husband's family, the Kahns, also had a foothold in the country. Two of his uncles, Isaac and Louis Kahn, having spent time in New Zealand and Australia, came to Palestine with the aim of establishing a shipping line between Haifa and Port Said. After this failed, Isaac returned to Sydney and Louis remained in Tel Aviv, hoping to succeed in cultivating pineapples. Fortunately, he had other sources of income. Because Louis's wife, Hannah, was British born and bred, their home in Tel Aviv became an "outpost" of the Empire. When my husband made *aliyah* in 1933, he kept close contact with them and with their sister, Ella, an unmarried aunt living in Tel Aviv, who taught English and did translations from Russian.

With the founding of the State in 1948, I told my parents that the moment of truth had come, that it was time to fulfill their and my own dream of making *aliyah*. I had obtained my BA degree at Melbourne University and was working for the weekly *Jewish Herald*. My parents would not let me travel alone, so in August 1948 I embarked on the s.s. *Maloya* with my brother Alec for Israel, leaving our parents alone. We had decided to spend some months visiting relatives in London and Paris, as we were sure that once we settled in Israel, traveling would be beyond our resources. We arrived in Haifa in February 1949 during the second truce and went to stay with our cousin in Tel Aviv, at 192 Dizengoff Street. The Izbicki family lived in one large room with their son Nachman, and shared a kitchen and bathroom with their neighbors, a common fact of living in those days.

Ita's half-brother Yosef was also there, having survived the war in Russia.

Although the Izbickis soon moved into a two-room apartment, my brother and I did not want to impose any longer and found other accommodation. Another niece of my father, Ida Weinstein, and her family had also arrived in the country with Yosef, having spent the war years in Siberia. Actually, we had already met them in Paris where they were waiting for their papers, so they were no longer strangers.

Today, nearly sixty years later, I can honestly say that these early years of the State were the most magical of all. In spite of the difficulties, the problems, the frustrations and deprivation, there was a special magic in the air, a tangible excitement. The country was full of young people from all over, who had come to fight, to settle, to bring new skills, to contribute and build the young country. Of course not all could survive the conditions and too many left disappointed after two or three years, some to return later in life. My parents returned in 1954 for their third attempt at *aliyah* and were blessed with another twenty-six years during which they saw the birth of their grandchildren and accompanied their development till early adulthood.

I was invited to speak this evening by Estelle Fink and would like to finish with a little anecdote about how we first met. I'm not sure of the exact date, but one morning in the 1960s, very early, I received a phone call. "My name is Estelle Fink and I am a friend of your cousin, Fritzie Gottesman. I have been looking around for an apartment and don't see anything suitable; everything is so small. Fritzie told me I should come and see your place so I should know there are really nice homes in Jerusalem." I made a swift calculation and invited her to come in the afternoon or the next day. "I'm sorry," she said, "but I am leaving today and now is the only time I have." I said that would be all right, but thought inwardly that only American women could have such *hutzpah*. I had barely sent the children off and combed my hair before she arrived. I don't know to what extent she was influenced but she finally succeeded in finding what she wanted and has been happily and productively settled in Jerusalem for many, many years.

Thank you for your attention.

Shabbat Shalom.

The Window

SHE SAT AT THE ROUND TABLE IN THE KITCHEN, A MUG OF COFFEE cradled in her hands. She looked at the window in the opposite wall, and thought what an integral part of her life it had been. It was a large window, with a pointed arch. The lower rectangular section was made up of two panes that opened inwards, as did the rippled glass of the upper arched section, which was divided into segments by a wooden frame. In the centre of each pane was a beautiful little round blue glass circle, an old-fashioned "bull's eye." It was a beautiful Arab-style window in a beautiful spacious Arab-built apartment, constructed in 1926, in what had once been the Christian Arab section of Jerusalem, Talbieh. Wooden shutters, matching in shape completed the character of the windows, but because they were outside, they had proved at times to be rather inconvenient, especially when it was raining. She had spent fifty years of her life in this apartment, had raised their four children there, and now, some five years after her husband had passed away, she decided that she must move.

She had taken the color scheme of the kitchen from the two little blue windows, blue-painted cupboards and pale turquoise walls. She liked the idea of the protection against the "evil eye," but they were also "her" colors, which she had always found soothing. Although the other rooms had undergone color changes over the years, the kitchen had always remained the same. When one of her friends had referred to it recently as "your blue kitchen," she was surprised, so used to it had she become.

However beautiful the window was, it was merely a frame for the view outside, a fine view of the Old City of Jerusalem and the surrounding hills. One could see the walls of the Old City, the Tower of David, the Dormition Abbey, the tower of the Augusta Victoria Hospital, the Hebrew University spire and countless rooftops with small domes and television aerials. On a very clear day, when the air could be absolutely crystalline, one could even get a glimpse of the Dead Sea and the mountains of Moab beyond. At night, besides the illumination of the Old City, one could see clusters of lights here and there in the background, proof that there were really people living "over there" (Jordan) in their villages. After the Intercontinental Hotel (today called the Seven Arches) was built in 1964 on the Mount of Olives, *Har ha-Zeitim*, its lights became a focus of our attention and wonder, and little did they (the Jordanians) dream that one day, in the aftermath of the 1967 Six Day War, we (the Israelis) would be going there for lunch or dinner as a matter of course.

The clear dry air had an unusual ability of carrying the sounds of the Old City: the pealing of the church bells and the muezzin calling the Moslems to prayer. She had noted once that if you could hear the muezzin during the night, it meant that conditions were right for a *hamsin* the next day, that very hot, very dry atmospheric condition which seemed to bleach one's very bones.

And so the view from the window kept her company through the days and the years, constantly changing with the moving sun and the flow of the seasons, always there. Her favorite scene was actually a winter one, when the sky could sometimes be a dark, threatening, leaden grey, and a sudden trick of the setting sun would infuse the ancient walls and buildings with a strange luminous light so that the stones seemed to glow with a heavenly light against the dark sky. It was breathtaking in its dramatic, ethereal beauty – spellbinding. Truly Jerusalem of Gold. She had even tried a few times to photograph the scene, but never succeeded in getting an adequate result. Though she had at times taken wonderful photos with her simple "idiot" camera, apparently neither she nor the camera was good enough for this job. But she knew that the scene was engraved in her memory, one of her most cherished possessions.

But that was all in the past. Now when she looked through her window there was no Old City, no mountains, no spiritual comfort or inspiration. Now she saw a concrete wall rising daily before her eyes, the rear of a huge apartment block imposing itself in the name of "modern progress" on the old picturesque residential suburb. The building would eventually be covered with the familiar Jerusalem stone, but that would not restore the space and the beauty which had been and was now lost forever. This was one of the reasons that had lead to her decision to close down her home, and that had softened the sadness of turning the key for the last time on the most important chapter of her life.

Asi by The Window 1983.

The Apartment in Talbieh

IN TIME, THE INVESTMENT GROUP TO WHICH MY HUSBAND ALEX belonged decided to extend its scope and build a pencil factory in Jerusalem, to be known as Jerusalem Pencils, Ltd. This meant that unexpectedly we would have to sell the apartment in Tel Aviv and move to Jerusalem, with all the attendant problems.

The acquisition of the apartment I decided to give up fifty years later was a story in itself. The joke of the matter was that although my husband was the businessman, it was I who had sold the apartment in Tel Aviv (a 76-step walk-up) while Alex was away on a business trip. Our lawyer friend had asked me anxiously whether I shouldn't wait for his return before closing the deal, but as there had been a dearth of buyers, I knew I must grab the opportunity and not waste time or money on expensive phone calls.

Similarly, I also found the Jerusalem apartment on another occasion when Alex was away, trying to develop export business for the new enterprise. It was difficult in those days to find larger flats. I had seen in Tel Aviv that although some families lived very comfortably, the average family lived in two or, at best, two and a half rooms, or perhaps even shared with another family. This meant that only the children had a bedroom and the parents slept on a pull-out sofa in the living room. The bed was made up in the evening and re-arranged in the morning.

We wanted a comfortable flat. We already had two boys and hoped for more, and also live-in help. In those days help was not a big problem. By the early 1950s there had been a large *aliyah* from Yemen. The miraculous Magic Carpet undertaking airlifted that community from Aden to Tel Aviv in a matter of days. There was also a wave of Holocaust survivors, who were anxious to find work with accommodation to help them get through the first trials in the new land. In particular, many young women wanted to realize their Zionist ideals of aliyah and were happy to be live-in nannies until they learned some Hebrew or found work more suited to their qualifications. Needless to say, they didn't stay too long on the job unless one had a serious contract with them, so at times there was a rapid turnover and sometimes no help at all.

So it happened that when it was time to move to Jerusalem, in the spring of 1954, the family had to rent a temporary, adequate enough apartment in Rehavia, which belonged to Itzhak Ben-Zvi, who was then President of Israel. It had been his family home before they moved into the official residence. I continued the search for a more spacious dwelling, and sure enough, while Alex was again away, I was shown two attractive properties. One was a detached villa with a walled garden on a very desirable street, and the other the second floor of a fine Arab-style house with an impressive outside staircase and a large terrace looking out over the Old City. It stood on a very large plot that had many trees, but only the vaguest suggestion of a garden.

I decided to take the latter, but when I asked our office to arrange payment of the deposit, they refused to do so without Alex's authorization. It was too complicated, they said. It was a case not of outright purchase but of "key money," an accepted legal practice at the time for gaining possession of a property by paying a sizable deposit, which guaranteed a set rent. It also meant dealing with the Custodian of Enemy Property, a government body that had taken over the properties of those Arab families who had left the country with the outbreak of the 1948 War of Independence. Our office thought we should get legal advice on the situation.

During the following years, some owners turned up to inspect their properties, and the tenants were able to arrange with them to buy their homes outright. Sometimes such transactions were made by meeting with owners living abroad. In all the years we lived in Disraeli Street, no one came to claim the house, but it took a very long time before we were able to purchase it. In time, the house was declared a "protected property" (which meant that no outside changes could be made), and a team came from a special municipal department to record the exterior and interior details of the architectural design. Eventually, the house appeared in David Kroyanker's book on architecture in Jerusalem.

But to return to my story, by the time Alex returned from his trip, the Foreign Office was also bidding for the apartment, which it wanted for one of their returning ambassadors, or as a residence for some future foreign embassy that would hopefully move to Jerusalem. It became quite a battle as to who had the first claim (why hadn't I put down that deposit!), and the question went right up to the Cabinet. When Prime Minister Moshe Sharett was called upon for arbitration, he decided that a foreign investor who was building a factory in Jerusalem which would provide employment had priority over a government official. Thus, the deal was formally closed, and we began to renovate. There was a lot to do.

The apartment was very spacious. There was a large dining room, an even larger living room, and a room destined to become the kitchen, of which there had been no evidence, but only three bedrooms, and of course a bathroom with a beautiful window, and an extra toilet. It was not the classical Arab layout of a central hall from which the other rooms opened, but was probably considered in the late 1920s as of modern design, albeit not very efficient. In one of the corridors there was a built-in original wardrobe/storage unit, about four metres long and reaching the ceiling. Another wide corridor ran from the front door through the entrance hall to the back covered porch, providing ample play space even for tricycles. Part of the original apartment, about a third of it, had already been portioned off for a smaller flat, which was occupied.

The tiled floor, which was in excellent condition, had a geometric design in grey, black and white, rather than the traditional floral patterns seen in other homes. Did this indicate a difference in taste between Moslem and Christian Arabs, or was it simply a matter of personal choice? The ceilings were four metres high, and the windows were large with pointed arches, which created a very gracious atmosphere. They could have been left uncurtained, but I didn't like the bare look which that created.

As it was we had few possessions, both of us having arrived in the country with a couple of suitcases, Alex from New York and I from Melbourne, Australia. Though we planned to live in Tel Aviv, we actually married in Jerusalem, for sentimental reasons, on January 20, 1950, at the home of our friends Mr. and Mrs. Al Friedgut of Canada. It was Alex's birthday gift to his mother, who had perished in the Riga Death March in the winter of 1941. In letters, she had often nagged him about his bachelor state. It was the height of the austerity period and there were just thirty guests. Rabbi Isaac Herzog, the chief rabbi at that time, officiated.

After the wedding we each brought over our books, personal belongings and such household necessities which my mother thought a new bride should bring to her marriage (the *nedunia*). We acquired the basics for the Tel Aviv flat, but that would not suffice for the new home.

Since it was early spring when we moved in, in 1955, it was not till winter approached that we discovered how cold the apartment could be. We had removed several of the old wood-burning heaters and their flues, thinking them to be impractical and unsightly, leaving only one in the dining room. Central heating was almost unknown in this supposedly subtropical country, and the main means of heating were kerosene (*neft*) heaters of various types, which tended to be smelly and gradually darkened the walls. I used to put a piece of orange peel on the heater to combat the smell, and a kettle placed on top of the heater created a cozy atmosphere. It also meant keeping a reserve tank of kerosene on the balcony, which was filled by the scruffy kerosene man who came round with his horse and cart, ringing his bell to announce himself. There were as yet no plastic jerrycans for easy transport of the fuel.[1] Other regular droppers-by were the old man

---

1 These were manufactured by Alex when he opened Duraplas, a plastics company, alongside the pencil factory.

who sharpened knives, the man who washed windows, the man who came before Succoth to ask for a *lulav* from the palm tree, the dues collectors from wizo and the Blind Institute, and other sundry seekers of charity. While in Tel Aviv I had become used to the melodious cries of the *"alter zachen, alter she-yech"* man (old things, old shoes) and the *"bakbookeem"* of the bottle collector, which added a lively note to the ambience, but I never heard them in Jerusalem.

Electric heaters were not very effective in the large rooms, and I soon found that the gas oven in the kitchen, the blue kitchen we had created, was a godsend. It became the warmest, most popular room in the home, and also taught me never to opt for an all-electric stove, and so we always had gas as insurance against the frequent electrical outages. The living room was never used in winter, when it was as cold as a freezer. Hot water was supplied by an electric boiler, but one had to be economical because of the cost, and the supply never kept up with the demand.

The supply of water generally was a problem because of the altitude of Jerusalem, and Talbieh was one of the highest points in the city. Sometimes during periods of high consumption there was not enough pressure to get the water to the city, let alone up into high apartments. To maintain a supply, water tanks had been installed on the rooftops, but these constantly needed the services of the *installator*, or plumber. Many years passed before the municipality was able to supply water directly into apartments, and with individual metres. The user-unfriendly water tanks were gradually dismantled, to the joy and relief of the tenants. In the summer of 1956, when our third child, our daughter Varda, was born, there was a long, hot *hamsin* and no water in the apartment. The maid had to take the nappies (cloth, not disposables) down into the garden and do the laundry there.

Fortunately, over the years the heating situation began to improve, with better electric radiators and heaters appearing each year, and central heating gradually becoming a must. Just a few years after we moved in, the flue of the wood-burning stove in the dining room exploded, showering soot over the whole room. This traumatic event brought on the decision to install central heating, even though it was a key-money apartment. Even so, the heating engineer, who was of the old spartan school, gave us the most minimal heat possible. Eventually, we had to correct his false assessment of our heating needs.

When we moved in, the other tenants of the house were the Touring Club at the raised ground floor level, a leftover from the Mandatory times, then presided over by Mrs. Aura Herzog; the social activities continued with lectures, dances, play readings and so on. In fact, we had attended a communal Seder there when we first arrived in Jerusalem. The Ben Ezras, a family from Morocco, occupied an apartment at the back ground-floor level, and the small apartment which had been separated from our apartment was occupied by the Rosner family, who had two boys. After a couple of years they left and were followed by the Dinitz family from the Ministry of Foreign Affairs, Vivian and Simcha and their three children. About a year later, an American family, Hadassah and Alec Aylat and their two children, moved in at the side ground level. When Simcha Dinitz was posted abroad and began his ambassadorial career, another Foreign Office family moved into that apartment, Ruth and Shaul Kariv and their two children. All the children got on famously and we parents became good friends and spent much time together, often playing canasta in the evenings.

A separate one-room building in the side garden was occupied at one stage by an employee of the club, or used for storage. Perhaps this had served as servants' quarters when the original family lived there, as such small accommodations were often seen amongst the Arab dwellings.

The Touring Club continued its social activities and also added a catering service for weddings and other celebrations, which were usually held in the large garden. It was very entertaining for the children to watch from the terrace, but the noise was sometimes impossible and kept them and the neighbors awake until late. Sometimes, the police had to be summoned. However, as more catering services began to appear on the Jerusalem scene, the Touring Club went out of business, and the Jewish Agency, the lessee, established an ulpan for new immigrants and offices for their organizations. Chief among these were the Association of Americans and Canadians in Israel (AACI) and the Association of British Immigrants, while other waves of immigrants added their names as they came along. With front-row seats on the terrace, the family kept track of all the new languages heard during their outdoor meetings and celebrations. Some years later, a generous donor contributed a tennis court which became very popular, though it meant that the neighborhood children lost their beloved football field.

This situation continued unchanged for many years, but eventually natural developments in the city and in the lives of the various families brought changes.

View through The Window with Asi, 1955

Jerusalem Then...

1950s, 1960s

THE DECISION BY MY HUSBAND'S GROUP TO START A FACTORY IN Jerusalem necessitated a lot of traveling back and forth, which was considered dangerous at that time, because the terrorists, then called the *fedayeen*, were active in the Jerusalem corridor, especially at night. The journey from Tel Aviv took at least two hours through Rehovot and Kibbutz Hulda, and cars were few and far between. There were as yet no cellphones, so that at times one could find oneself quite isolated. Even in the daytime, counting cars was an exciting game for the children when we were driving, and the rusting chassis of military vehicles along the Bab-el-Wad Road, eerie witnesses of the War of Independence, were material for history lessons.

Jerusalem in the early 1950s was a sombre town divided in two by a high wall, making the Old City inaccessible. Jordanian soldiers, who could be seen on the walls and at lookout points, sometimes fired into nearby Jewish homes, causing casualties.

Austerity was still the order of the day, and tourists brought their own instant coffee and breakfast cereal with them. People generally were always looking for a place where they could get a decent meal if they wanted to eat out. The siege and intermittent fighting of 1947–1948 were still fresh in people's minds. There was little scope for relaxation except movies and occasional concerts by the Israel Philharmonic Orchestra. These were held in the Edison Cinema, which was situated in the old Zichron Moshe quarter near Meah She'arim.

Jerusalem had the reputation of going to bed at 10 p.m. Tel Aviv wits used to say that the best thing about Jerusalem was the taxi back to Tel Aviv, but in fact a busy social life flourished, primarily in homes – visitors to be entertained, new *olim* (immigrants) to be welcomed, luncheons, dinners, receptions, Purim parties, and so on. Occasionally, musical evenings were arranged in order to present new young talent, and some of these performers, such as Yefim Bronfman, went on to have important careers. Also customarily, Jerusalemites hosted the musicians of the Israel Philharmonic Orchestra at after-concert receptions given in private homes, with dinner provided for the artists.

Apart from the well-visited historical sites, Jerusalem was an intriguing town to explore, so different from the new white city of Tel Aviv. The first impression was of the beautiful Jerusalem stone reflecting varying tones of beige to pale pink in bright sunlight. A municipal law passed by the British Mandatory administration had decreed that local stone was the only building material to be used in the city and, indeed, it played a great part in shaping its visual aspect. Here and there were some exceptions, but they did not disturb the general picture. The Arab stonemasons crouching at the building sites, chipping away at slabs of stone, added to the uniqueness of the scene, and it was interesting to note the many different ways in which the facing stones were dressed.

Besides this element of color, the buildings showed a strong Middle Eastern influence, such as grand stairways, arched windows, doorways with unusual fanlights, and elegant balconies featuring pillars and columns. The decorative iron work, wooden shutters, rounded corners and bay windows contrasted sharply with the square, bare look of Bauhaus Tel Aviv. There were many imposing mansions along Hebron Road, some owned by and some rented to embassies and consulates, or to national organizations. Some were overcrowded with many more families of newcomers than had been planned for. Above all, there were still remnants of Mandatory glory and British manners, and everyone seemed to speak excellent English. This was partly due to the influence of the Evelina de Rothschild School, which had been built by her husband the Baron Ferdinand as a memorial to her after she died in childbirth in 1866. The school had an excellent reputation, carrying on the traditions of British education. Growing up in Melbourne, I was often told by my mother that she regretted that I couldn't get my schooling there. My family had spent time in Jerusalem when I was a baby and knew the city well.

In contrast to the Islamic architecture were the original Templar houses seen in what came to be known as the German Colony along Emek Refa'im Street, and also seen in Haifa, Tel Aviv and rural areas. Members of the Christian German religious sect who wanted to fulfill biblical prophecies by rebuilding the Holy Land built these houses in the late nineteenth and early twentieth centuries. Although the houses look simple, unadorned, puritanical, like a child's drawing, they are highly prized.

The district of Talbieh, where we settled, bordered on Rehavia and was a little gem; homes there were much sought after. Well-to-do Christian Arabs built the neighborhood in the early twentieth century, and a small number of Jewish families lived there, among them the German-born philosopher Martin Buber. There were many grand two-storey homes, but most of the houses were small, of one or one and a half storeys, roofed with red tiles, and set in gardens. Many had been built over water cisterns to solve the perennial problem of an intermittent water supply. In later years, when expansion and additions were in demand, the cisterns were emptied and converted into additional rooms or small apartments.

The population of Talbieh was made up in part by those who worked in or were associated with the large national and government organizations, chiefly the Foreign Ministry, the Jewish National Fund (JNF) and Keren ha-Yesod, the Jewish Agency, the Hebrew University, Hadassah Hospital, and new *olim*. The young families who had taken over the abandoned houses after 1948 had lots of children. There were three large kindergartens, two elementary schools, Beth Hayeled and Henrietta Szold, and two nice parks with playgrounds. One of the fanciest buildings, decorated with blue and white ceramic tiles in Persian fashion, was used as a home for disadvantaged children, Meshek Yeladim Motza. Situated on the corner of Disraeli and Alkalai Streets, its intake of twenty-odd boys and girls greatly increased the child population. Their voices, singing or at prayer, drifted through the open windows and added to the hubbub of the streets during playtimes. A newly built Sephardi Metivta (synagogue and yeshiva) was located on the corner of Alkalai and Jabotinsky Streets, and a small Ashkenazi *shul* or *shtiebel* occupied the corner of Disraeli and Marcus Streets. This became one of the first victims of the "raze and rebuild" drive which soon hit the area.

Ha-Zvi Yisrael Synagogue on Hovevei Zion Street was only completed for use in 1975, though the nucleus of founding members had prayed together for many years before realizing their ambition of building a new Ashkenazi *shul*. This was achieved by the combined efforts of two groups; veterans led by the publisher Reuven Mass and bank director Dr. Daniel Frankel, and newcomers from the States led by Drs. Hillel Blondheim and Erwin Gordon. It came to be affectionately called "the Hovevei." Rabbi Yehezkel Reich, a survivor from Hungary, served the district and the synagogue for more than thirty-five years. He was followed by R. Avigdor Burstein. Today, Ha-Zvi Yisrael has a large, mainly Anglo congregation and several separate *minyanim*, differentiated by age and style.

With few cars and little traffic on the inner streets, it was natural for the children to go out to play without the parents being too worried about what they were up to. The girls skipped rope, played hopscotch, "Jacks" (Five Stones), or organized "concerts," while the boys played street football or a ball game called *stanga*. Another game, called *ajouim*, involved the collection of apricot pits, apparently used as "currency," or even as marbles. Consequently, we always had bags of them lying around the house. Also, many empty lots and new building sites provided places for the boys to go foraging or organize their own adventure stories.

There was a small home for the blind in the vicinity, and the inmates who took their walks in twos were part of the scene. The Hansen Leper Hospital, behind high walls, was a little further away and less intrusive.

Two new large housing blocks were soon built in the area – the Soldiers' Shikun and the Journalists' Shikun – both on Pinsker Street. The latter occupied almost a whole large block, bordered by Alkalai and Oliphant

Streets, and was so-called because a group of journalists had founded it. About forty families lived there, including writers, Foreign Office personnel and academics. Among them, the poet Haim Gouri was already known for his poems and writings about the "young and beautiful" Palmah soldiers and about their camaraderie and bravery. Many of the poems, such as "*Ha-re'uth*" ("Friendship"), were set to music and became the classics of the period, almost national anthems, played on memorial days or at other official functions.

Among his other prolific writings was a poem which could have been called the anthem of Talbieh at that time, and which became one of my own favorites. It was called "*Ha-panass ha-boded*" ("The Solitary Streetlight"), and was set to haunting music by Sasha Argov. Haim and his attractive wife, Aliza, had three daughters who used to gather with their friends at the streetlight right under the balcony of their apartment. Quite a horde mainly of little girls, my older daughter included, soon developed a special circle of friends who played together, went to school together, lived in each other's pockets.

It was always a problem to get the children home, and after six o'clock in the evening the streets would begin to resound with the mothers' calls: "Shmulik, Danny, *ha-bayta!* Miri, *ha-bayta!*" And in the words of the poet, the children would protest: "'Just one second, *Ima*, just one minute more,/ You are always spoiling things just when .../ We have hardly started with the game ...'/ But all their anxious pleading was in vain" – words surely heard wherever children gather to play. I decided I didn't want to stand on the stairs shouting for my children, and took to using a small Swiss cowbell, which I would ring furiously from time to time. If they didn't hear or heed it, someone else always did and reminded them to go home. The scenes under his balcony, repeating over the years, and combining with his own early memories, inspired Gouri to write his poem.

It happens sometimes that a number of individuals gather by chance at a particular place and time and develop a wonderful and special kinship. So it was with this particular group of girls. Their friendship lasted through the crises of school and adolescence, through a year's volunteering in a development town, Kiryat Malachi, which grew out of their activities in the Scout Movement, and until they finished the army. They continued on to The Hebrew University and then began to go their separate ways. Some left the group following the call of career or marriage, but others remained and continued to keep in close touch. They studied, paid condolence calls when tragedy struck, went to memorial ceremonies for friends who had fallen in the line of duty; they married, brought children into the world, enjoyed watching their progress and kept up contacts into the third generation.

Till today the wistful, haunting melody of Gouri's song touches some deep emotion within me and brings tears to my eyes, and I'm not sure why. Obviously nostalgia, but nostalgia for what? For my own younger and creative years? For the warmth and togetherness of a growing family? For the vanished childhood of my children and its challenges? For the memory of a simpler, happier time, happy in spite of political and economic upheavals? It was a paradise lost, a time and a way of life that no longer exists, except possibly in kibbutzim and rural villages. Children could play outside, rush about and expend their energy, could invent games and stories, make friends, share experiences, survive fights and arguments, could socialize and explore the world about them without having to be watched over night and day. Terrorism and exploding buses have changed all that, have destroyed a lot of these essential elements of "growing up" and maturing, while television, computers and new impersonal mechanical gadgets rivet the attention of the young and destroy their span of attention, their imagination and creativity . . . .

Their emails won't be considered as social documents preserving the spirit of our times, or providing evidence of how it was to grow up in Israel in the turbulent twentieth and twenty-first centuries. In Talbieh.

The Solitary Streetlight

by Haim Gouri

Once there was a solitary light at the end of the road
Which lit up the small world of our childhood
And shed its light on games of hide and seek,
And by its haze the Indians to the camp would creep.
Just when the cops had almost caught the thief,
Mothers' voices echoed bringing grief;
"Time to come home, time to eat, it's late,
It's nearly bedtime, tomorrow school at eight."

"Just one second, Ima, just one minute more,
You are always spoiling things just when . . .
We have hardly started with the game."
But all our anxious pleading was in vain.

Once there was a solitary light at the end of the way,
And nearby was a hedge, a garden and a gate;
There I told her all that young men say throughout the world,
When standing near the doorstep with their girls.
I plucked a million leaves while standing there,
But my hand wanted just to touch her lovely hair.
She said, "I'm sorry, I have a big exam tomorrow,
I must be up early, now I really have to go."

"Just one second, Rina, just one minute more,
 You are always spoiling things just when . . .
 We have hardly spoken yet today . . . ."
But all my anxious pleading was in vain.

Once there was a solitary light – the years have flown,
A different light shines now around the town.
Some neighborhoods have found their niche in song,
But here the same voices in the streets and parks go on.
And when some youngster leans upon his bike below,
And fills the air with shouts and whistles, such a flow.
I go out on the balcony and shout,
"Go home before I come," but then
 I relent and say, "Okay,
"Just one second kiddo, just one minute more,
 You can still play a little but,
Just more quietly than before."
As if I actually wanted to scare him off –
But I never really thought of getting tough.

Poem translated by E. Rafaeli and published with the
permission of the author, April, 2008.

We Took Them With – to the Rome Olympics

Summer 1960
Part I

THE WHOLE THING STARTED TWO YEARS PRIOR TO THE EVENT, when my husband decided that under no circumstances was he going to miss the 1960 Olympics in Rome. He felt that if he didn't fulfill his lifelong ambition then, when the games were just a few hours flight from Jerusalem, there was little chance that he ever would.

And so began a campaign, long before the Olympic Committee itself knew anything about the setup and organization of the games, which my husband set in motion with determination and strategy – to get tickets and to find suitable accommodation, because you couldn't have one without the other. Letters and cables flew to Rome and to New York, till in the end we found ourselves, through the help of friends, with a private apartment in the district of Parioli, rental paid, and scores of tickets for the games.

When Alex first broached the project to me, I said, rather absently, "Yes, it's a wonderful idea," and looked on rather unbelievingly at the volume of international mail his plan occasioned. When the children learned about it, they insisted, in their budding enthusiasm for sport, that they just had to see the Olympics too. In any case, they thought it was time they saw the big outside world, where mummy and daddy went "abroad." Asya, aged ten,

Lonny, seven, and Varda, four, did eventually have to come along for lack of any other suitable arrangement.

Time sped by, the apartment was reserved, the tickets secured, and still the whole project had an air of unreality. I suppose I didn't really want to consider the possibilities and delights of taking three young children to Europe. The scheme began to take on new dimensions. If we were going to the Olympics, we might as well go to Europe for the summer. Shall we do a car tour? Shall we not? Where to stay? Everything will be so crowded. The kids? The boys could cope with summer camp, but what about Varda?

When it looked as if our daring plan might really come off, I began to get apprehensive. Two and a half months in Europe with the kids! Were we crazy? It was simply a refined form of torture! But the hotel reservations were made, the *kinderheim*, a well-known Jewish school and summer camp, had accepted our brood and the plane reservations were secured. Our long-time friends in Rome, Ernst and Dr. Eva Lewin (Landsberger), were expecting us.

There was no turning back. As I bought shoes and sewed name labels, I kept telling myself it would be all right – they could behave decently when they wanted to – if only they won't fight and squabble all the time – perhaps they'll try not to be so fussy about their food and bed times – maybe it could work out nicely.

After a mad week of last-minute shopping, celebrating Alex's fiftieth birthday, of partying, goodbyes, packing and hoping desperately that I would survive it all without collapsing, we arose on July 4th at 3 a.m., and arrived in good time at Lydda (now Ben Gurion) Airport. Here a new surprise awaited us. The passport control authorities insisted that the children needed exit permits, a rule then in force because of prior kidnapping cases, while we had been officially assured in Jerusalem, twice, that this wasn't necessary. But the control officials stuck by their book, and we waited with growing impatience and nervousness as they rushed back and forth trying to clarify the situation.

The passengers passed through one by one, the clock moved monotonously forward, the children began to cry. It was already takeoff time, and we were delaying the plane. Finally, with a frenzied scramble, everything was arranged; we were rushed through customs, boarded the plane amid enquiring glances from anxious passengers and collapsed into our seats. We had made it! We were on our way!

The flight was reasonably good, except for a very rough hour after Athens. Lonny, Varda, my mother, who was traveling with us, and I were off our lunch. Strangely enough, Asya, who is the most susceptible in a car, felt fine and ate enough for all of us. But Varda found the flight rather tiresome, and after the initial excitement wore off, would insist now and then that she wanted to get out!

The weather in Zurich was quite pleasant, though each day was overcast, and there was always a sprinkle of rain. But the boys found it rather cool, and asked what kind of a summer was it? They had never seen rain in summer and were shocked that they needed jackets and long pants. "How can we swim?" they asked, and we had to explain that they would have to wait until we got to the Italian seaside. But if they were unimpressed by the weather, they were very impressed by the luxurious green of the grass and the cleanliness of the cars. ("Mummy, I haven't seen one dirty car, who cleans them?") The trams, the escalators and the posters calling for less noise fascinated them. And they consumed delicious dark cherries by the bowlful.

We felt that we ought to introduce our children to that institution known as "good food," and so the second day we ordered blue trout for lunch. Everyone enjoyed it immensely, until Lonny suddenly complained he had swallowed a bone. We fed him hard crust, soft bread, mashed potatoes, drinks, but nothing helped. Finally, I looked in his throat and sure enough there was a little fish bone in his left tonsil, sticking out at right angles. It seemed to me that any efficient chemist would be able to remove it, so we went round to the pharmacy next door. I explained the situation to the pharmacist and was politely invited to the backroom. I was presented with large tweezers and a torch and told to go ahead! Of course, I was much too inept and Lonny, much too nervous for me to be able to do anything, so we gave up and decided it was really a doctor's job.

Now Lonny got really upset, because he didn't want to miss the Charlie Chaplin film we'd promised them that afternoon, so we agreed to wait until afterwards.

We got to the cinema and bought the tickets but when we got to the door, a new surprise awaited us. Children under six years were not permitted; they wouldn't let Varda in. She cried pitifully, but it didn't help; my mother and the boys went in and we parents had to take Varda shopping with us. Buying a new toy at Franz Carl Weber's incredible toy shop helped to calm her down.

After the cinema, I took Lonny down to the throat specialist. He took a look, then placing a tongue depressor on Lonny's tongue told him to pant like a dog; he had the bone out in less than half a second and offered it as a souvenir! Fifteen francs please! I told Lonny that was certainly the most expensive fish he had ever eaten, and he vowed he would never eat fish again. So much for learning to appreciate good food.

There is nothing like bringing one's children to Switzerland to realize how ill-mannered they are, especially if they are sabras. The quietness of the Swiss merely accentuated Varda's habit of talking at the top of her voice, especially when she needed to go to the toilet. She also astonished them with her habit of lying down on the floor and having a tantrum in practically every shop we entered. People tut-tutted in sympathy saying she must be very tired, and glowered at me for my cold indifference. They didn't know that what she really wanted was an ice cream cone or a tram ride. We also had occasion to wonder who had thought up the theory that children learn good table manners by observing their parents.

Each day of our brief stay in Zurich we sallied forth, en masse or in division, to savor the delights of Bahnhofstrasse (Station Street). One of the first necessities we had to buy, since the children had come without jackets, was the classic blue blazer with brass buttons. The minute they donned these, they seemed magically transformed from wild sabras to civilized children. Clothes certainly help to make the man! But they did not enjoy "shopping," and were merely bewildered by the profusion of such stores as the Franz Carl Weber toy emporium.

This mad rush of shopping, and entertaining the children as well, (the zoo, the ride on the lake, the trams, etc.), was quite a strain after all the excitement of the last weeks, and I was already longing to be alone in the mountains with Alex. We saw my mother off on her plane to London to visit my brother, and were due to leave ourselves the next day for the *kinderheim* at Celerina.

But the day dawned wet and miserable, and our trip into the Alps, which was supposed to introduce the kids to the glories of the Swiss landscape, was marred by steady rain, low clouds and mist. I couldn't resist some poisonous looks at Alex, because he had argued vehemently against taking sweaters and warm clothing. Luckily, I hadn't listened to him, but even so had taken less than I had wanted to. When the heating came on in the train, I felt completely vindicated.

Once again, Varda found the long journey tiresome and kept wanting to get out, but an hour's sleep helped her see it through, and finally we arrived at our destination. In my mind's eye I had imagined a gracious, charming and antiseptically clean home, filled with flowers and pleasant nannies, the epitome of what is implied in the words "Swiss childcare." We were in for a shock, for the *kinderheim* we had selected so carefully, observant and well-recommended, was everything but. Dark and gloomy, even smelly. In a moment of panic, I felt like gathering up my brood and taking them away again, but at the same time I knew it was essential for Alex and me to have some time for ourselves. So I blinked back the tears of disappointment and frustration and proceeded to get the children settled. After half an hour or so, Asya and Varda seemed quite absorbed, and Lonny was the one who dreaded the prospect of parting with us. Seeing his misery made us both miserable too, so we hastened the goodbyes.

Varda waved nonchalantly from her chair where she was already busy; Asya asked us not to embarrass him by coming into the common room, gave us a quick kiss and was off. Then we both stepped out in the cold rain, with an hour to kill before our train for Schulz-Tarasp-Vulpera arrived.

I was worried about having left Lonny crying, and astonished at Varda's behavior, which I secretly felt was too good to be true. Altogether, the whole incident had been quite difficult for it was the first time we had left them alone in a strange place. Sitting later in our little red toy-like country train to Engadine, we both found ourselves reaching for handkerchiefs. "Good heavens," I burst out after a few minutes, "they've gone for a holiday in the Swiss Alps! Why are we carrying on like this?" Parents!

It was early evening by now, and getting steadily colder and wetter. I took off my damp shoes, wrapped my feet in a sweater, and was grateful when the conductor turned on the heat. At last Alex grudgingly admitted that it was a "little cool."

We arrived tired and cold at the Waldhaus in Vulpera and wasted no time getting to bed as fast as we could. I snuggled deep under the big down comforter, despite the fact that the heating was on. Next morning we woke to a beautiful view of smooth green Alpine slopes, pine forests and tended flower gardens. I couldn't help but sadly compare it with the arid Jerusalem hills, and hope that perhaps one day they too would get to look a little like this.

We feasted our eyes on the tranquil scene, and felt it gradually permeating into our very souls. It made us feel good. But at the same time, I couldn't relax completely. After the intense activity of the past few weeks, it was fantastic to wake one day and find oneself with nothing to do. No children to dress and hustle, no shopping to shop, no cooking to cook, no laundry to launder – no packing, no appointments, no plane to catch. The prospect made me faintly nervous and I was sure I'd never last the three weeks we'd allotted ourselves in the Vulpera spa.

We were anxious about the children and in the evening when we phoned, my apprehensions about Varda were justified. Whereas Lonny and Asya had settled down, she was giving lots of trouble, screaming and crying for Mummy. Perhaps they wouldn't be able to keep her if it continued. Our hearts sank. On the one hand, I felt deeply for her unhappiness, but on the other, knew too that this holiday was much needed by us. Alex was already anxious to arrange for her to come to us, but I forced myself to be firm; it was only a matter of three weeks and in a few days she would get used to it. She was being fed and cared for and was together with her brothers, so it wasn't really so terrible. How hard we had to work to convince ourselves.

Sunday, July 10

I am still having difficulty relaxing and enjoying the feeling of having nothing to do, but I think I'm making some progress. We began to explore the surroundings and found many attractive walks through the pine forests. I am reminded at times of the bush country near Melbourne, especially by the smell of the damp green undergrowth.

I began my "cure," which consists of drinking specific amounts of evil-tasting (and smelling) mineral water, and have difficulty downing the stuff. Alex derides my pulling faces, but he doesn't have to drink any "Lucius," as this particular water is called. I hope my digestive system will really benefit.

News about Varda is a little better but not yet wholly reassuring. Asya, it seems, suffers from her quite a bit and has to spend a lot of time with her; he was very upset on the phone and begged us to take her away!

Monday, July 11

In the morning we woke to a day of glorious sunshine and I breathed a sigh of satisfaction. I am not conditioned to cold European summers, and must still wear sweaters while the natives "sun bake." It was a day to make one's heart sing, a beautiful, to us, spring day. The mountains stood out boldly against the clear blue sky; the green was greener, the flowerbeds brighter, and the scent of the pine forests filled the air. For a moment I wished I were a horse so I could roll in that luxurious green.

Immediately after lunch, we went over to Schulz and took the *Seilbahn* (cable car) up to Motta Naluns, a ride of fifteen minutes. The little red cabin, seating two, rose slowly, vibrating, from 1,400 to 2,150 metres. Behind me, the Alps unfolded themselves in all their grim grandeur against a now-clouding sky, while the remnants of last year's snow reflected the sunshine. Above the pine forests, there was nothing but barefaced rocks and crags. We passed over sturdy peasant women mowing and gathering the grass and children at play nearby. Below us, the rich pasture lands were sprinkled with a gay profusion of alpine flowers, and pine trees brushed at the windows. Alex looked warily down, and said he felt more comfortable in an airplane, but I pointed to the rescue rope cunningly packed over the door, and felt quite at ease.

We got out at the top and from vantage points admired the view. This was the valley of the Inn River with clean and tidy Swiss villages nestling on the slopes, each with its characteristic white chapel and square, tall-pointed steeple. And we were fascinated by the flowers. I had previously been in the Alps only in the wintertime, and was amazed at this vast variety of little flowers, ferns and grasses, spread all about in an infinite profusion of color and shape. But the flowers had no smell.

We wandered about for an hour or so, studying the view, picking flowers, admiring the stamina of the old women we passed, and shuddering at sign posts, which pointed out walks of anything from one to six hours. We were also bothered by swarms of flies, which were more numerous here than in the valley. Then like true city-corrupted dwellers, we scorned the one and half hour descent by foot, and climbed back into the tight little red cable car.

Faithfully we took the daily pilgrimage to the *Trinkhalle* by foot, and had a pleasant half-hour's walk through the forest alongside the river. We enjoyed the rich smell of still-damp undergrowth and wished that Israel had such abundant and swift-flowing rivers as the turbulent, pale-green Inn River.

By the time we returned to the hotel, we were quite enchanted and exhilarated with our day of freedom and exercise, and regretted only that we were not made of sterner stuff (particularly I) to do this more often.

We decided not to phone the children.

I think, above all, I enjoyed that most characteristic of things Swiss, the three-note horn of the little yellow post bus. All day the countryside resounds with this alpine music as the bus heralds its arrival, and gives warning at sharp corners.

Tuesday, July 12

Steady rain and low clouds cover the mountains, coming right down into the valley. I spent the morning writing letters.

In the afternoon the rain stopped so we walked to the Schloss Tarasp, a slightly muddy 45-minute walk. But there was a delicious scent as we walked through the fields of mown grass, alongside the pine forests, and again there were the delightful masses of alpine flowers, but growing much taller than those higher up.

After a steady climb, we came to a cluster of houses, each decorated with window boxes of geraniums. An open door revealed a modern harvester inside a big wooden shed, and here and there were outdoor religious shrines, also decorated with fresh flowers. A strong, unmistakable smell of cows pervaded the air.

At last we reached the castle, perched high on a crag, only to discover we had made a mistake in the time and had missed the guided tour. The gates were locked with a massive key. We inspected the view there, and then went back down the slope to the *Gasthaus* to have some tea. Our appetites were good so we ordered rolls and cheese. The woman brought us thick slices of brown bread and freshly churned butter, and an enormous slab of Tilsiter cheese, which we demolished with ease.

I looked through the window to the small square, where there was an enormous drinking trough and pump watched over by the figure of St. John the Baptist. Some children were playing hide and seek and there was one little toddler garbed in an enormous red wind jacket that almost reached the ground, and out of which he managed to peer with one eye. The mountains beyond stood out sharply against a clouded sky.

The *Gasthaus* itself was furnished in typical peasant style, but a grand, modern jukebox stood on one side, suggesting that the populace gathered here for its revelry. When I went to the inside of the house to find the toilet, I nearly finished up in the cow-room, a space in the house used in the winter for the animals, and indeed the whole house was permeated with the smell of cows. This was certainly the closest I'd been to seeing the "real" Switzerland.

In the evening we heard more bad news about Varda and we decided that we'd have to bring her over the next day. There's no point in her carrying on so much. Though I'm sorry that it's so difficult for her, it means the end of our holiday: I was nervous and on edge for the rest of the evening. Perhaps we'll be able to find a girl to help take care of her.

Wednesday, July 13

The morning was cloudy but by the time we left to fetch Varda, it had cleared and the sun was shining enthusiastically. As we drove towards St. Moritz, the world about us seemed to be a magnificent composition of blue and shades of green – the emerald pastures, the pale green river, the dark pine forests. There were touches of silvery white in the sky and on the bare brown peaks. Everything reflected the brilliant sunshine, even the perspiring backs of the road workers. We passed through one village after another, with their narrow cobbled streets; in some, women were doing laundry at the village pump, in others we passed peasants with gleaming scythes over their shoulders. Women going out to the fields carried long-handled rakes.

Everybody seemed to be taking advantage of the weather. We passed many picnickers by the roadside, modern picnickers with chairs and tables and cookers, while in the fields we saw families of peasants, including young children, haying. In some places, they were merely turning the mown grass to dry or hanging it over wooden frames; in others, where it was already dry the women were raking it together in mounds, which the men tied in bundles.

When we arrived at the *kinderheim*, we found the children happily occupied in the garden. We were told Varda had been a perfect angel since learning we were coming to take her away. They were excited to see us, Varda immediately started crying, "Take me home, take me home," but as soon as I reassured her, she was all right again. We spent some time listening to their stories and meeting their friends. Asya told how much he'd suffered from Varda and about their trip in the *Seilbahn* (cable car), and how he'd established his position among the boys. Lonny chattered about his football games and assured us several times that there was plenty of food; it just didn't taste as good as at home. Finally, we gathered up Varda and her possessions and began the trip back.

As the afternoon drew into the long twilight, which is quite unknown in Israel, the brilliant colors of noontime softened, though the sun retained its pleasant warmth. The distant mountains merged in a high blue haze and as the shadows lengthened across the valley, the sun picked out each little white village with its black pointed steeple, crowning it like a jewel in a sea of green velvet.

Well, we had had four free days and though Varda is trying hard to be charming and behave correctly, our holiday and my mood have taken on a different aspect. Still, we've been lucky to find a nice young girl named Crystal, the daughter of one of the staff members, who was happy to earn some money.

The countryside is very beautiful as we climb into a hilly region with mountains in the background. The wheat harvest is just beginning here, so the scenes are familiar, but still lovely. We see many haystacks, also many vegetable gardens. The mountains and valleys are completely terraced, and the heavy soil needs no retaining wall.

Now we are moving at the foot of steep mountains, not cultivated but quite green, while plains stretch away. Villages and factories, large housing developments, trees and more trees dot the countryside. Young cypress saplings have been planted on the mountainsides and brilliant sunshine accentuates the colors. Marvelous craggy peaks rise to form the skyline, a different aspect.

Monday, July 18

The weather is highly unreliable. For everyday of bright sunshine, there are two to three heavy with cloud and rain. Even Alex finally gave in and went and bought a heavy sweater.

Yesterday we took Varda on the cable car to Motta Naluns and she enjoyed it immensely. I thought she'd be afraid in the little cabin but she wasn't at all. She enjoyed running about on the mountain slopes, and picking flowers, but as usual got quickly bored.

Vulpera is one of a group of three villages situated in the Inn River valley, at the foot of snow-capped mountains. It consists of two big hotels constituting the spa, some smaller pensiones, a golf course and swimming pool; a post office, pharmacy, photographer, watchmaker, handicrafts, antique shop, lingerie shop, hairdressing salon, newspaper stall and most important of all, a shop specializing in Scottish cashmere sweaters and mink and chinchilla stoles. The clientele of Vulpera seems to be such as to support all of these adequately.

The village people speak German, French and Italian, but the native language is Romansh and it betrays itself in the soft 's', almost 'sh', which the natives repeat in all other languages as well. The houses in many of the surrounding villages bear inscriptions, both biblical and lay, in this language, and it also appears on shop signs, but even with a knowledge of French or Italian, it is difficult to understand. The popular greeting is "Gruss Gott," said to one and all, in the shops or out walking.

"Why does God make it rain all the time?" asked Varda.

"Why don't you ask Him to stop it, and make the sun shine instead?"

"But He's way up in the sky – I can't shout so loud."

Thursday, July 21

After lunch, a group of village children came to entertain us with Swiss songs, music and dances. They were charming in their spontaneity and the guests kept them for more than an hour.

About midday, the skies began clearing and we decided to take the two-hour walk to Avrona, through the Clemgia Gorge. We walked down to the bridge where the Clemgia tributary joins the Inn River, then turned to follow it upstream through the gorge. The narrow cleft between the mountains was filled with a rushing noise as the waters tossed and tumbled turbulently over the enormous rocks and boulders. We crossed back and forth over the stream by a series of footbridges, at times almost hypnotized by the swift flow of the water. Rounding one corner, we had to walk carefully around a little brown and white field mouse sitting unconcernedly in the middle of the path. The path took us steadily upwards, and as we progressed further, the thick growth covering the mountainsides began to thin out, and we discovered a new landscape of bare rock and spare greenery.

Here and there we passed under rocks dripping with water, or stepped over little rivulets which materialized from under stones, and slowed down to feed the larger stream. Quite often we passed other walkers of various ages, for hiking seems to be the Swiss national sport. Finally, after about an hour's walk we turned away from the gorge and climbed up and over the brow of the hill. Suddenly we were in a world of silence, a forest of tall trees and lush, inviting green grass. The noisy river could no longer be heard. A ten- or fifteen-minute walk brought us to Avrona, and after a cup of tea, we completed the circle, which brought us back to our hotel.

Sunday, July 24

Yesterday afternoon, there was a sudden winter chill in the air, much sharper than the coolness of the last few days. Sure enough, when we got up this morning, we saw that the surrounding peaks were all covered with snow. Even the 2,150-metre high peak of the lower Motta Naluns, where we went on the chair lift, was liberally dusted with white. This was one thing I never expected on a summer vacation.

Bad weather kept us quite inactive. We didn't go golfing or play tennis, and the forest paths were too slippery with mud for pleasant walking. For the first week or so, the very inactivity made me tense and nervous, but as our stay came to a close, it scarcely bothered me at all, and we ate, slept, read and chatted, greatly relaxed. We enjoyed doing nothing.

The focal point of the day was the afternoon trip to the *Trinkhalle*, the drinking hall or pump room. This is a long, low building, by the river, with a central hall where the curative waters are enshrined. A pavilion of shops leads off from the hall and supplies some entertainment and interest while one sips one's quota. Here gather daily an assortment of people of all colors, shapes, sizes, ages and nationalities bent on the serious business of getting down two hundred milliliters of "Lucius," "Bonifacius" or "Emeritus" without betraying too strongly their inner distaste for sulfurous water.

The cold weather persists, and I begin to feel rheumatic pains in my back and shoulders. I am beginning to look forward to leaving here. With the onset of the aches, I thought it wouldn't do any harm to try *fango*, a mud pack. Try anything once. I tried a Scotch shower last week, a combination of alternate strong jets of hot and cold water, but found the aftereffects unpleasant, so didn't continue though it's said to be good for the circulation. This time I came into the cubicle and undressed, unsure of the procedure. In a few minutes, the younger of the two attendants came in and put down layers of plastic and old sheets on the bed. Soon after, the older attendant came in with a bucket of steaming gray-black mud. Neither of the women had been selected for beauty or charm. I was rather startled, as I hadn't expected it to be hot. With one hand, she scooped up some of the mud and smeared it over my back. It was very hot. Then I lay down for a second to make an "outline," which she proceeded to cover with a thick layer of mud. She spread some more over my back and shoulders, then I gingerly lowered myself onto this steaming mess, and was wrapped in a cocoon of sheets and blankets, my arms inside, so that I was completely immobile. I could have been nailed down.

Gradually the mud began to cool off, while at the same time my own temperature began to rise. I couldn't move, couldn't read, there was no one to talk to. Just relax, relax, don't look at the clock, relax. Between the warm mud on my back and arms, and the weight of blankets on top, I began to feel like a pot simmering on the stove. Finally, the half hour was over and the younger attendant came to release me from the cocoon, inquiring solicitously whether I had managed to raise a sweat. I had.

I knelt in the bathtub while she scraped and showered away the mud, and though I felt pleasantly warm and "good," I was quite exhausted and had to lie down for some time. But I was prepared to try it again.

❖

Varda: "Asya and Lonny are in the *kaitana* [summer camp]. They have to eat everything that's given to them and have to do what they are told. But I'm here with you and I don't have to eat everything or do what I am told!"

❖

Friday, July 29

Great excitement this morning as Alex and Varda went off to meet Asya and Lonny. She has been talking of nothing else for the last few days. Alex was worried because they were making their first train journey alone. "Don't stand near the door, don't lean out of the windows, and don't get out till you see us."

It was a shock to see them again. Though it had been only two and a half weeks since I saw them, they seemed changed, grown, more mature, and their expressions were different. Lonny looked exactly like my brother Alec, and they both looked healthy and happy in spite of their tales of woe. They behaved beautifully, spoke quietly and intelligently and didn't fight or argue. I thought surely that they couldn't have achieved such polish and culture in such a short space of time.

After lunch we loaded our suitcases into the hired car and said a fond goodbye to the New York couple, Mr. and Mrs. E. Lieberman, with whom we had become very friendly. He had noticed Alex reading the *Ha'aretz* newspaper one day and introduced himself. We spent many pleasant hours together and kept in touch for several years.

We started on our way to Meran in Italy. It was a brilliant day, the first good weather in two weeks. We went northwards and crossed the border at Nauders, cut across a corner of Austria to the Italian border at Resia. The

Austrian landscape was not much different from the Swiss, but seemed much gentler with wider valleys and softer slopes. There was much traffic on the roads and much activity in the fields. The peasants, as in Switzerland, were busy bringing in the fodder for the winter. Whole families were out at work and we were surprised to see ox-drawn carts in use. Crossing into Italy, we soon found ourselves in enchanting surroundings. The road ran for some distance beside Lake Resia, which in turn flowed into the Adige River. The mountains rose on each side of us and ahead of us in the distance, we could see the snow-covered Dolomites against the blue sky.

We drove steadily southwards, and here too saw the peasants busy at work. Unlike Switzerland, we found haystacks here, and saw whole fields full of rows of small yellow stacks, like regiments of soldiers. The yellow fields provided a colorful contrast to the green. Our eyes occasionally caught sight of medieval castles perched on seemingly unapproachable crags, some in ruins, others restored, and still others turned into hotels. Here and there a church or convent also caught our notice, but most of all we were impressed with the farms clinging to the sides of the mountains, or unexpectedly in the midst of the pine forests. What difficulties and years of toil must go into the development of such a farm, and I personally shuddered at the thought of having to spend winters up there.

The children noticed the numerous roadside Catholic shrines and wanted to know who and what they were for, so Alex explained to them the rudiments of Christianity and the history of Jesus. As he spoke, I noticed that the pine forests gave way to acacia and poplar trees, apple orchards, and then there were vineyards, also situated mostly on the difficult hillsides.

We arrived in Meran after driving three and a half hours, and were immediately struck by the heat, though it couldn't have been much more than 26°C. Our three weeks at 1,400 metres above sea level, and the cold we had experienced there, had made us completely unaccustomed to the heat at a lower altitude. The air seemed heavy and impure, and I suddenly thought how the air at Vulpera had been clear and pure like crystal, as refreshing as a glass of cold water on a hot day. I hadn't realized it while we were there, but now both Alex and I were longing for it.

47

By the time we found our hotel, unpacked and settled down, we felt tired, cranky and headachy. We put it down largely to the change of altitude and climate.

Saturday, July 30

The children seem to be getting back to their normal selves. Already they look as they always looked, and have begun to talk and behave as they always did. Three weeks' discipline wears off very quickly. We wandered round the town, got tired, partook of ice cream, and lost tempers. In the afternoon we took them swimming, as conciliation for the shopping trip of the morning. Asya seems torn as whether to remain with us or return to the *kinderheim*. Life with us was too quiet and dull, it seemed. "If you come to a place you have to have a plan. What are we going to do here? I'm tired of looking at trees and mountains and houses. They're all the same. You have to have a plan; one day shopping, next day swimming, next day *téléphérique* [cable car], and so on." I was quite overwhelmed by his outburst, and gave him a little lecture on the necessity of being adaptable in life, particularly when traveling.

Sunday, July 31

All got up feeling grumpy, headachy, dizzy, and depressed. Good heavens, I thought guiltily, what a way to feel on a holiday like this! Is it possible that Meran just doesn't agree with us? Finally, I decided that we were simply de-acclimatized to heat and humidity after our weeks in the high mountains. We could find no other explanation, and no doubt that it had some influence, for my veins, which hadn't bothered me in the cool Alps, immediately began aching after a few hours in Meran.

However, to change the mood we decided on an expedition to the Vigiljoch, a nearby 1,400-metre high peak. We had completely forgotten that it was Sunday, and arrived at the funicular station to find a crowd of about eighty people ahead of us. After Alex had bought the tickets, we discovered we had about half an hour's wait. We were already in the press of the crowd and I wondered if the children could survive it. Alex and I looked at each other questioningly, and the boys began to look ready to complain. What would we do with them if we changed our minds now? At the crucial moment, Varda said she didn't want to go back and wanted to ride in the *téléphérique*, and that was the decision.

Later on we discovered that it was a special holiday, The Day of the Church, and perhaps that accounted for some of the crowd, but even so, this was obviously a popular outing for everyone. Many of the girls appeared in what I took to be the traditional peasant clothes, and this set them apart from the others; a long-skirted dirndl, blue or pink with a small floral pattern seemed the most popular. Often it was worn with an embroidered black velvet bodice, a little white blouse with lace edging round the collar and sleeves, and a freshly starched apron, which generously covered the skirt. Stout shoes and socks, the hair done up in curls, kept tidy in a hair net, and tiny gold earrings completed the picture. No lipstick, of course.

I was naïvely surprised to find, despite this ever increasingly sophisticated world, that young women wore these as their normal daily clothes, and dressed their daughters similarly. Indeed, they were pleasant to look at, and one or two looked as if they had stepped out of tourist posters. The men too were of a new type, fair, tall and slim, and one could easily pick out the land dwellers from the city tourists.

I remarked to Alex that they didn't look Italian at all and he said that indeed they still considered themselves Austrian and were determined to remain so in spite of now being part of Italy. German was the language most heard, but I found it quite difficult to understand the local dialect.

A young man, who had obviously spent much of the morning in the bar, enlivened our waiting time. It was now about 10:30. He kept wandering through the crowd joking and yodeling. Fortunately, the tickets for the overhead cable car were numbered, so there wasn't much pushing and shoving, and eventually our turn came, and we boarded the aluminum car, which had standing room for about twenty-five.

The boys regretted that the "happy" man had gone in the previous car, but when we got to the top, in a stupendous steep climb of one thousand metres (one kilometre) in seven minutes, we found him there in the café happily entertaining the customers. At least he seemed happy, but certainly the three middle-aged women to whom he'd attached himself were not.

When Asya saw him downing three glasses of wine in quick succession, he began to realize that the man was drunk, and got panicky. Previously "drunk" was only a word to him but now for the first time he saw the reality and it frightened him. "How can he allow himself to behave like that in front of people? Maybe he's really only clowning to entertain?" When Asya saw him going around and talking to everyone, embracing and kissing them, he ran out of the café and wouldn't come back. We left the café and went to look at the chair lift, which continued up another four hundred metres. The children were a bit apprehensive of the open chair, so we decided to walk a little instead.

We continued upwards for about half an hour and then we were all hungry and tired so we entered the first restaurant we came to, which proved to be a very simple establishment indeed. Inside we found a group of young peasants, boys and girls, and amongst them, again a drunk. Poor Asya – it was a difficult day for him altogether. At first he again thought the man was just being jolly, but then realized, when the others refused him more wine, that he was really drunk. Had we not already ordered, he would have fled. Somehow, the sight of this uncontrolled, uninhibited behavior set off a powerful reaction in him and unnerved him. He was fascinated and kept asking dozens of questions about the whys and wherefores of drinkers and their drinking habits, whether they drank to entertain company and not when they're alone.

We had a simple meal of eggs, bread and cheese, then started the return trip. It was a good day for such an outing, warm and sunny, but unfortunately a heat haze enveloped the more distant mountains so that we couldn't see the real grandeur of the landscape, but the closer view of the valley of the Esch River, with its vineyards and apple orchards was enchanting to behold. Coming to the *Seilbahn* for our return trip, I spied our happy friend of the morning stretched out fast asleep in the corner of a meadow. Once again, Asya was intrigued and baffled by the eccentricities of the drunk, and I suspected at the time that this whole encounter had made a deep impression on him.

Monday, August 2

Today turned out to be clear and fresh, after a tremendous storm and rain all yesterday. We spent the morning at the hairdresser with Varda, who also insisted on having her hair cut, and then cried because the razor cut was painful. She looks charming with her short Italian-style hairdo.

In the afternoon we risked taking the children on a short tour of old castles in the district, specifically the Furstenburg and Schenne Schloss. They were most impressed with the medieval weapons and armor displayed and even I shuddered at an item called the *Morgenshtern*, or Morning Star, which was a heavy, spiked, iron club, used for beating both animals and people. In the first castle, we saw a collection of old musical instruments in one room, and as I touched the strings of something that looked like a zither, Asya began to get very excited and said, "Why are you touching everything? It's embarrassing." He was almost in tears, and I thought to myself, "My God, I've got a son who's already ashamed of my behavior!"

In the same castle, we were surprised to see sliding windows, with the panes made of little circular "bull's eyes" set in four sections, and also sliding wooden shutters. It was amazing to see that these modern features dated back to the fifteenth century. Here too were examples of some of the earliest clocks made, striking wall clocks which were still working, while another timepiece consisted of four hourglasses, with the sand falling at different rates to mark the hour, the quarter, half, and three-quarters of an hour. This had to be turned over every hour, but what happened if the timekeeper forgot his job, or was unpunctual?

We also noted that the beds were somewhat shorter than today's. Enormous tiled Dutch ovens were used for heating, and were fuelled from the kitchen. There were raised thresholds to prevent draughts, cooking implements reminiscent of some used today; enormous jewel cases for the ladies, patterned terra cotta tiled floors, and leather water buckets, presumably for the horses.

The tour included a charming drive to Fragsburg, the highest point in the vicinity of Meran – a mere eight hundred metres, but as it was a narrow, winding road leading through the vineyards and apple orchards, the bus had to sound its raucous horn most of the way, which made the kids rather nervous.

It was quite a successful afternoon, even though it ended with heavy rain. And as usual, I did wish that the Rafaelis could all want to go to the toilet at the same time!

The next day, if the weather were fine, we hoped to take the Five-Pass Tour of the Dolomites. We have a babysitter for the boys, who had said, "What'll we do there? Look at more mountains, more houses, more trees?" But Varda insisted on going. We, the beleaguered parents, hoped it would work out all right.

One of the things that the kids enjoy most are the slot machines dispensing colored chewing gum. Every time we go out, we have to be well stocked with ten-lira coins. One of my "precious" moments in Meran happened when I took Lonny and Varda to play ball in the park. A little girl sat nearby and looked so enviously at the ball that I invited her to play with Lonny. It was charming to watch them, unable to exchange a word but playing with serious concentration and quiet enjoyment. It seems a ball is the best passport for making friends.

Thursday, August 4

All our efforts to dissuade Varda from accompanying us were of no avail, so we set off in the morning at eight, looking skywards in trepidation, because it was cloudy and rain seemed to threaten. The boys looked a bit disconsolate at being left behind, but they'll have a better time.

Our "babysitter" turned out to be quite an interesting person, and it was an unexpectedly stimulating meeting. She was an attractive, intelligent looking woman in her mid-forties, spoke cultured English, and seemed to have a way with children.

When she learned we came from Israel, she seemed taken aback for a moment, and then told me she had a daughter on a kibbutz near Haifa whom she hadn't seen for more than three years, and who was shortly to have her first baby. Now it was my turn to be surprised, for our child minder certainly didn't look Jewish, but I didn't pursue the subject.

Later on, she told me she was originally German, but had been married to a Dutch Jew and had lived in Holland. She managed to protect and save her husband and baby daughter from the Nazis, although most of his family lost their lives. But the strain and difficulties of those years cast a long shadow, and after the war they eventually separated. The daughter grew up in Holland, fell in love with a Jewish boy who wanted to settle in Israel, and followed him there to be married. Now the mother was living in Meran, not in easy circumstances, and was waiting anxiously for news of her daughter and grandchild.

I had liked her on first sight and on sudden impulse asked if she wouldn't like to come to us as a nanny in order to be near her daughter. Though she was openly overwhelmed by the idea, she had to turn the offer down because of health reasons. We were both sorry. I would have liked more time to get better acquainted but that wasn't possible.

By the time we left Bolzano, with the CIT bus at full capacity, the sun was shining brightly and the sky was delightfully blue. We turned off onto the Dolomite Highway 48, and were soon in a deep ravine with steep granite cliffs rising above us. At times we felt almost imprisoned there. We passed an occasional stone-cutting quarry, where the rocks were chiseled down to building size.

Occasionally, we passed a pleasant little hollow, where people were camping by a stream in what looked like an idyllic location. Coming out of this ravine, we began gradually to climb upwards through the hills. We noticed that here, as in Switzerland, the land was completely cultivated, not an unplanted corner to be seen anywhere. Here and there, we would pass a cluster of wooden houses, and see women hanging washing, or little children looking after the cows or bringing in the hay.

After about an hour's driving in which we covered only twenty-three kilometres, we had a long stop at the Karer Zee, which lies at the foot of the Rosengarten massif of the Dolomites. This charming little volcanic lake at an altitude of fifteen hundred metres reflects the colors of the sky and forests about it. Legend has it that once upon a time an angry giant threw the rainbow into the lake when a beautiful wood nymph escaped him, and the colors one sees in the lake on a fine day are the shattered fragments.

Continuing upwards through the Latemar Forest, logging camps and saw mills abound all along the road. At this point, once again we saw that our pleasure in the trip was being threatened. It was getting cold, heavy clouds were piling up and without doubt it was getting set to rain. What a pity we would not get our "postcard" views. It occurred to me that professional landscape photographers can wait weeks and months for those rare brilliant days one sees in their pictures and color slides. We were amazed at the number of "little" cars that were successfully tackling these mountains.

Soon we began to get our real close looks at the Dolomite rock formations, the Marmolada range being the first really impressive one. This is an enormous round mass of rock poised on the horizon. For a moment, I felt as though I was looking at the new Guggenheim Museum in New York, and wondered if the architect Frank Lloyd Wright had found his inspiration here.

Soon, too, Varda began to complain that she was tired and that she wasn't feeling well. I understood only too well how she felt, for the constant vibration of the heavy bus and the endlessly twisting roads were upsetting me too, and the cigar-smoking passenger behind us certainly didn't add to our comfort. It was too cold to open the windows properly for fresh air. Finally, Varda settled down and I hoped she would fall asleep.

The mountains were really awe-inspiring: great primeval masses, rising alien, bare-faced from the green meadows, of a shape and structure not seen anywhere else. At every turning they presented a different view, a changing aspect, so that it was difficult to understand how the guides remembered the names of the many distinct groups. Here and there, jagged edges and peaks jutted into the air like enormous stalagmites, and one could fancy human figures amongst the various shapes, as if people were sitting or crouching on the ridges.

The clouds were lowering, a light rain began to fall, and it got very cold. Varda had not fallen asleep, and after a quiet spell, she began to get really upset, crying bitterly that she wanted to stop, get out and go home. She felt nauseous, but fortunately for us, and unfortunately for her, she had eaten nothing, so couldn't get any relief. It was still a good half hour to our luncheon stop at the Pordoi Pass, and one of the longest thirty minutes I have ever spent. "Lucky that Asya and Lonny stayed home; they would have been sicker than me," she consoled herself.

Alex and I agreed it would be wise to leave the bus if we could get a taxi for the return trip and luckily, we were able to do this. Lucky, too, that taxis were reasonable in Italy. By now, at an altitude of 2,150 metres it was bitterly cold, and the sweaters we had taken, with foresight, were nevertheless inadequate. The clouds came down in a heavy mist, with wind and rain, and when we arrived at the luncheon stop, we were thankful for the heater the hotel provided.

It was a pity we couldn't see the full grandeur of the scenery, yet in a way the grayness of the clouds simply accentuated the unearthliness of the surroundings, and I imagined one could make many trips to these mountains and see them differently each time.

After lunch, our taxi, carrying a refreshed and happier Varda, took us on a shortened trip through the Sella Pass, then down the Val Gardena through S. Christina and Ortesei. This is the district of the Ladins, who still speak Romansh, of the famous woodcarvers and of winter sports. It could almost be Switzerland in its architecture and greenness. Wooden chalets were numerous, and occasionally a house would be one half brick for living and one half wood for storage.

We stopped at Ortesei for tea and I darted into a shop to buy some woolen socks for my cold, cold feet. After Ortesei the mountain slopes began to take on a more cultivated look, and as we came lower, vineyards began to appear again, and the Dolomites behind us gradually dropped out of sight. After a brief stop at Bolzano, we then finally got back to our hotel in time for supper. Varda vowed to listen next time she was warned to stay at home.

We decided to cut short our stay in Meran and to cram in a few days in Florence, so we'll leave early tomorrow for Lake Garda and Verona, to pick up our rented car there.

Friday, August 5

After a flurry of phone calls last night, we arranged and confirmed to take a hired car to Verona, spend the night there, pick up our rented car and drive down to Florence for a few days before going to the seaside. This wasn't in the original plan, but somehow Meran wasn't quite what we'd expected, and for the children it was dull. Though our stay had been pleasant enough, we never really felt "well" there, and we came to the conclusion that the inconsistent weather and/or the too-soft European beds were to blame.

The weather played us false again. From the minute the porter called us at six instead of seven, the day didn't go as expected. We managed to get away by 8:30 as planned. I've decided that the worst thing about traveling with three children is the eternal packing and unpacking and trying to get rid of the rubbish they manage to accumulate on the way. And soon, too, the overcast skies fulfilled their promise and it began to rain. The clouds were so low we couldn't even see the closest mountains. In any event, it meant we didn't have to concentrate on the landscape and could tell jokes and sing our way to Verona. It was on this trip that Varda adopted our holiday slogan, *Muchrahim lehiyot sameah*, to the words of that old Hora classic, "Hava Nagila" – "Let Us Rejoice: Awake, brothers, and be happy."

Traffic was very heavy in both directions, and in thirty minutes we counted five crashes in which the cars had skidded onto the shoulders of the road. Our route took us through Trento, where we planned to have tea on the piazza after looking at the twelfth-century cathedral. Here we discovered that if you order toast, you get a toasted ham and cheese sandwich, which we were able to exchange for plain toast. On to Riva at the northern tip of Lake Garda; this looked a very charming spot.

The rain stopped and the sun was making valiant efforts to force itself through the clouds, but all the same, it was gray and overcast so we decided to take the shorter drive down the eastern side of the lake. Though it was still a pretty sight, I imagined that on a sunny day it looked much more picturesque. Nevertheless, there were many hardy northerners determined to get in their summer swimming and sunning. We were amazed at the number of campers who congregated in the special camping areas with their bright orange, blue or green tents, because I had never thought of camping, or even caravanning, as a European pastime before.

We also saw some very grand estates, and some exciting modern villas, particularly in Garda. Finally, after being told by the driver for almost an hour that Garda was "just round the corner," we actually got there, and decided it was high time for lunch. Now we really began to feel ourselves in Italy. German-speaking Meran hadn't made us feel that way, in spite of the Italian delicatessen and food shops, and I had many times come to realize the truth of what Alex had told me of the complicated history of that region. The people who were originally from the Austrian-Hungarian Empire felt themselves different, apart, and spoke scornfully of "the Italians," who did this or that in their efforts to promote the homogeneity of the country by bringing "Italians" further north.

One interesting place we noticed on the way was an enormous quarry where slabs of porphyry were being cut, still by hand, into various-sized blocks, and heaps of each different size – larger square, large oblong, thin oblong, small cubes, tiny cubes, thin slabs, etc. – were piled along the roadside. The driver told us this stone was to be used for building, but it was now a state concern and the stones were mainly used for piazzas, decorative building, repairing old roads, etc.

I was also intrigued by the roadside markets we often passed, under marquees or tents, but we never had a chance to patronize them. I had decided to do my shopping in Florence.

Back to Garda. We sat down at a promenade café for lunch and watched the crowds of holidaymakers. Without doubt, this was a very popular holiday resort, and many sailing boats plied their way around the little breakwater. But just as I was planning to finish eating and have a look at the street stalls, sure enough, it began to rain again. Indeed, it poured. We saw people walking about in bathing suits and umbrellas and raincoats! We dashed to the car and headed off for Verona, with the rain bucketing down in torrents.

By 3:30 we got to our hotel, the Grand, and when the rain stopped at about five o'clock, we decided we'd have a quick look at Verona. I took my umbrella as a precaution and off we went to the Roman arena, where preparations were in progress for a great opera festival set to begin on the sixth of the month (August).

It is amazing, the instinct one has to improve the minds of one's children. Though we knew full well that the kids did not care much for sightseeing and wouldn't remember much of the trip, neither Alex nor I could resist an occasional little lecture on the appropriate subject – medieval history, Roman art of building and way of life, etc. I suppose we hoped they would salvage something of this great experience.

After the arena, we wanted to stroll through the Via Mazzini, a pedestrian-only shopping centre, and visit Juliet's house, of course. And what happened – again it began to rain, in earnest; and to top it all off, my umbrella wouldn't open. Well, to make a long story short, I left my umbrella to be repaired, and after searching for half an hour for a taxi, we got back to the hotel soaked through and through. The taxi driver almost drove us up the lobby steps and this cheered the kids up very much, for their spirits were about as damp as their clothes. And I had been afraid we would swelter in Verona! And I can't forget those opera settings standing about in the open arena.

Saturday, August 6

This is the first time we couldn't get connecting rooms, so there was much traffic back and forth through the corridor, especially at bed time and in the morning. Our rented car was delivered on time, and we were ready to leave at 9:30. However, we decided we couldn't be in Verona and not pay our respects to Juliet, so went to visit the Franciscan monastery where she is supposedly buried. At this golden opportunity, we, of course, told the children the story of Romeo and Juliet. Asya thought it was very sad; Lonny said laconically it was the parents' fault. Asya, with his logical mind, wanted to know where Romeo's tomb was and how did they know this was the place, and so on. The vault has actually served as the model for stage and screen productions, and with family vaults in the floor and plaques on the walls, it looks very authentic. We threw coins in the well, and wondered at the numerous notes from the lovelorn, seeking help from Juliet, which filled a special box.

We headed south for Bologna, the flat landscape a change after the mountains. We made slow time because the kids didn't feel too good, so we decided to stop and eat at Modena. We had an excellent lunch at the Crestes Restaurant on the Piazza Ducale, looked at the twelfth-century Campanile and then continued on our way. During lunch, we had made a realistic reappraisal of the situation, decided the kids couldn't care less if they saw Bologna or not, and as we had seen it before, we decided to take the new autostrade direct to Florence. The boys were very impressed with this speedy six-lane highway and we all enjoyed skimming along it for miles and miles in a ruler-straight line.

Unfortunately, the second half wasn't open to traffic yet, so we had to transfer to the Pistoia highway at Sassa Marconi. This was quite a good road and it took us over the Apennine Hills. It was a pleasant scene with the sun shining over the green fields and throwing the cypress trees into relief. But the driving was rather marred by the enormous heavy trailer trucks, which seemed to flood the road that Saturday afternoon. One would have thought there were no goods trains in Italy. We had one narrow escape when an oncoming truck was overtaken by a second truck trailer on a curve – and we swerved by with only centimetres to spare.

We made good time and arrived in Florence at 6:30 in the evening. Our trip to Florence was partly of a sentimental nature, for we had fond memories of our first visit there some eight years earlier. Naturally, we had booked in at the same little hotel, the Berchielli, by the Ponte Vecchio, and of course, as usually happens in such cases, it wasn't quite the same. They couldn't give us a room with a bath, or connecting rooms. The large rooms were furnished simply and rather drably. Our oldest took one look around and said, "Aren't there better hotels in Florence?" But of course, we said, "You're lucky we could get this." We settled down comfortably. The boys were pleased they could play football in their room – it was so large – and we had a pleasant little patio off ours, even though it looked onto another building. We were early to bed.

Sunday, August 7

This morning I was domestic, catching up on some washing and sewing. Then we went out for a nice lunch, and a walk. Sunday's a bad day for window shopping as most of the shops are shuttered, but it was satisfying to walk the streets of Florence just studying the names and old buildings. We looked at the Duomo and Giotto's Campanile, found a flock of hungry pigeons in the Piazza Saint Lorenzo, which the children enjoyed feeding, and then took a fiacre across the river to the Piazza Michelangelo. I think the kids couldn't quite understand why there should be a statue of *David, Melekh Yisrael*, in Florence, but they sang the song anyway in his honor. Some pranksters had hung an empty bottle of Chianti on the right hand of the statue and it swayed and clinked in the breeze, an irreverent, but very funny, jape.

Everyone voted it a successful day and we returned happily to the hotel. Florence seems to be full of students and beatniks, mostly Americans, mostly female. I eyed my three kids and thought fleetingly, how nice to be young and studying in Florence!

One of the nice things about traveling with the kids as against some of the less nice is to watch their reactions and adaptations to the whole experience. We enjoyed the aplomb with which Varda took to fingerbowls, and the way she threw new words into her vocabulary, like *téléphérique*, bidet, the ladies' and men's, etc; and, always so enthusiastic and insistent about changing for dinner! Her biggest linguistic achievement is to count in German: *Eins, zhwei, drei . . . .* Lonny is quietly adaptable, accepting any situation without great difficulty, interested in the foreign languages, and trying to acquire and use some of them. But he has no feeling for antiquity or history, and on seeing the Palazza Vecchio, he said, "That's not interesting, it's an old building." Asya is quite cultured, as he already knows a little from his reading and is old enough also to remember the salient features, but I think he misses his friends and his home surroundings and would gladly go home tomorrow.

Florence is a city of church bells, and we find ourselves listening for them as the hour approaches, trying to identify them as each chimes in its turn. I am especially attracted by one that has an odd fading-away stroke, and I wonder if it has any special significance.

Our efforts to widen the children's knowledge and appreciation of food were to no avail. Varda subsisted largely on a regular diet of melon, spaghetti or potatoes, cold chicken and ice cream. The boys are only slightly better, preferring steak or veal cutlets to chicken. But Lonny has developed a liking for trout and sole, in spite of his first bad experience in Zurich.

Alex and I were happy to get to know *fedora*, a delicious cake dessert soaked in wine, filled with whipped cream, and heaped with enormous chocolate flakes on top. It looks fascinating on the *dolce*, or sweets trolley, and is just as fascinating to eat, even though the kids steal the chocolate shavings from the top. The rest of it is too rich for them. We have also discovered a new salad ingredient, a little pointy dark-green leaf with an onion flavor. It is called rughetta, but no one knows the English name for it.

Wednesday, August 10

Our four days in Florence were drawing to a close and the next day we went off to Forte dei Marmi for ten days of sea and sand. The kids were eager, since for them, summer is not summer without swimming.

It had been nice to come to Florence for the second time and be able to enjoy just being there without feeling under obligation to cram in all the "musts." This was frankly a shopping expedition with just a sprinkling of general sightseeing and education, but I did feel a need to go to the Academia to see for myself, and to show the kids, Michelangelo's original *David*. I felt quite excited at seeing it again, and was overwhelmed as at the first time, by the sheer beauty of this serenely quiet but powerful work. Varda insisted on singing "*Ve-David yefe einayim*" – but fortunately in a quiet voice. I think the boys were impressed, and their curiosity was aroused too by the unfinished works displayed. It is one thing to see the completed statue, another thing to see the figures partly emerging from the rock. These unfinished works of Michelangelo's always make me feel as if the figure is already there in the rock; one has only to brush away the superfluous stone to reveal it.

When Asya realized the fact that the magnificent buildings of the Duomo, Giotto's Campanile, the arena in Verona were all done by hand, his modern-age mind was amazed that such things were possible.

I love watching the traffic police in their white summer uniforms and white gloves. They control the traffic like a conductor leading a symphony orchestra and woe betide if you misread one of the signals.

I have been amazed in Switzerland and in Italy at the attention paid to young children. In Zurich the children were offered sweets or some little toy or sample in every shop we entered. In Italy the gifts weren't so many, but everyone always has a smile and a word, and often a sweet for children. This must be the traditional Italian love for children, for I see it coming spontaneously from waiters, shop girls, saleswomen, etc. Varda's ego is having a lovely time, for with her fair hair, light coloring and blue eyes, she is quite a sensation wherever she goes.

Charming the way some Italians have of answering "yes" when asked if they speak English, then look at you blankly when you tell them what you need. This was especially true of waiters, who knew little more than "meat and potatoes." I regretted that I hadn't made good my resolution to learn Italian before coming here, but I did begin to pick up some functional words and phrases.

Suddenly, we realized we hadn't seen a movie for about two months! Incredible – but usually by the time we'd finished our shopping or sightseeing and got the kids to bed, we were too tired and too late for anything. Our efforts to find babysitters, more for day than night, were quite fruitless. There just wasn't such a thing among the Italians, who have large families on whom to call when necessary. This was also one of the contributing factors why we didn't do much serious sightseeing and gallery visiting.

Friday, August 12

We got away early from Florence yesterday (Thursday). It was a good day for driving, the children were happy to be going to the sea, and it had been one of our best days so far. They especially enjoy driving on the autostrada. We made Pisa in good time, and on seeing the Leaning Tower, they really sat up and took notice. Here was something which really fired their imagination: How did it happen? Why doesn't it fall down? What will happen if it falls down while we're sitting here? And so on.

It was now mid-morning and getting quite hot. There must have been several hundreds of tourists there, and we especially noticed one clad in bathing trunks. Finding a parking space was very difficult but finally we managed it. The children all demanded to go up to the top of the tower, so Alex and I took a deep breath. We'd been up once many years earlier, but what doesn't one do to further the education of one's offspring? Against my better judgment, we took our place in the queue of people climbing upwards in the semi-gloom.

The boys began to get some idea of the force of gravity as they toiled awkwardly and dizzily upwards. By the time we got to the sixth gallery,

I felt I couldn't go any higher and when the boys looked out at the view, they agreed that it was enough. Alex and I then suggested we walk once right around the gallery. Asya replied that he just wanted to take pictures. Lonny didn't mind admitting that he was afraid, but with Alex's help and persuasion, he eventually inched himself round, hugging the wall all the time. Varda skipped along with me quite unconcernedly. "She's just not old enough to understand. That's why she's not afraid," said Lonny. We made our way down again and noted that the turnstiles counted the number of people going out as well as going in. We wondered if anyone had ever attempted suicide. We were glad to sit down and have a rest, and I was very much aware of my leg muscles.

After a visit to the Duomo as well, we decided we'd better continue on our way. First, though, we had toilet troubles with Varda. I could usually get her to use the old-fashioned standing toilets so common still in Italy, for minor needs, if they were reasonably clean, but it was time now for "big business," and what were we to do? Finally, we espied the very elegant new Grand Hotel and decided a drink at the bar would be worth the use of the toilet facilities. And it was!

This business of the toilets has given me many moments of guilt when I see how vital it is to Varda. She so dreads the standing toilets that she always tries to utilize the "nice" toilets when available, and then is upset if she can't perform as she wishes, in case she'll have to use a "not nice" toilet later. It is difficult for children to grasp that they can't always be finicky when one has tried to train them to a reasonable degree of orderliness and cleanliness.

The drive from Pisa to Viareggio led through miles and miles of inviting pine forests. But at Viareggio the scenery changed abruptly: brightly painted houses, a wide ocean road with planted shrubs and flower beds, forests of beach umbrellas, flocks of sailing boats and crowds of holidaymakers in casual and informal clothes on the beaches and in the streets. In the bright sunshine, against the blue sky, it looked utterly enchanting.

We arrived at our hotel in Forte dei Marmi for lunch, and in the afternoon I got down to the eternal task of unpacking and getting straightened out while Alex took the kids for their first dip. By evening we were all ready for an early night. The accommodation belies the grandeur implied in the name of the hotel, the Grand Hotel Imperiale, and our two rooms and bath together are not as large as the room the kids had in Florence. It's a tight squeeze. It also never occurred to us, when asking for rooms overlooking the sea, that the main state highway would pass under our window and the traffic is considerable. However, we all slept very well that night.

But this morning! Quite a different story! As soon as I tried to get up, I found I could scarcely move. I was hurting, not just aching, all over – my calf muscles, my thigh muscles, my back, my head – I felt completely exhausted and miserable. That Tower of Pisa! I knew I shouldn't have climbed it. I felt so low; it needed only the squabbling and arguing of the kids to bring on the tears. A complete depression took hold of me. I realized that we'd had the kids on our hands fully and completely, without a break, every minute of the day for the last two weeks and this wasn't the end yet. We hadn't been out alone or to a show or for one meal. Some holiday! Then to top it all, the skies were overcast. A cool wind was blowing – no bathing. By lunchtime a real storm was brewing, the skies so heavy there was really "darkness at noon" and soon the rain came down in torrents. At least I got some sleep and gradually began to feel better, though my leg muscles were very sore, especially when we had to walk up or down the steps.

There was a brief respite in the late afternoon, but then the wind came up again and as I was writing these words, a real gale whistled round the building and down the corridors. It was so strong, it should surely blow itself out by morning, we said, hopefully!

Saturday, August 13

Day dawned inauspiciously, with gray skies and gray angry seas. Immediately the cry was raised, what are we going to do today? So after breakfast we sallied back and forth to see what there was to do, and we found it. Just a short distance from the hotel was a pleasant, tree-filled park, covering about two city blocks, where for a few hundred lire the kids had an enjoyable morning on a merry-go-round, a toy train, bicycles, pony carts and battery-driven cars. Lonny amazed us by getting on a two-wheeled bike for the first time and just riding off. They had more fun than they've had for some time.

By the afternoon, the skies had cleared sufficiently for us to venture onto the beach, though the sea remained uninviting. This was one of the nicest beaches I have ever seen. Fine clean sand, no rocks or stones, no orange peel, ice cream sticks or lunch remnants. Whether this is due to the good habits of the clientele, or the watchfulness of the concessionaire of that part of the beach, I couldn't say. In either event, it was a pleasure to behold, with its neatly arranged rows of chairs, umbrellas and play area. Another pleasure to behold were the young Italian women, who have a distinctive style and seem to be made to wear sports and casual clothes. They can be easily distinguished from the tourists, who tend to fussiness in their sportswear, and wear the kind of clothes they shouldn't. No wonder Italy excels in this branch of fashion.

Sunday, August 14

Gray day, cold and wet. We began to long for the consistency of the Israeli sun. The beaches were deserted, the park and the shops, full. It was amazing how "shopping" became automatic when there was nothing else to do. It seemed like one develops a kind of conditioned reflex at the sight of an interesting shop, even if it's only window shopping.

It began to clear in the afternoon, so we took a ride into Viareggio. What a hustling, bustling little town. The cafés were crowded, the shops were crowded, the streets were crowded; we saw gay, casual clothes and heard the clack of wooden beach sandals. Traffic was very heavy, though its being Sunday and a holiday weekend may have partly accounted for this. We were glad we'd selected Forte dei Marmi.

Asya has started seriously with tennis lessons, and we hoped he'd be able to keep it up when we got back home.

Don't know what we'll do if the weather doesn't improve.

Monday, August 15

It literally poured all day. Kids very despondent and irritable; want to go home. Almost agree.

Tuesday, August 16

The day started un-optimistically, but by mid-morning the sky was blue, the sun was shining, the sea was inviting. Quickly the beach blossomed forth again in a forest of gay umbrellas and a bevy of bright bikinis. The water filled with swimmers, colorful water mattresses, motorboats and sailing boats. Our mood improved just at the sight.

Wednesday, August 17

Another delightful day; the sea and the beach were at their best. A flock of sailing boats came down to the sea, and even a yacht appeared. Music drifted through the air from transistor radios, and a variety of beach vendors made their rounds: the lady with the fresh iced coconut, "*Ko-ko, fresce, ko-ko*"; the "*pizza-pizza-pizza*" man; the tablecloth man with his wares done up in a big black bundle; the towel man with his big basket; the walnut man; the marble man with imitation fruits; and last but not least, the ice cream man.

Excursions into the local night life were not very rewarding. Though there was a string of bright lights along the seafront and crowds on the streets, dressed as informally as on the beach, the main occupation seemed to be shopping, strolling, coffee-ing, or the cinema. The stores stayed open until 10:30. One night, we finally decided to see a film, naïvely taking for granted that there would be English subtitles. But we were wrong, and the comedy was consequently quite dull.

We have investigated the "hinterland," lying behind the main seaside promenade, and found that Forte dei Marmi has a large pleasantly green, residential area, with lots of modern new villas and some beautiful "stately homes" as well.

Varda threw a tantrum tonight at the dinner table. One advantage of a hotel where there are lots of families with kids is that no eyebrows are raised when a child has to be sent, or taken away from the table. Rather there is an air of sympathy for the parents. Probably Varda had too much sun and sea today.

. . . At its best, Italian cooking is absolutely wonderful, but at its worst, it is unforgivable.

Saturday, August 20

The weather was bad again yesterday so without any difficulty we decided to shorten our stay by the seaside and start out for Rome. Again I was packing. It always took half a day to get everyone ready. I looked forward to staying put in Rome for three weeks, not having to pack and unpack till we go home.

Today was a good day for traveling, sunny but cool and fresh. Without undue pressure, we managed to make a good start, even though Alex discovered he'd lost the key to the gasoline tank and it had to be found. We had thought of returning to Florence and visiting Sienna, but then decided instead to take the coastal road directly south. We wanted to make the trip in two days and decided we'd stay overnight at Grosseto. We thought 180 kilometres was about all the kids could comfortably take in a day.

We passed by Pisa, seeing the tower and cathedral again from a distance, and made our first stop in Livorno, or Leghorn. After Livorno we were pleasantly surprised; driving along the coast through some of the best and most exciting country we had seen yet was a real delight. The thickly wooded, hilly land fell directly into the sea, where the turquoise-blue water swirled and tumbled around the boulders and rocks. Here and there, as the road turned and twisted, we caught glimpses of a little cove where gay umbrellas were set on a tiny strip of beach and people were swimming. On a winter's day it may have looked rather sinister, but that day in the sunshine it was beautiful. Here and there, a castle perched picturesquely on a cliff overlooking the sea. We decided if we would ever come again to Italy in the summer, that this would be the place.

This area stretched for not more than a few kilometres, ending at Castiglioncello, which has the look of a popular resort. After that, the landscape flattened out and became less interesting and less beautiful. We stopped for lunch. We have discovered that the romantic notion of "just stopping somewhere nice" has its pitfalls. We always seem to pass the "interesting" places when we're not hungry and then we finish up in a barely passable eating house.

We made good time to Grosseto, the road being almost empty and we presumed everyone else was siesta-ing, so we decided to keep on for another hour. We found on the map a little place called Orbetello, which seemed to be romantically situated on a peninsula, and decided we'd make our overnight stop there.

On our arrival we found it to be somewhat less romantic than we'd imagined. Strictly not for foreign tourists, though there were many local holidaymakers. The only accommodation we could get was two rooms at opposite ends of the corridor. This occasioned a wild discussion as to would sleep with whom, because the kids wouldn't stay alone. Finally, we decided on a division of the sexes, and Alex slept with the boys in one room, and Varda and I in the other. Before dinner we went for a little stroll, while the boys stayed in to watch a nice film about the Russian circus on television. Their rabid interest in television brands them surely as coming from an underdeveloped, TV-less country.

We circled the whole place in about twenty minutes and found it consisted of quite nice residential streets and a parallel shopping street. The two were connected with little lanes here and there, where we found for the first time, ravages of the war. People were still living in half-destroyed houses, the ruins disguised or beautified with boxes of flowers and plants. There seemed to be a kind of inland lake or lagoon, or perhaps there was an island (St. Stefano) connected by two outer strips of land, while a causeway for cars crossed the middle of the lake. I don't know if it was a natural formation or whether the land had been reclaimed. We would have liked to cross the causeway and visit St. Stefano, but were rather tired.

We had dinner in the hotel restaurant, which opened onto the street, while listening to the sounds of an Italian village relaxing on a Saturday evening. One could hear music from radios, the swelling tones and moods of conversation as the populace spilled forth from their homes, the clack-clack of wooden shoes, the rattling of colored chain-curtains swinging in the open doorways, and occasionally the pealing of the church bell. It seemed as if the little street would burst asunder, that it was too small to contain the vibrant sounds of its humanity.

It wasn't a very special little village, yet it was the kind of place one might come, if one wished to live and learn Italian, and get the "feel" of Italy.

Sunday, August 21

The next day, having only one hundred and fifty kilometres to go, we took it easy and set off at around ten o'clock. As we moved further south, the country was taking on a distinctly "end of summer" look: the low, dry, yellow hills rolling away into the distance, although plenty of green trees relieved the monotony. Soon we noticed a fascinating silhouette of square towers against the sky, and as we came closer, it became even more fascinating and we could make out the remains of a medieval town called Tarquinia, dominating the landscape and famed for its Etruscan antiquities. We couldn't resist it. The guide book said one should devote about four hours to it.

Unfortunately, we couldn't afford the time and we didn't think the kids would take kindly to a necropolis, so we left the latter and just drove into the village, and visited the medieval quarter. The town was certainly picturesque, situated as it was on a plateau overlooking the surrounding plains, with the typical narrow, cobbled streets, old palazzos and piazzas. The medieval quarter was well populated, though much of it seemed to be in ruins, in contrast to a few new little houses dotted here and there. But it was medieval only in layout, architecture and convenience; water was drawn at a pump in the square, and many women were busy doing laundry in dark little rooms, or hanging the wash in front of their houses in the street. Aside from this, there were TV antennas sprouting from the rooftops and the roar of motorbikes split the air. It was the most incongruous place we'd seen and certainly more impressive from the distance than within.

Now that we were coming closer to our destination, the kids, and we too, I must admit, were getting more and more excited with the idea of Rome and the Olympics. Then almost before we knew it, we were right in that labyrinthine city, trying to find our way across the town to the apartment where we were to stay. Flags fluttered colorfully in the breeze and the city seemed geared up for the great event with policemen everywhere in the city, numerous direction signs and lots of banners and bunting. At last, in spite of the confusing efforts to direct us, we reached our destination. *Due cento novanta*, 290, via Salaria was our address, and we made sure the children had memorized it. We were glad to be staying in a private home with a landlady to feed us, and to feel again like a normal family.

Though we had had a relatively easy day, the midday heat, reminiscent of Tel Aviv at its worst, was already having its effect and we were exhausted. By the time I'd finished unpacking and arranging, I was glad of a light supper and the opportunity to get to bed early.

Monday, August 22

Alex is overwhelmed with new problems, as friends unable to attend the Olympic Games have asked us to get rid of tickets for them. This would appear to be easy, but as is always the way in such cases, the tickets are too cheap, too expensive, too few, wrong days or heaven knows what. He went off with the car and I decided to take the kids to the Borghese Gardens. It didn't seem to be far according to the map, but by the time we got there we were quite hot and exhausted. I am too literal-minded and if someone says "just a few minutes," I mistakenly believe him.

We spent a little time in the park, and then managed to get to see the American Nursery School where I'd been advised to send the kids. It seemed a nice, cheerful sort of place, though catering more for the four to six-year old age groups. Varda agreed to attend, and the boys were willing to be left there some afternoons.

In the afternoon, again I made the mistake of taking Varda for a "little walk," intending to make the Villa Savoia, but it was a bit too far and we turned back. The day was saved from being a dead loss by a very pleasant evening spent with Eva and Ernst Lewin, old friends living in Rome, who had invited us for dinner. We dined, Italian-style, late at 10:30 in a little restaurant in Trastevere. Once again, getting there was the problem, and it took us more than half an hour to cross Rome, which was now ablaze with neon lights and aswirl with fast currents of crazy traffic. The Coliseum and Foro Romano were beautifully floodlit, and we felt we ought to take the kids out one night to see this spectacle. It was the first "night out" we'd had for three weeks, and we thoroughly enjoyed it.

Tuesday, August 23

Of course, Varda refused to go to the kindergarten today, so I finished up taking them all to the zoo, while Alex was still busy with tickets. We had our photos taken fondling a live lion cub, though the kids were at first reluctant to sit down with him. They had a lovely time feeding the seals while I took movies of them. We all enjoyed the antics and playacting of these peculiar animals, and were also much taken with the wonderful assembly of variously colored parrots, and especially with one who kept shouting *"Prego, prego."* We saw two bears having a fight, which scared everyone, and fed biscuits to the bears and elephants, who amused us with their ways of retrieving food that fell outside the cage. It was a most successful morning and we all enjoyed it.

Wednesday, August 24

I spent the morning at the kindergarten with Varda. She had quite a nice time and I think that after another day or so, she'll be prepared to go alone.

In the afternoon we drove out to have a look at the Olympic area. The village itself looked very elegant and spacious and there were hundreds of people milling around looking for celebrities and autographs. Roads and parking areas seem to be well organized, but the question is how it will work tomorrow, for the opening ceremony. There seems to be an ample presence of policemen, who are invariably charming and helpful, especially when it comes to finding a taxi. Then we went to look at the swimming pool and sat in a terrace café having tea, while we watched the divers and swimmers trying out the open-air pool.

In the evening Eva and Ernst invited us to bring the kids for supper and to see the Olympic flame entering Rome. The kids were overjoyed at such a grownup invitation, and from people they are fond of! Our friends live near the Terme de Caracalla, and at about 8:30 we went down to the main road to see the great event. The streets were thronged with cars and people, but there was still room to stand and see in comfort. We didn't have long to wait. First came the police, then movie vans, then police outriders on motorcycles, almost forcing a way through the crowds who had rushed to the middle of the road. Then the young runner approached, protected on each side by a motorcyclist, bearing the orange-glowing torch. It was a short moment of excitement and applause, and then he was gone, with a stream of reporters' cars, official cars, and Vespa riders following in his wake.

We went back to the apartment, and had our supper in a little walled garden, typically Roman. The Romans love terrace and patio gardens, and nearly all the apartment houses show greenery and box plants. Suddenly, a bell began striking and I asked our hosts what church was so close by. "That's no church," they laughed. "It's the opera!" Sure enough, a few minutes after the warning gong had sounded, we began to hear the opening aria of *Aïda* being performed at the Baths of Caracalla. It was a delightful accompaniment to our dinner. Though we stayed until about 10:30, the children behaved very well, and only betrayed the extent of their tiredness when we got home; they were in bed and asleep in record time.

On Alex's 50th Birthday

by Esther Rafaeli
July 1960

A FORMIDABLE TASK THE HECHTS HAVE SET US
To thank them for the greetings they penned us,
For we're not used to writing in rhyme
And indeed it's taking us quite a long time.

And so we appreciate all the more
The thoughts they expressed when they left our door,
To convey to Sacha without delay
Their warmest friendship on his 50th birth day.

(*Left*) Alex and boys at Lake Garda

(*Middle*) Ice cream on Via Veneto

(*Right*) At the Games

Best wishes too for a happy vacation
Which we're spending now at an Alpine location.
While you in Jerusalem complain of the heat,
We're sitting in Engadine and I have cold feet.

For this mild mountain climate is summer they're sayin',
But it's filled with grey clouds, and even some ra'in.
Most of the time we're suffering chills,
But when it is sunny we walk in the hills.

Or take the *Sielbahn* right up to the tip
To admire the view, alpine flowers to pick.
Curative waters I drink night and day;
The taste is awful and yet one must pay.

Three weeks of this, we'll be so healthy,
Then pick up the kids, and down to Italy;
For we are heading to the Olympics in Rome,
The jewel in the crown, before we go home.

This poem acknowledges birthday greetings from the late Carola and Ariel
Bin Nun, which was written in German, in rhyme.

Rome: Our Olympic Adventure

Thursday, August 25

AT LAST THE GREAT DAY CAME, AND THE OPENING OF THE OLYMPIC Games was indeed a wonderful spectacle. The children behaved irreproachably, and we enjoyed ourselves thoroughly. A little careful planning brought us smoothly and comfortably to the stadium, and by half past three we were in our seats with plenty of time to spare. I wonder if there is any other stadium in the world so beautifully situated as Rome's – surrounded by trees and smooth lawns, the famous Marble Stadium on one side, the Olympic swimming and diving pools on the other, and all approached through spacious, elegantly designed piazzas. "Grand" is the only adjective to describe every aspect of this comprehensive sports centre.

We sat and watched the tribunes filling up with visitors from all over. Masses of people, speaking a variety of languages, dressed in colorful national costumes. The flags of the participating nations fluttered in the breeze, massed bands supplied music, and helicopters whirred low to get the nearest possible closeups of the scene. Ice cream and cold drink vendors were doing a roaring trade; a buzz of excitement filled the air.

Suddenly a gasp went up from the crowd, and we saw that a young man, clad only in shorts, was running on the fresh red-clay track. For a moment we thought it was a workman hurrying to some forgotten last-minute job, but it soon became obvious that he was actually bent on making a circuit of the field. He was more than halfway round by the time the spectators grasped the fact, that here was a daring young man determined to win some bet, or bent on satisfying some private ambition. They began to cheer him on, and photographers rushed to snap him, which pleased him considerably. Belatedly, some officials began to give chase, but he finished his round well ahead of them, vaulted the partition and vanished into the crowd of standees. The officials found no trace of him, but he received a hearty round of applause, and everyone felt this was a good omen for the Games – a spirit of daring, of individual effort, of good humor.

The opening ceremony in itself is a simple event. A flag is presented, the Games are declared open, and the Olympic torch is lit. What makes it exciting and moving are the associations underlying the symbols, the spectacle of the thousands of parading athletes in their variously colored uniforms, the color of the massed national flags against the emerald-green field at the centre of the red track with its fresh white lines. After three cannon shots reverberated through the air, completely scaring the kids, hundreds of pigeons were released, representing, as they wheeled in the air, man's eternal desire for peace. And when the runner bearing the Olympic flame came in, circled the stadium and lit the enormous torch atop the stands, one could not help but be moved by this impressive reminder of a centuries-long tradition.

When the Israel delegation marched by, the children cheered so vociferously that everyone turned to see who the enthusiastic supporters of this little no-sport-distinguished country were.

When the formalities were over, we wanted to leave quickly to avoid the rush, but the children insisted on staying to the very end. We were glad we gave in, for just before the close came the nicest moment of the afternoon, that typical "Italian" touch. As the host country was marching out to a tremendous ovation, we suddenly noticed a little spurt of flame in the crowd at the other side of the stadium. It surely couldn't be a fire! We realized that people were lighting torches made out of newspapers and programs to fete the Italian sportsmen, and as dusk fell the whole stadium was a mass of little glowing flames. It was one of the most charming spontaneous gestures we had ever seen.

Leaving the stadium was not as easy as getting into it. We were caught up in very vocal traffic snarls and were constantly diverted from our planned course so that we kept on finishing up somewhere else. Suddenly we saw a little restaurant, just a few tables on the pavement, not crowded *and* with a parking place right in front. We lost no time in discussion and immediately pulled in and had supper. It was well after nine before we arrived home, and tumbled, tired but contented, into bed.

The first week of the Games was wisely devoted mainly to swimming and diving. Many spectators took advantage of the broiling sun to strip to the waist and suntan, and many girls wore bathing suits or brief sun tops. We had good seats, and the children were quickly caught up in the racing fever. Several times during the week, we made a "big day" of it, staying right through from the afternoon to the evening events, and having a quick supper at the cafeteria.

The swimming and diving events were a thrilling sight at night. Illuminated from the bottom, the diving pool took on a deep turquoise blue, and the swimming pool looked a clear, translucent green. Floodlights lit up the whole area and were reflected in the water, and the stands on both sides were filled with cheering and barracking crowds. There were Japanese *en masse* with little Japanese flags, numerous Germans (the largest number of tourists from any single country) with their organized rhythmic cheering, the English with their enthusiastic clapping and quiet "come on there" and the Italians excitedly jumping up and down as they shouted encouragement to their compatriots.

One felt sorry for those competitors from faraway places who had no crowds to cheer them on. The night the Israeli, Shefa, swam in the 400-metre heats, the children nearly went out of their heads with excitement, shouting "Shefa Yis-ra-el" till they were hoarse. An American sitting behind us leaned forward, perhaps a little embarrassed by their noise, and said,

"What are you shouting for? He's not even winning!" "We know, but we have to encourage him," they answered.

The main struggle for swimming honors was between the Australians and Americans, though some surprises were provided by other countries; it was tremendously exciting, especially as my sentiments were still with Australia. One evening, we were surprised to find the Echo satellite moving majestically across the sky (though everyone called it a Sputnik), clearly visible to the naked eye. It was the first time we'd seen any of the satellites, and it was very exciting to behold, though rather disturbing at the same time.

Another evening we had a big surprise when a group including Elizabeth Taylor, Eddie Fischer and writer Art Buchwald came in not far from us. What a buzzing and standing and craning of our necks! We couldn't really get a good look at them, but it was interesting to watch the reactions of the crowd, especially to Ms. Taylor's décolleté. I was fascinated by the ice cream vendor, who just happened to be standing by the row where they sat down. This fellow looked so typical, with his plump face, small mustache and cheerful eyes; he could have played a part in a movie. He stood transfixed as he realized who he was looking at, and couldn't bring himself to move away. And when Mr. Fisher actually bought ice cream from him, he absolutely radiated with glory. It was a good ten minutes before he managed to continue on his way.

The heat continued to be quite exhausting; in fact, it seemed to get worse. Why on earth did they choose Rome in August for the games? The spectators ought to have received medals for attending.

We had assigned seats at the swimming, and began to get acquainted with the people around us, particularly with an attractive woman who sat in front of us. She told us she's Hungarian, but has lived in Italy more than twenty years. I felt she must be Jewish.

The swimming moved into its final stages and became even more exciting as more and more finals and victory ceremonies were held. It is interesting to find that there are many moments of beauty, aside from the competitive aspect. In races where the swimmers are evenly matched, they move down the pool in a perfectly straight line, as if performing a ballet. It was delightful to watch the performances of champions as they put in that extra tremendous spurt and surged forward to victory, sometimes only by inches. In water polo too, a sport which demands stamina and strength, but has an *Alice in Wonderland* air about it, there were some moments when the teams look like shoals of flying fish diving after the ball, or swooping off to protect the goal. These moments of real style and beauty are more relished, since they were so unexpected in competitive sport.

One of the most extraordinary races was the 100-metre freestyle, which was fought out between Devitt of Australia and Larsen of the USA. The crowd was shrieking and yelling as they swam the last fifty metres neck and neck, and it was impossible to see who had won. Larsen and the crowd thought he had it, and he was photographed and congratulated. The jury gave the photo-finish to Devitt, to his own and everyone else's surprise. There was an appeal but the original decision held.

I finally solved the riddle of the tapless washbasins in the cloakrooms. The water is operated by a foot pressure mechanism! So modern that I, and many others, didn't think of looking for such a thing and thought they'd just forgotten to install the taps. It took me a week to notice the chrome button on the floor. There also seems to be a strange shortage of toilet paper in Italy, as it is never supplied in public toilets, but is thrust at you, rationed by the attendant, as you enter.

Thursday, September 1

The athletic events started, and our sons are very impressed by what they have seen; they were just beginning to get an idea of what "serious" sport means. Like most Israelis, they thought sport begins and ends with football, but now they see that there are many other fields for magnificent individual endeavor. The children have begun to ask for milk, so even if only for this, the trip has been worthwhile. One of the most exciting events so far was the high jump, which turned into a tense and dramatic struggle between three Russians and the American favorite, Thomas. By the time it entered into the final phase, all other events were over, and the attention of the one hundred thousand spectators focused on this one spot. A gasp went up when Thomas failed to clear at 2.14-metre height and only made third place, when he had been expected to set a new Olympic and world record. Obviously, against three Russians he was at a psychological disadvantage, but it is also true that form alone is not enough for competitive sport. One must also have nerves of steel and tremendous self-control to withstand the pressure and excitement.

Friday, September 2

This was a day of tremendous excitement and incredible performances on the track. The Americans took all three places in the 400-metre hurdles as if in revenge for Thomas's defeat the day before and, indeed, before the race we had seen them clasp hands as if in a pact to do so. The unknown American Wilma Rudolph, who never walked until the age of eight because of polio, made a magnificent sprint in the 100-metre dash to defeat the Russian favorite, Itkina, and became the fastest woman in the world. New Zealand surprised everyone by taking two gold medals in the 800-metre and 5,000-metre races, and the senior member of our family got so carried away with Halberg's performance that he began a persistent one-man cheer for him – there not being many New Zealanders to encourage him. But after a few moments, a group of Germans began to shout him down, but it didn't help their man and Halberg won beautifully.

The German cheer, with its "Hi-hi-hi-cha-cha-cha," has become the joke of the Games and has provoked others to follow suit. The Americans counter by insisting on singing their anthem right through to the end at each medal awards ceremony, and they had many opportunities last night when they won the men's high diving, the women's mixed relay, and the men's 200-metre butterfly. We also saw the Australians Jon Konrads and Murray Rose win their heats in the 1,500-metre freestyle.

During this race, which took over seventeen and a half minutes, we had plenty of time to enjoy the perfection of Rose's style, the easy grace of his strokes in their unfailing rhythmic steadiness. One could also hear, for the first time, in the quiet which accompanied this swim, the soft splashing of the water as hands dipped and rose, like soft waves against an island shore. It was an unexpectedly aesthetic pleasure, but probably the final will not be so quiet.

My feelings about the Hungarian lady were right after all. This evening she inquired after relatives who live in Jerusalem, a well-known academic and religious family, who originally came from Frankfurt. She told us that she is married to an Italian and we have now met the whole family.

On Sunday we finally had time off from sport to take the children to those "musts" for Jewish visitors to Rome, Michelangelo's statue of Moses and the Arch of Titus. Just as we started up the romantic-looking stairway, which leads from Via Cavour to the Church of St. Pietro-in-Vinculi, we were surprised to see emerging from the shadows above us a grand-looking Hassid with a long grey beard and satin *kapote*, accompanied by two young yeshiva boys with long black *peyot* twisted behind their ears. It was a most unexpected sight, and I am sure they were equally surprised when we said "Shalom" as we passed. Could it be they were on the same mission upon which we were now bent? I suspected we would meet the same trio at the Arch of Titus, and sure enough, we did.

The children were fascinated by Michelangelo's *Moses*, as they had been by his *David* in Florence. When the middle one, aged seven, turned to me and said that the works of Michelangelo (he pronounced it in Hebrew) were the nicest of any he had seen, I once again felt our whole summer trip had been justified. We spent some ten to fifteen minutes at the Arch of Titus, making that symbolic pilgrimage which has grown in significance since the establishment of the State, and which demonstrates the history of the Jews more forcefully than any number of books or lectures. Judging from the scratchings on the stones, it is the rendezvous of Jews from all over the world, and in the few minutes we were there we met two Hebrew-speaking couples from Israel, an American couple on their way to Israel, and the aforementioned Hassidim.

We are well into the second week of the Games, and we went off early yesterday morning to see the *Grand Prix de Dressage*. One has to know a great deal about horse riding and training to understand and appreciate this event, and it was interesting, but not quite our cup of tea. However, it was an odd sight to see the Russian entry appear in full riding habit, including that supreme symbol of corrupt aristocracy at leisure, a red hunting jacket. Eventually, he actually won this event.

Friday, September 9

The weather has turned quite cool, and we went off to the stadium armed with raincoats and umbrellas – we just couldn't miss the 10,000-metre race or the finals of the relays! The temperature dropped steadily and soon a steady rain set in, but the spectators remained faithful and sat through the events under a forest of umbrellas. This was the afternoon that the American team, though they finished first, was disqualified in the 400-metre relay. In the evening we took the boys to basketball, as promised, our daughter having graciously consented (with bribery) to stay home. It took almost an hour to reach the Palazzo del Sport and in the crazy Italian traffic, I was surprised we got there at all.

What a delightful surprise the Palazzo turned out to be, surely one of the most elegant of indoor sports venues. It was a beautifully modern circular building, while the inside revealed an enormous, subtly illuminated umbrella-like roof, no pillars to block the view, and comfortable cushioned seats. It was our first experience of basketball, and we found it a fast, enjoyable game, but I would place it in the same category as water polo – somewhat incomprehensible. The umpire whistles constantly, for no apparent reason most of the time. The 20-minute half could stretch to an hour because of the arguments and penalties, and the players can be changed at will. We had thought the spectators at the water polo were vocal, but here – my goodness!

The last two days were devoted to the finals of the individual gymnastics, which were held in the Baths of Caracalla. At the women's final we witnessed one of the most extraordinary displays of spectator rebellion against the judges, which was matched in intensity by the uproar when the Russian in the long jump refused to shake hands with the American Negro whom he had defeated to third place. The Russian was so thoroughly booed that he actually broke down and wept.

At the gymnastics, the crowd was much taken by the originality and flair of the Japanese gymnast and completely outraged by the low points allotted her. They were really angry and kept up a frenzied booing, hooting and whistling for more than fifteen minutes, preventing any announcements from being heard and keeping the competitors from continuing. Perhaps it was not a sporting demonstration, but the judges were not "sporting" either. It was obvious from this and later events that the judges (the majority being from Iron Curtain countries) were not impartial. They sat through the demonstration like graven images, though it seemed possible that they might be lynched at any moment.

Eventually order was restored, but the crowd lost no opportunity of showing Miss Ikeda that they thought she had been mistreated. Gymnastics is a beautiful and graceful form of sport, and the Russian girls in royal blue, low-cut leotards were slim and attractive. We were fascinated at the men's finals by the Russian called Yeheskel Portnoi. Somebody told us that there were eighty Jewish sportsmen in the Russian delegation, and we thought what a strong group it would be if they, and the Jewish competitors of other countries, had appeared in one delegation. We had also learned from someone who sat closer to the German bloc than we did that the amusing cheer is actually a corruption of the old Nazi salute, *Sieg Heil*, with the "Cha-cha-cha" tagged on for fun, disguise or what-have-you.

The Seventeenth Olympic Games finished. And the Rafaelis, too, were just about finished. "The tumult and the shouting dies . . . ." The races have been run, new records established, medals awarded. The closing ceremony was preceded by the finals of the horse jumping in which the horses proved they could be as temperamental as athletes, and the Russians were booed off the field for whipping their animals.

The closing ceremony was perhaps not as spectacular as the opening, but nevertheless was beautiful in its own way. Twilight approached as the flag bearers marched into the stadium and as night fell, the great floodlights were lit and the whole scene took on a special glow under the night sky. The flags of Greece, Italy and Japan were raised, in honor of the originating country, the host country, and the next host country. When the respective anthems were played, the Italians proudly joined in singing theirs, which sounds like an operatic aria and is certainly the most musical of any we have heard in the last two weeks.

Again, as at the opening, people began to light thousands of little flames that flickered in the dark. Suddenly, six projectors shot beams across the sky making a backdrop for the three flags and the Olympic flame, and welding into one single entity all the various elements of the wonderful scene. Then the lights went on, the cannon roared, the flame was extinguished and the Olympic flag was ceremoniously carried out.

It was all over. The suitcases were packed and our summer adventure had come to an end. Two Olympic expressions have taken root in the family vocabulary – *a vostri posti*, meaning "on your marks," and *tutti sedutti*, meaning "Hey, you in front, sit down." The boys have learnt to identify lots of flags, and have decided they must one day win a gold medal for Israel. And we felt we deserved a medal ourselves for having survived our summer project without major mishap.

At the Games.

A Poem for Varda, Aged 3+

by E. Rafaeli, 1960

ONCE SHE SAW THE SUNLIGHT ON THE DIMPLING WAVES,
And said, "Look, Mummy, the water's smiling!"
I wondered at the imagery her three-year mind brought forth.
She often gives me cause to wonder, this child of mine.

My daughter.

How did I create this sprite?
This happy, jumping, laughing one –
Blue eyes sparkling, long legs dancing –
Summer skies disrupted now and then
By short-lived storms.

My daughter.
What fascination in the contemplation of her,
To spy the innate femininity in her little ways.
The dress and socks selected with such care –
"I looked and looked, I haven't a thing to wear!"
And off she runs to show her Daddy and her friends
How nice she looks.

When I Consider...

**(Inspired by John Milton's poem "On His Blindness")
by E. Rafaeli, 1961**

WHEN I CONSIDER HOW MY DAYS ARE SPENT
From morn to night twixt babies, laundry, stove,
And those dreams and visions to which I strove
Lodged with me useless; though I once was bent
To tend that precious flame which could transform
The daily drudge that is the housewife's thrall.

Is this it, the why and wherefore of it all?
I bewildered ask. But Nature to refute
That restless grumbling does provide
Some moments' joy which pierce one to the core:
A baby's loving smile, a husband's caring touch,
These are the stuff of which we make our lives;
Labor and love, sorrow and joy, said the wise king,
A time and season for everything.

Questionings

ca. 1968

LONG AFTER THE LAST GOODBYE HAD BEEN SHOUTED AND THE last slamming of the front door reverberated through the house, she remained seated at the breakfast table in the kitchen, her head resting on her hands, her eyes gazing into the empty coffee mug. Of late, she had often found herself in this posture, much troubled by this mood. For some time she had gradually become aware of a deep malaise creeping into every limb, into her very existence, more pronounced each day, making the simplest of tasks difficult to perform.

She surveyed her emotional discomfort and wondered how she had come to this point. Her relationship with her husband was tense and troubled, with her children hardly more satisfactory. True, there were some external factors partly responsible. The Six Day War had created complications in the export schedule of the factory, just when it was so important to stabilize the market; there were worries whether their oldest child would finish school with good grades before going to the army; she was between maids, which meant physical and mental stress. There was no lack of young immigrant women looking for work as au pairs, but they never seemed to stay very long, moving on to greener pastures. As for the children, it was difficult learning how to cope with teenagers, to maintain discipline without warring all the time.

Had she also been such a horrid teenager? she wondered. Had her own mother breathed a sigh of relief after she had gone off to school? Had her mother suffered these spasms of doubt and agonized whether she was following the right course for her children, whether her relations with them were "positive" and "rewarding?"

She doubted it. Her mother had always seemed so sure of herself, knew what she wanted; *she* was less inhibited, and apparently not given to introspection. Though her life had certainly not been a bed of roses, she always seemed have a positive outlook on matters. "Find a solution and get on with it," her mother always said. This was a principle she tried to instill in her children.

Her daughter rose from the chair and began to gather the breakfast dishes and clear the table. She felt and often said that her life was going down the kitchen sink; meals and dishes followed each other endlessly because there was no uniform school day, and each child came home at a different time. True, she had managed to do her second degree at the Hebrew University in English literature and Special Education, but it had not led to the beginnings of a career. After graduating, she had been somewhat afraid to take the plunge and go out to work. And then there was the baby.

Because there was an eight-year gap between the two girls, and the boys were already teenagers, her maternal instinct didn't allow her to leave the little one too much alone and out of things. In her own childhood she had not liked coming from school to an empty house and being alone till her mother came home from work, so she made a point of being at home when her youngest came from kindergarten, and later from school. She kept this up fairly consistently till the last year of high school. What had happened to the hopes of her youth? How had she come to this pass?

She took a few minutes to look through the window at her view of the Jerusalem hills, and suddenly a different scene sprang to mind. She recalled a vacation she had taken many, many years ago with three of her girlfriends. They had gone away for a brief respite to one of their favorite hangouts, Olinda, not too far from town (Melbourne), yet sufficiently into the country so that they could enjoy walking along tree-shaded paths and breathing the damp, earthy smell of the thick fern undergrowth. It must have been the year of the final matriculation exams.

On this particular occasion, while staying at the guesthouse, they met a pleasant, youngish man, a pilot or navigator back from the war, World War II. Probably for lack of other company in this off-period at the guesthouse, this Vic (funny that she remembered his name after so many years), a married man but holidaying alone, seemed to enjoy walking and talking with the four exuberant girls. They developed quite a camaraderie. On the last evening they were busy chatting away about themselves, and their expectations of life, trying as it were, to form some self-image and to speculate about their plans for the future. Teenagers.

Victor seemed to enjoy listening to their deliberations, and at some moment volunteered to share with them the impressions they had made on him during the week. They were all agog. "Well," he began, "if I wanted a girl to go out on the town with, I would take Joan. She has lots of go and a vivacious personality. As a career woman, I would select Jeanette; she is the most seriously intellectual of you all. As a wife I would choose Rae; there's something capable and comforting about her. And you," he said turning to the fourth girl, "you I would select as the mother of my children."

They had burst out laughing, but inwardly she had felt disconcerted and a little peeved. She would rather have been the good-time girl or the career woman, for domesticity was the farthest thing in her plans for the future.

Had Victor been entertaining himself and quietly making fun of them? Or had he really had an intuitive eye? Although they had gradually gone their own ways and eventually lost touch, she did hear about her friends from time to time. Joan, the good-time girl, became a nurse, married and presumably had children. Jeanette became an active member of the Communist Party, took her Liberal Arts degree, married, and after her children grew older, went into local politics. Rae became a pharmacist, married, and had a child. And she, the "mother" candidate, took her Arts degree, moved to Israel, married, and became a full-time mother of four! The irony of it! To have finished up in apparent fulfillment of Victor's assessment!

She turned from the window with a smile on her lips at the long-forgotten memory. Funny, she should think of it just now, when her real life was so removed from those idyllic days. For various reasons she had subordinated her personal ambitions to the needs of her husband and children, and thus arrived at her present situation, a somewhat frustrated, somewhat depressed full-time mother, with some volunteer work thrown in for good measure.

Was there some message hidden here? Was it time to accept her mother's philosophy? "Find a solution and get on with it." Time to accept the reality of her life?

She saw no other option for herself, and this is what she set herself to do.

Rome zoo, 1960

No Unknown Soldiers

by Moshe Shamir
Translated from the Hebrew by E. Rafaeli

WE HAVE NO UNKNOWN SOLDIERS.

When we pray for the life of our army, for its victory, each of us adds a specific name. In his heart and on his lips he adds the name of his father or son, his brother or his friend.

We have no unknown soldiers.

Each of us knows that someone is protecting his life, and he knows exactly who that someone is. He can tell you his name.

We have no unknown soldiers.

The clear skies above our heads – we know exactly whom to thank for that. Even though he turns his back to the camera, we know that pilot. His speech gives him away; his modesty and simplicity give him away.

We have no unknown soldiers.

The children know exactly where the nature teacher is serving and to which tank unit the sports instructor belongs.

And in the neighborhood everyone knows who was called up and when, and to which unit. Throughout the country spreads the network of messages, from mother to mother, from settlement to settlement – the most widespread and continuous underground web of love and anxiety in the whole world.

❖

Our soldier is not an unknown soldier, because our citizen is not an unknown citizen.

We know him very well, so well that sometimes he gets on our nerves. He has a high degree of self awareness, he sticks to his opinions. He asks questions, he wants to check everything meticulously – no one is going to sell him a story. He cares, for himself, for his family, for the organization and for his party. And always for something which stands for justice, logic, honesty.

He doesn't give in. He sticks his nose in everyone's business, likes to be in the know, on the inside where the decisions are made. He doesn't want to remain unknown.

Throughout the year we suffer quite a bit from these characteristics – but in wartime they turn into resourcefulness, versatility and self-sacrifice. In wartime these characteristics create special qualities, the dedication and heroism of the Israeli soldier.

Our soldier is not unknown, because the country he defends is not unknown.

It is not a country in which he just happened to be born. For the great majority of us the choice of this homeland is still the focal point of a vital personal experience. The great majority of us have been reborn here, by choice, by decision, by the struggle to get here. Or is still living his parents' version of this experience.

This is the land we wanted, with which we made our Covenant; this is the land which taught and is teaching us that there is no other, that she is the savior of our souls, that she is our only home. Others are born into their native lands as naturally as the oak and the grass and the insects. We prefer the choice, the conscious acquisition, the making of the Covenant, choosing our own fate.

We prefer a homeland, which is not unknown, which has a name, and the name is our name.

Our soldier is not an unknown soldier because our nation is not an unknown nation. She was not formed by geography, not tempered by climatic conditions, not welded by historic pressures.

Self-awareness, giving the name and knowing the name – that is its essence.

> The nation chooses to be a nation, to remain a nation; after and against a thousand ordeals and being asked, "Who are you?" In fire and flame, in extermination and expulsion, thousands and thousands of times he returned and insisted, "I am a Jew!" Thus he said, "I want, I acknowledge, I choose to be – a Jew."

> This is a person with endless self-awareness, which reaches into the depths of his soul. This makes life more difficult, more frustrating, sometimes embarrassing; it means self-criticism and weighing every step and what the apathetic, happy world citizens call "unnaturalness."

But blessed is He who made us Jews.

And because of all these factors, we have no unknown soldiers.

We know them, we identify with them, every minute and hour of the day.

They know us, they identify with us, every minute and hour of the day.

We breathe together, fight together, fall and rise together.

We have no unknown soldiers.

(This article appeared in *Ma'ariv* shortly after the Yom Kippur War, 1973.)

Wars...

WE MOVED INTO OUR NEW JERUSALEM HOME IN 1955 AND IN JUNE a year later I gave birth to Varda, our first girl and third child. There was a terrible *hamsin* for about eight days, and no water in the taps in the house. The maid at that time, a woman named Miriam, had to take the cloth nappies (no Pampers in those days) down into the garden where there was water, and do the washing there.

After a few months when life was progressing normally, my husband had to make a trip to the States, and soon after, at the end of October, the Sinai Campaign took place. There was no immediate danger to Jerusalem, but we were told to protect the water tanks on the roofs of every building, which we did with sandbags. Alex's office staff was very helpful in getting this matter organized, and Alex phoned every day from the States to check on the situation.

The Six Day War of 1967 was a very different matter. Three weeks of uncertainty, caused by Egypt's closing of the Tiran Straits at the entrance to the Red Sea and the withdrawal of the UN observers from Sinai, preceded the outbreak of the war. There were endless discussions on television and in the newspapers, and an ill-prepared appearance on TV by the already exhausted Prime Minister Levi Eshkol, caused more dismay than reassurance. Apparently, he was advised on short notice that he should talk to the nation to calm and encourage the people, about the prospect of an impending war, but he had no time to read the script in order to familiarize himself with its content. He became nervous and uncertain of himself, and made a disastrous impression, upsetting the nation even more.

There was time to lay in food, and bomb shelters were prepared for private and for public use in the event of war actually breaking out. In our house, it was decided that we and the Karivs, the other upstairs tenants, would move down to the Aylats, who were on the ground floor and had some inner rooms that were considered safe. Their neighbors, the Ben Ezras, were in a similar situation and could stay put. The Touring Club would presumably not hold any functions. There was plenty of time for speculation as to what was going to happen and what we should do.

On Monday, June 5, we found out. The day started normally, people went to work and the children went to school. Karni, aged two and a half, was still at home, not being fully toilet-trained yet, as was demanded then by the kindergartens.

The morning news of the air strike on Cairo, which wiped out the whole Egyptian air force, had cheered everyone. Attention was focused on the south, and no one really expected that anything would happen in Jerusalem. After all, it was the Holy City of three religions! Nevertheless, we obeyed the instructions for any eventuality. At 9:20 I went to my gym class situated in a nearby building, and as I was walking home an hour later, the first Jordanian shells exploded over Jerusalem and the sirens sounded.

Within seconds I was home. The maid, Zilpa, was very worried about her two young children, who were at home with their grandmother, and we considered what we should do. It was too dangerous for her to go home, and we thought it best to sit in the inside corridor leading to the bathroom, since our apartment faced east, in a direct line to the Old City. The very first shell had damaged our cables and there was no electricity. We prepared candles for the evening, brought chairs into the corridor, and worried about the children.

After an hour or so, Lonny and his friend, Haim Confino, arrived. They were eighth-graders at the nearby Henrietta Szold School and were permitted to run home during a lull in the firing. Haim knew his family was not at home, so he came with Lonny. They joined us in the corridor and thought it all a great lark. After a while Varda, the fifth-grader, was brought home by the father of one of her friends. However, our oldest boy, Asi, who attended the Boyar High School in Kiryat Yovel on the other side of Jerusalem, had to wait quite a while until Alex was able to fetch him.

Zilpa and I prepared some sandwiches and fruit, and fortunately could boil water on the gas stove and make tea, that most essential drink. Zilpa had been with us for more than a year and fitted in extremely well. We developed a very good relationship, and in fact she stayed with us for almost forty years and came to be considered one of the family. After Alex arrived with Asi, he took Zilpa home. However, a barrier had been set up near her home, which was not far from the Old City walls, so he had to let her off at some distance and she went the rest of the way on foot. Young Haim also managed to get to his home, which was just a block away.

Later in the afternoon while there was still light, we packed tooth-brushes, pajamas, towels, etc, some food for the evening meal, and made our way down the outside stairs, into the street and round the building to the Aylats. After a noisy evening, we managed to get the kids settled in sleeping bags and folding beds, listened to the news and got to bed. Alex, of course, went back to sleep in his own bed, saying the situation was nothing compared to the bombardments he had survived in Europe while serving in the American army in World War II. The next day, Tuesday, we stayed at the Aylat home or close by, as shells were still falling and fires were break-ing out. We spent the time glued to the radio or phoning friends. Except Alex. He just had to go out and see what was happening. He had to check if the factory in Mekor Baruch was okay, and to see where his workers had been posted and if they needed anything.

The main fighting took place beyond Meah She'arim to the north, near the Jordanian Police School, in the area known as Ammunition Hill, and also in the southeast around Government House (Armon ha-Natziv) in Talpiot. This building served as the UN headquarters and was close to the Jordanian border. Alex came home and reported that the UN staff had been evacuated by the Israelis to the President Hotel on Ahad ha-Am Street, not far from us. They were standing about in the street with their suitcases, waiting for accommodation to be arranged, just like any bunch of refugees. They looked quite embarrassed, not only because of the situation in which they found themselves, but also for being exposed to the Israelis who came out of curiosity to see this unusual scene.

I had in the meantime taken the first opportunity to run upstairs and see what was happening in the refrigerator. Electricity had not been restored and it was a complete mess, with the ice cream in the freezer already melting and the meat beginning to defrost. In fact, our apartment was the last to have electricity restored, three days later, shortly before Shabbat. There was no option. I took the meat downstairs, and for the duration, we had to eat schnitzel and filet steak! The lesson I learned from this episode was that it was essential to have a gas rather than an electric cooker, and that emergency rations should consist of food that does not need to be cooked.

Wednesday, the third day, was much of the same but with an improvement in mood. We heard that the army in the south was advancing rapidly and taking the whole Sinai Peninsula. We knew there was heavy fighting around Jerusalem, and that Israel was gradually capturing the towns of the West Bank. At that time Jerusalem was situated at the end of a long "corridor" from the west and was being attacked on three sides, but the IDF fought well and began overcoming the enemy. Would the army also try to take the Old City? The direct shelling had stopped and we felt safer to go out. In fact, we only came downstairs to the Aylats for company or to sleep.

This historic Wednesday afternoon we were at home, and I was preparing supper for the younger children, one of whom had a friend visiting. We were listening to the radio, at least I was, and suddenly there was a special announcement – "Har ha-Bayit be-yadenu!" – "The Temple Mount is in our hands! We are broadcasting from the Western Wall!" Then came the sound of the shofar, blown by the army chaplain at the time, Rabbi Goren. There was a moment of disbelief, then a great wave of emotion swept over me, a mixture of relief, of exultation, of spirituality and fulfillment, and I burst into tears. Years later, during an Independence Day celebration, I asked the children whether they remembered that historic *shofar*-blowing event, and they said, "Yes. You cried."

Early next morning we all went up on the roof. It was a beautiful, cool June morning, very quiet. As far as we could see the land was in our hands. The war was over, except for the battle in the north for the Golan Heights. Peace was a dazzling prospect. We inspected our apartment for damage; a couple of the windows facing the Old City were cracked, and on the terrace we found a generous amount of shrapnel, fallout from the firing from the Old City. We gathered it up and I thought we could make up some paper weights as souvenirs. (I never got around to doing this, but still have the shrapnel – E.R., 2005) On the festival of Shavuot, June 14, it was permitted to visit the Old City along an organized, guarded route. Tens of thousands made the "pilgrimage" in spite of the fierce *hamsin*, while the Arab inhabitants watched us from the doors and windows. When the authorities eventually allowed us to do so, we Israelis began to travel like there was no tomorrow – to Bethlehem, to the Dead Sea, to Kuneitra and to the battlefields in the north and south – because of the general feeling that we would quickly have to give up the territories that had fallen into Israeli hands. We simply had to see as much as we could, and my father went with us on some of the excursions. He was thrilled to see parts of the country he had never visited, and felt that the days of the Messiah had come.

One new development was to hear our planes flying over, as they had been banned for some time from using Jerusalem air space.

The so-called War of Attrition began some months later by Egyptian attacks on the Bar-Lev Line on the southern border. It was limited in scope but there were many casualties, among them a close friend and schoolmate of my boys, who lived in the neighborhood, Mickey Czasnik. His father, Fred, was a well-known news photographer. The army delegation, which came to break the news to the family, could not bring itself to do so. They left, and returned later to fulfill their sad mission. Also among friends from our area was Arik, the older son of Vickie and Danny Angel, of the well-known bakery. This was the closest encounter with the realities of war that my sons had experienced, and it was a great shock. Asi was also doing his military service at this time, but in a different part of the country. This war lasted a couple of years before a cease-fire was achieved.

Between wars civilian life continued in its usual chaotic way. In 1970 or 1971, there was a short interlude when my blue kitchen served as a temporary schoolroom. The high school teachers waged a protracted strike and worried parents began to organize a few hours of tuition a day, taught by adults who had something to offer from their own knowledge. I undertook to introduce Varda and her friends to English literature, in which I had majored at university. For weeks, we discussed the works of Keats and Wordsworth at the round breakfast table, and the poem "The Daffodils" was learned by heart and became a sort of mantra among the girls. It was a minor event soon forgotten, but years later two of the girls who had gone on to study English literature told me, on separate occasions, that those hours of poetry in my kitchen had piqued their interest and inspired them to take up the subject seriously. I was quite flattered.

The Yom Kippur War followed in 1973, and came upon us like a thunderbolt – a completely different story. Yom Kippur fell that year on Shabbat, October 6. Lonny, who was on leave from the army, went downstairs with Alex to the Touring Club, where Yom Kippur services were being held. At about 9:30 or so there was a knock on the front door. I opened to find a soldier on the step who asked for Lonny. When I replied that he was downstairs at prayers, he was reluctant to disturb the congregation and asked if we could call him out. I sent Varda with the message, and noticed a jeep with soldiers parked below. Lonny came running. He changed into uniform, took his gear, and with a quick hug and the information that there was a call up because of an emergency, he was off. It all seemed rather strange even though we knew the army was on alert.

The morning services finished just before two, and as the family gathered and I prepared to feed Karni, the sirens sounded. We looked at each other in amazement and froze. Sirens! On Shabbat! On Yom Kippur!! What could it mean? We rushed to the radio which was always silent on this holiest day, and heard the two o'clock signal coming on the air, and then the news. Egypt had attacked us, had crossed the Suez Canal. Syria was attacking in the north. We were at war.

I thought of Lonny rushing off in a state of fasting. I thought of Asi, our oldest, who had finished a business trip to Europe and was spending Rosh ha-Shannah in London with my brother before returning. What a state he must be in. Would he manage to get a seat on a plane? The phone lines were constantly busy and it was almost impossible to make an overseas call into or out of Israel.

Soon the radio was broadcasting the army code words and telling those who were involved in auxiliary or Home Front services to report for duty. There were far fewer men in the synagogue for the afternoon and closing Yom Kippur prayers, and there was a sense of apprehension in the air. In the evening, Lonny called to say that he had just broken his fast and was waiting for his assignment. The TV showed pictures of rabbis in their prayer shawls digging ditches.

In the first days, the news was very bad. Lists of casualties were already being published and a heavy cloud of gloom began to settle over the country. All social life stopped, and one only met people while doing essential shopping at the grocery. One became afraid to ask about sons and husbands who had been called up, because the casualty lists kept getting longer and longer. The phones were very busy and anyone who had a scrap of new information – that is, those who were "in the know" would quickly pass it on. From time to time, Lonny would phone to let us know he was all right. Asi managed to get back after some ten days.

The gloom became deeper with the ever-growing announcements of the fallen, the temporary funerals customary in wartime, and the need to make *shivah* calls. Everyone had a relative or friend, a neighbor or acquaintance, who was serving. These were days of fear and anxiety. Sometimes, I was even afraid to answer the doorbell. Some women took up volunteer work, but I felt that my war effort was to be at home so that I could be in touch with everyone and keep the family going and up to date.

The war lasted three weeks in Jerusalem and the south, much longer in the north where a war of attrition continued for six months, but it took many months before life began to return to its normal routine.

For our family it wasn't too normal. From this period on, in fact, for more than a decade, from 1969 into the 1980s, we were busy with the army. The three older children successively did their service and sometimes overlapped. Asi, who started in February 1969 serving until February 1972, was in an elite unit. He had spent a couple of his high school years at the military academy in Haifa and was partially prepared for his new adventure. Lonny began his service on August 1971 till June 1974, also in Sayeret Matkal, and in 1977 he added a fourth year to his service as a team commander. He had some interesting experiences of which we knew little until long after the war. There was a lot less idle chatter in those days.

During the first Lebanese war, which broke out in June 1982, fifteen years to the day after the Six Day War, Lonny was called for reserve duty with his unit. A year later, in 1983, he volunteered for four months on a special assignment and was proud to receive an officer's commission for merit from the then Chief of Staff Moshe Levy. One thing led to another, and in 1985 he served for a year as a deputy commander of his unit. As I said before, we knew nothing about these developments because of the strict secrecy in which the army conducted itself in those days.

Asi returned to the army because of guilt feelings that he had not served in the Yom Kippur War and served two more years, from May 1974 till February 1976. Varda was called up in 1974, after having volunteered for a year in Kiryat Malachi in the framework of the Scout Movement. She and her group of friends were busy helping disadvantaged children of the Moroccan community there, and developing the Scout Movement. In 2008, Varda's younger son did a similar year in the bombarded southern town of Sderot, and was discovered by a daughter of the same family with whom Varda had worked in Kiryat Malachi. She is now married and settled in Sderot. This coincidence caused much excitement all round. Varda did a course in the army called Yediat ha-Aretz (literally, "Knowledge of the Land") and her army stint was in the educational field, taking soldiers on various tours of the country. She went on to study archaeology at The Hebrew University. She also took another course in Egyptology and became a guide for tours to Egypt, which lasted several years until tours were curtailed by the Egyptians.

With the children so involved in military matters and the volatile situation, I did not leave the country during the first decade of this whole period, in case something should happen while I was away.

During the first Lebanese War of 1982, Asi was called up for reserve duty. From time to time, he spent many months in Lebanon, where he had two narrow escapes from death in the course of one day.

Then came the Gulf War in 1991. Gas masks. Scud attacks. Alex went to hospital for a corneal transplant, which did not succeed, and suffered a light heart attack, which kept him in Hadassah Hospital longer than planned. It was weird having to carry the gas mask about everywhere and having to take shelter when an alert sounded. Artistic women decorated their gas-mask boxes in bright colors and set a fashion. The trips to and from Hadassah, especially in the early dark of winter days, were full of tension.

During this time, the idea of "sealed rooms" (*mamadim*) was conceived, and a great amount of wide wrapping tape (nicknamed "*seret Saddam*," or "Saddam ribbon") was sold for taping up windows. This helped to prevent glass shattering, and also sealed up cracks around windows and doors against the feared poison gas said to be threatening Israel. Jerusalem did not actually come under attack, but the sirens and radio broadcasts were heard, and all precautions were taken just in case.

It was winter and the nights were long; social life abated. There was the occasion when the siren went off during an Isaac Stern concert at the

Jerusalem Theater. The orchestra, the Israel Philharmonic, took time off to don their masks, as did the audience, and returned to play the full program. The scene was rather surrealistic, and gave public morale a great boost. I was not at this particular event, but such concerts were part of the effort to keep a semblance of normality and an expression of the artists' identification with Israel. Of course, it was very encouraging when top flight musicians such as Stern and Leonard Bernstein came to perform for the public and for the army in open-air sites. Guest artists who left immediately or cancelled their scheduled appearances were objects of scorn.

The Gulf War, which was a by-product of the American-Iraqi conflict, necessitated long periods of reserve duty for both boys, until 1996 for Asi and 1999 for Lonny, after which they were no longer called for active duty. Karni did her military service from 1982 to 1984, serving in an intelligence unit, but with no unusual happenings. After this, we had some respite until our grandsons began to come of military age.

The War of the Terrorists, the two Intifadas, went on concomitantly throughout these years, from one atrocity to another, from one bus explosion to another, from one plane hijacking to another. Smashing Israeli car windows was a popular pastime for young Palestinians.

The 1976 Entebbe rescue was the outstanding event of this period, but it was only a brief moment of joy set against the death of the leader, Yoni Netanyahu, an against the harrowing suicide bombings, especially the bus explosions. Children became terrified of traveling on the buses, and this started the need for parents to drive their children to and from their destinations. They became their children's chauffeurs, and the children took happily to the new arrangements, which eventually were difficult to shake off.

Reunion of NY Etzel supporters 1978 ▼ From left: Shoshana Raziel, Miriam Chaiken, Alex, Sam Dubiner, Eliahu Lankin (captain of the 'Altalena'), Nat Horwit.

Alex prepares Itamar's birthday 1992

Alex surprises granddaughters at entrance. From left: Tal, Inbar, Carmel

Death in the Family

MY FATHER DIED IN NOVEMBER 1979, ALONE IN THE HOSPITAL IN Gedera, angry and fearful, fighting to the last. An event I had dreaded for many years had finally happened. For the first time in my life, I was bereaved of a member of my innermost circle. My strong, active, temperamental, opinionated, emotional father, the man who had instilled in me the values by which I live my life, was no more. I had often clashed with him, but his influence on me, both positive and negative, had been decisive. I was truly the daughter of my father, but without his excitability, his "short fuse." I now had to face the fact of his death and deal with the minutiae that it involved.

Death had always been an enigma to me, a frightening one, as I imagine it is to everybody. All my life it had lurked in the shadow, never far away. As a child I had heard half-whispered stories of unnatural deaths: the small daughter of friends died of cancer after a black spot appeared on her forehead; the daughter of Mr. Miletski, the shoemaker, slipped on the stairs one night when going down to open the door and broke her neck; the youngest child of friends was killed when the lorry behind which he was playing backed up unawares; drowning and car accidents took their toll of acquaintances young and old. Moreover, the war years and anxiety over what was happening to our families in Europe served to intensify my own anxiety about death and violence.

How could people endure such physical suffering, how could the survivors survive the emotional anguish, how does one cope with the seeming nothingness of Death? My parents, strong believers that children didn't have to know everything, never prepared us for such eventualities and never involved me in the rites and rituals. I never actually attended a funeral until I was a young married woman. My own children, who grew up in the stark realities of Israeli life, can't understand such a background at all. In their teens, they were already losing friends who fell in battle and making their own *shivah* calls. But now my own father had died. Now I would no longer leave the synagogue when *Yizkor* was said.

Father's death was a severe shock to my mother because she hadn't realized how very ill he was, or perhaps she hadn't wanted to realize. He had become very difficult in the final weeks of illness, and when he was unable to eat with his usual good appetite, he became very critical of everything she prepared. A lot of food was thrown out. He was both angry and depressed by his growing weakness, and the fact that he couldn't even make the effort to go to *shul* meant that he was really very ill. The doctors we consulted dismissed his complaints of dizziness, weariness, and lack of appetite as problems of old age, for which there was no medical cure. "You must be philosophical about it," they said. "Keep busy, take up hobbies." Father was infuriated and deeply insulted. He hated not to be taken seriously; he hated to be called old even though he was nearing eighty-eight. "What difference does it make how old I am? I'm a *mensch* like everyone else; they should pay more attention!"

My father had always been an active and healthy man, and had made remarkable recoveries during a bad period some twelve or thirteen years earlier, when he suffered a heart attack and underwent a cancer operation. His looks still belied his age and he enjoyed being taken for a younger man. Up to the last few weeks he still had lots of energy. But now the day had come when I could see that he was truly seriously ill, and I persuaded him to go to the hospital for a thorough checkup. My fears were confirmed. His liver was affected and enlarged, but it was too late for anything to be done. The doctors gave him two to three months to live and sent him home, warning me that it would be advisable to get him into a nursing home within a few weeks.

I called my brother Alec in London and told him to come as soon as he could, even for the shortest of visits, and not to wait for the Hanukah trip he had already booked. My father's birthday was on the sixth Hanukah candle, and we always tried to arrange a family get-together on that day. In fact, we never knew the exact date of my father's birthday until we had to work it out for the tombstone. It was, and always had been celebrated, on the sixth light of Hanukah.

My brother arrived within the week, just as Father's condition was beginning to deteriorate more rapidly. We tried to smooth over the situation and act in our usual way, but Father recognized now that he was gravely ill. We later learned that on our very last visit when we took the children, he had dictated to my husband the epitaph he wanted inscribed on his tombstone. Within a few days, we were advised by the geriatric hospital that a bed had become available. Torn by emotional conflict and heartache, we managed to persuade my father that he would be better off there.

We were all depressed by the sight that met our eyes, which is when I think my mother realized the situation for the first time. The doctor, himself a good candidate for the geriatric ward, assured my brother that he could return to London the following morning and still see his father on his return for the scheduled Hanukah visit. He hustled us out, barely giving us time to say our goodbyes. We sat in one of the lobbies for a few minutes to overcome our agitation. Alec broke down and went out on the balcony to pull himself together. Mother shed some tears as she faced up to the reality, which was staring her right in the face. I simply felt sick.

I visited Father again the next day. He was weaker but still fully conscious and complaining that the nurses were not giving him proper food or medicine. He hated the place, and the terminal cases around him upset him even more. "*Nam mich aheim,*" he pleaded. "Take me home, I want to die at home, not here." I promised (I still spoke Yiddish with my parents) that I would speak to the doctor about it, but my anxiety for my mother and the desire to spare her this drawn-out agony prevailed. I had accepted the prognosis that Father still had a couple of months, and did not see any way of keeping him at home for such a long time. I did not have enough experience to see that the end was closer than that.

The next morning, Thursday, at 8:45, I received a call from the hospital. The doctor informed me curtly that my father had passed away, and hung up. I had to call again three times before I was able to find out what I had to do. Fortunately, my husband and older daughter were still at home and we made a plan of action. First, we had to find Lonny, our second son, who had already left for appointments in Tel Aviv. His sad task was to break the news to my mother, since I saw that I would not be able to get to her (in Tel Aviv) for two to three hours, and I was afraid she might be advised by the hospital. I had to phone my brother and find out when he would be able to come before I could fix the time of the funeral.

My brother was shocked at my news. It was seven in the morning in London; he could not do anything for a couple of hours. He had not even unpacked his bag since coming home the night before. My older son insisted on driving me to Gedera and Tel Aviv, as the weather was very stormy. The gray overcast sky, howling wind, and heavy rain were a fitting accompaniment to the events of the day. I felt they reflected perfectly the storm and anger of my father's last days, perhaps even of his life.

After the shock of the funeral and the busy-ness of the *shivah*, a period, incidentally, in which the children gathered around and were a great source of comfort and support, mother seemed to hold her own. She insisted on returning home to Tel Aviv and busied herself with her household. She was determined to be independent. I phoned her daily and visited her often, but after several weeks she began to complain. Her asthma had come back after a long absence, and she was constantly short of breath. The doctors were confusing and unhelpful, so I decided to bring her back to Jerusalem to stay with us.

I thought she had become depressed once the reality of being alone began to force itself on her, and I knew that I myself had experienced quite a "down" when the thirty-day mourning period was over and all the formal duties attended to. I hoped she would rebound to her usual, practical self and find some source of interest to sustain her. The doctors prescribed the same medicines again, assuring us that her condition was not dangerous and did not require hospitalization. We celebrated her eighty-fourth birthday with magnificent pink roses.

One day I got up early to find her in the throes of a severe asthma attack. She had been suffering for several hours, unable to call out for help. I immediately called the cardiac unit, and within fifteen minutes she was getting oxygen, injections, and all necessary treatment. The young people of the cardiac emergency unit were superb in their quiet efficiency. They stayed for over an hour and confirmed that hospitalization would not be helpful. Nothing more could be done.

Mother was utterly exhausted after this attack and stayed in bed most of the time. She fretted that she was a burden to me and insisted she would go home as soon as she felt better. I agreed laughingly, but secretly I was becoming anxious. She was very weak, and talked a great deal about her father and her childhood in Łódź, Poland. I dreaded the thought that she might be slipping into senility. On the other hand, she was alert and read the papers, and argued with me about my daughter living away from home. She had always had the curious habit of sleeping with her eyes partly open, yet every time I looked in to see how she was, my heart skipped a beat on observing this. I had to look quickly for the steady rise and fall of the blankets for reassurance.

Two days later, a Friday afternoon, she looked and felt much better, and decided she would dress for dinner, but she announced that she would not talk to my brother when he made his usual Friday night call from London because that was too much of an effort. We had a very pleasant dinner, in the kitchen as usual, the whole family at home except for Lonny, who had gone to Tel Aviv for the weekend. It was Tu bi-Shevat and we sang songs and gossiped. Mother ate with good appetite, which I regarded as a good sign. After dinner, she watched the news with Alex, and Varda and I began to clean up.

After ten or fifteen minutes mother suddenly returned to the kitchen and sat down, breathing very heavily. I asked her what was wrong, thinking perhaps that she'd eaten too much. She didn't answer and went into the bedroom. She sat on the bed, tugging at the neck of her sweater. I said I would call the doctor. She still didn't answer. Now I thought she was having another asthma attack and ran to the phone. The Magen David switchboard told me that both cardiac units were busy for some time and that they would send an ambulance without a doctor. I ran back to the bedroom and found mother lying across the bed, Varda sitting next to her.

"Sit up! Sit up!" I cried. "You can't breathe like that!" I pulled her up, but she just slipped through my hands to the floor – she was so heavy. Varda tried to help, but even together, we couldn't lift her, slight as she was, and I suddenly realized that she must be unconscious. We called Asi, who was in his room, getting ready to go out. He was able to lift Mother onto the bed, and began to check her pulse and eyes. Hearing the commotion, my husband came to see what was happening, and I went again to the phone to call our family doctor. I had realized that an ambulance without a doctor could be of no help. The doctor asked if someone could fetch him, as he was too tired to drive even the short distance to our home, and my husband went immediately.

There we stood in the bedroom, Karni's room, and looked down at Mother. There was no pulse, no reaction to light in her eyes. Then suddenly, she went completely limp, her jaw dropped, and a tiny bubble of blood appeared on her lips. I knew now that she was dead, but couldn't grasp the enormity of what had happened. Only five minutes before, she had been watching TV and arguing some point with Alex – and now, without a sound, without any of that terrifying death rattle or suffering one reads about or sees in films, she was gone.

I became aware of Karni, our fifteen-year-old daughter, standing in the corner watching. I wondered how long she had been there. The doctor came in with Alex, and the ambulance driver just behind. After a brief examination, the doctor confirmed what we already knew. My mother was dead. The driver said that he was very sorry, but he was not permitted to move dead people. Since it was the eve of Shabbat, we couldn't call the

Burial Society either. Mother would have to remain at home until the following evening.

The driver left. The telephone rang. Asi picked up the phone, and hearing my brother's voice, hung up because he didn't know how to break the news. I sat down near my mother and tried to take in the enormity of what had happened. My mother was dead, barely two months after my father. He had died at 8:45 on a Thursday morning, she at 8:45 on Friday evening. I, who had always been so afraid of death, had just seen my mother slip away from me, with a minimum of fuss and bother, in her own efficient and practical way, determined not to be a burden. I, who had never seen the face of Death, would spend the Shabbat knowing my mother lay lifeless on my daughter's bed.

They say that only *zaddikim*, the just and righteous ones, die on the eve of Shabbat. My mother was not a *zaddikah*, but perhaps after a long life of turmoil and struggle, after the eventful journey from a comfortable Hasidic home in Łódź to the inhospitable Palestine of the 1920s, thence to the distant and alien Australia; an unsuccessful return to Palestine in 1935–1936; back to Australia once again, and finally a more successful *aliyah* in 1954 – perhaps this *mavet bi-neshikah*, or "death by Divine kiss," was her reward. Perhaps this was her blessing for following her husband for more than sixty years in his constant struggle to fulfill his Zionist dream. Her reward, too, for her unflagging love of Israel through thick and thin. Not that she was a passive, compliant wife, but this, this strong love of Zion, my parents always had in common.

The doctor tapped me gently on the shoulder and asked me to help fill out the necessary forms. Alex called Lonny in Tel Aviv to break the news and then took the doctor home. I went to look at mother again, lying so still under the fresh white sheet, and then sat down at the kitchen table. Suddenly, I noticed that the candles she had blessed at the onset of Shabbat were still flickering. They still had life in them. Through sudden tears I realized this was a moment I would never forget. Death was in the house. A great void had suddenly opened in my life, and yet there was a strange, indefinable element of beauty in the events of the evening, in the hush that enveloped us all. Death did not have to be violent and ugly and painful. He could come quietly, kindly, as a friend, if one were fortunate. Why hadn't my father been equally blessed to die at home peacefully, amongst those whom he loved and who loved him?

I went to the phone and with a heavy heart called London. "We've been trying to reach you all evening," said my sister-in-law. "The line has been terrible. How're things?" "I'm afraid I have bad news," I said. "Mummy died suddenly, just an hour ago. Will Alec be able to come again?"

Ze'ev and Fruma Shapiro, my parents, at the Kotel, 1967.

To My Father Alex, on His 70th Birthday

By Lonny Rafaeli
July 1, 1980

As a glass of water cannot sum up an ocean, so I am
    not summing up a life,
merely expressing some memories, some nostalgia.

Some seventy years ago, in the month of Sivan (July 1, 1910),
In a little town, Drissa, close to Dvinsk,
My father was born, in a good hour, under a lucky star.
I had searched for him for many years . . .
So he could play Cops and Robbers, or Indians, in Latvian . . .
And read Pushkin and Tolstoy in the original Russian . . .
And interrogate Nazis in Germany in German . . .
And curse roundly in English as an American GI . . .
Order in French in fancy restaurants . . .
And tell spicy jokes in Yiddish . . .
And in Hebrew, to work and build factories in Israel.

I had dreamt of a father with an adventurous spirit –
But not so many and of such variety;
As a child he was brought during the Revolution to Riga, the capital;

Hence the school years during war and revolution.
His mother a socialist and father a capitalist,
They compromised on the Hebrew High School.

Filled with boundless energy, he sought outlets after school,
Always in training and developing his form –
For his legs are not long, and he's not very tall –
He ran the 400 and 800 with might and main,
As if the pride of the nation depended on it.
Days and nights he spent with his friends in the Movement, for don't
     forget that Betar was founded in Riga.
So in sport and Betar he went from strength to strength –
And fell asleep over his books almost every night;
Even so, in his twentieth year he was already far from home in
     Heidelberg,
Where he studied and ran and lived the good life with spirited friends.
But the rise of the Nazis was already in progress,
And at the age of twenty-four, Ph.D. in hand,
He sought his fortunes in a new land.

By ship to Palestine, the Motherland.
With Professor Ruppin on Mt. Scopus, and against the attackers
In the Shapiro Quarter,
As a night watchman, research assistant, journalist or insurance agent,
He became deeply involved with the beloved land.
Then he joined the Underground and served many arduous years with
     faith and enthusiasm.
By the end of the Thirties, filled with ominous forebodings,
He is crisscrossing Europe, buying arms and sounding the warning
Of the approaching cataclysm.
Soon the forewarnings turned into terrifying facts,
And body and soul rose up in protest.

Undeterred by his age, by now thirty-two,
My father joined the American army;
In spite of diplomas, experience and years,
He enrolled as a private,
Stubborn as a mule, he succeeded in adjusting,
And landing on the shores of Europe,
He knew he would fulfill his pledge.
From town to town he progressed and took note
Till the cup of hatred overflowed.
He fought his battles and took his revenge
For the fate of his brother, his parents and friends.

The war finally ended and the embers still smoldered,
Yet the gallant band renewed the battle to establish the Jewish State.
The dream comes true. So passed the years . . .
And the overcoming of grief and relentless work became
A sign and symbol that would stand for generations.

Now nearing forty, and having left a trail
Of broken hearts in various lands, during
Exciting days and mysterious nights –
Finally, the war fox realized he must resume responsibilities, this time to
    himself.
With typical thoroughness, he undertook to learn about business.
Two whole years he worked tirelessly,
Constantly raising his sights further and further.
The land of milk and honey, for which they had fought,
Waited far away for promoters, for newcomers, for fresh blood.
The first steps did not put him off. On the contrary,
Industry was brought to the land and began to flourish.

But, ladies and gentlemen, time off for a pause,
For finally, we find father in the society for broken hearts.

One day, he saw my mother in the office of WIZO.
He lost his heart – and so ended his hesitations and deliberations.
He was trapped in a net that hadn't even been spread.
And the rabbi blessed them – and since,
Thirty years have passed in bliss.
The new generation began to appear,
Four of us, one after the other.
Thus, my story comes to an end, with the hope
That tomorrow or the day after, on the heels of this celebration,
The impulse will come and with pencil in hand
Abba will unburden his heart and his memory,
And many wonderful tales will come forth which will
Remain forever inscribed in history.[1]
Although this is a story two thousand years old,
Which begins in the Diaspora and ends in Jerusalem,
He is the one and only, he is my dad.
As my friends say, we wish we had one like him.

Asi and Lonny in army, 1972–02

---

1 Alex's book, *Dream and Action*, was published in 1993 and also translated into Hebrew.

Forty Years On

> "Forty years on when afar and asunder
> Parted are those who are singing today;
> When you look back and regretfully wonder
> What you were like in your work and your play."

IT WASN'T EXACTLY FORTY YEARS ON FOR EVERYONE WHO ATTEN-
ded the UHS (University High School, Melbourne) reunion on May 5,
1980, but it was about the average between the older "old boys" and the
younger "old boys," not forgetting of course the "old girls." The call had gone
out for the first official reunion of this kind in Israel, although many of
those involved meet quite often in the regular course of their lives, being
friends from way back.

BRING WHATEVER SOUVENIRS YOU MAY HAVE! was the order
of the day.

And so we all converged on the Meerkin home in Beit Meir, an agricultural village on the outskirts of Jerusalem. Signs directed us along the way,
as if we were really going to our old school – Storey Street, Royal Parade,
Parkville, Kangaroos. Newspaper cuttings carrying football and cricket
results. Someone wore her old hat ribbon with the green and tan colors.
Many brought copies of the school magazine, *The Record*; old photos, old
Speech Night programs, but, oddly enough, no school ties. Memories and
associations long undisturbed suddenly sprang to life.

It is extraordinary how such gatherings have a dynamic of their own. Do you remember . . . the school assemblies, the sports days, the teachers? The time Miss Horton's panties fell down in the middle of the class? The school socials where mixed dancing was allowed, and the tuck shop where mixed queues were not allowed?

We studied the photos to see whom we could recognize, to see how we looked then, to check who was present this evening. We tried to imagine our Israeli sons wearing the funny little school cap, and wondered if it was still in use. Someone recalled that he had actually worn a straw boater as part of the summer uniform – class of '38.

The years fell away as each contributed his particular memories of "Weary" Wannon, the history master, of "Potty" Noalls, the drawing teacher, of the young biology teacher, Miss Crofts, on whom all the senior boys had a crush, and all wanted to hear her talk about the reproductive system.

But above all, we recalled that most beloved principle, Stanton Sharman, who led the school for twenty-six years and who could have served as the model for Mr. Chips. We were heartbroken when he retired, and felt sorry for Mr. Brookes, who was taking his place – an impossible task. The girls recalled the headmistresses they had known – tall, thin Miss Gainsford, who wore long pointy shoes when they were not in fashion, and tiny Miss Schmeltzer, who would not allow "powder, paint, puffs, or perms," and taught us that "manners maketh man."

And the songs! Where had the words lain hidden all these forty years? School songs and sports songs, the school anthem, came surging forth as one person or another remembered a verse here, a chorus there. It was exciting and moving to hear it all again. The deep sentiments had educated generations to loyalty, sportsmanship, and comradeship. "What clichés," someone remarked, but isn't that the trouble with clichés – that their sentiments are true and valid? Certainly, they had inspired all of us with a deep loyalty to the old school, with an appreciation of the good memories and pleasant and unpleasant times we had known there.

Surely our children have missed something in the casual, informal style of today's education. No ceremonies, no school traditions, no beautiful Speech Nights (graduation) to remember. When the "old boys" in the audience used to stand up together with the pupils, to end the evening singing "The Best School of All," there was hardly a dry eye in the stately Town Hall. Is it the same today? Was the school different, better, more colorful, more satisfying in those days, or is it our distance from it that lends the enchantment?

Whatever the answer, we enjoyed our get-together and regretted the absence of those who were unable to attend. We enjoyed reviving our youth for a few brief hours and wondered how the present school, currently celebrating its seventieth anniversary, would like the idea of our school songs being sung with great gusto in a little agricultural village on the outskirts of Jerusalem, Israel.

> "It's good to see the school we knew,
> We keep her honor yet."

Reply to my article from UHS

The University High School,
Story Street,
Parkville 3072
1.7.80

Dear Mrs. Rafaeli,

So many people have been interested in your letter of May 12. I salute you and your co-signatories, and assure you that the old school is continuing to flourish.

I had intended to wait until the Minister of Education's return from overseas, before replying. Any day now he is expected to change the status of the school. There has been a period of conflict. I guess it really is a choice for him between declaring the school a district high school (with a zone) and encouraging mediocrity in education or declaring us "special" with examination entry (no zone) and fostering academic excellence.

To you the choice will seem obvious; here, politics has clouded the issue. It is true, as you say, that there is a "casual informal style" to today's education. However, there remains, within these buildings, enough of the past to affect us. Tradition is strong.

Next week, the class of '55 meets to celebrate. It goes on. You will be interested to hear that UHS has been chosen to educate 30 pupils from 1981 (and thereafter, 30 each year) in an experimental program for "gifted children" chosen, by tests, from the whole of Australia. The aim is to sandwich six years of secondary education into four years. Universities will accept these students at the ripe old age of 15!

Do write again after subsequent re-unions. The present generation is intrigued by the reference to Miss Horton's panties. No mention occurs in "The City Built to Music." For obvious reasons.

Sincerely,
Jack S. Clark
(Principal)

Varda in the kitchen

Esther and Alex, 1989.

Map of Our Journey

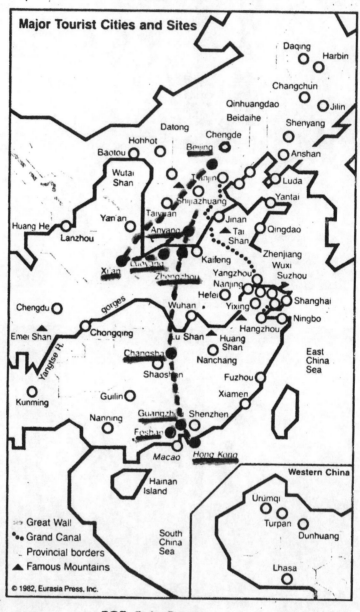

Major Tourist Cities and Sites

Daqing
Harbin
Changchun
Qinhuangdao   Jilin
Beidaihe   Shenyang
Datong   Chengde   Anshan
Hohhot   Beijing
Baotou   Luda
Wutai   Tianjin
Shan   Yantai
Shijiazhuang
Yan'an   Taiyuan   Jinan   Qingdao
Anyang   Tai   Zhenjiang
Huang He   Shan   Wuxi
Lanzhou   Kaifeng   Suzhou
Xi'an   Luoyang   Yangzhou
Zhengzhou   Nanjing   Shanghai
Hefei   Yixing
Chengdu   Wuhan   Ningbo
gorges   Hangzhou
Emei Shan   Chongqing   Lu Shan   Huang
Shan   East
Changsha   Nanchang   China
Shaoshan   Sea
Fuzhou
Kunming   Guilin   Xiamen
Nanning   Guangzhou   Shenzhen
Foshan
Macao   Hong Kong

Hainan
Island   **Western China**

Urumqi
Turpan   Dunhuang
South
China
Sea

Lhasa

»» **Great Wall**
•• **Grand Canal**
- **Provincial borders**
▲ **Famous Mountains**

© 1982, Eurasia Press, Inc.

■■■ **Trip Route**

Our Trip to China

Introduction

EARLY IN 1982, MY EYE CAUGHT A SMALL ADVERTISEMENT IN THE *Jerusalem Post*, announcing organized group tours to China from London. The idea quickly fired the imagination of my husband and me, but we couldn't carry our plans through that summer.

Later in the year, we heard that the same agents were organizing a tour out of Israel for the summer of 1983, and we quickly signed on. This group came to be known as the Museum Group, since the initiative had come from Rivka Bitterman, Curator for Far Eastern Art at the Israel Museum. In fact, fewer than half of the twenty-six people were connected with the museum, being volunteers and docents, as I was, and the others came in answer to publicity. The only prerequisite was a foreign passport, since there were no diplomatic relations between Israel and China at that time.

The company included three doctors – an eye surgeon, an orthopedic surgeon and a GP – a fact which made us feel better about possible health problems. The tour leaders from London were Laura and Cecil Kline.

The character of our group naturally influenced our choice of itinerary – it was to be an Art and Archaeology tour. In the three weeks we covered a great deal of territory, and while the emphasis was on museums and excavations, we of course saw the major places of interest in the towns we visited.

In the months before our trip, we met several times for background lectures on Chinese culture and history. Many of our group were very knowledgeable, having studied the subject at university level, or were seasoned travelers and art collectors. There was also much anxiety and trepidation about the unknown aspects of our great adventure, arising from the terrible stories we had heard about standards of hygiene and accommodation. There were moments when we almost gave up the idea, but thank goodness we didn't, because most of our fears were not substantiated.

Since we were a Jewish group from Jerusalem, we asked for a visit to Kai-Feng. A Chinese Jewish community had flourished in this town for well over one thousand years, unknown to the outside world until the seventeenth century. The original settlers, traders from Persia, maintained their customs and religion, but gradual assimilation into Chinese life eventually took its toll, and by the nineteenth century the community had virtually ceased to exist. Our enquiries assured us that nothing Jewish remained now, not even the memorial stelae, which stood in the grounds of the synagogue, so we cancelled that visit, although Kai-Feng was quite close to Zhen Zhou, one of our major stops. The story of the Russian Jews, who settled in Manchuria at the beginning of the twentieth century, is a separate short chapter, lasting only forty to fifty years.

We saw a great deal during our visit, but China is so vast, there is still so much to see, that we would happily return for further exploration.

PART I

Monday, May 30, 1983

Here I am, spending my fifty-something birthday in Hong Kong, on our way to our adventurous first trip to China. We arrived here exactly twenty-four hours after leaving home on Sunday, the 29th, at 3:15 a.m., feeling somewhat worse for wear. The trip with Lufthansa was actually twenty-one hours flying time, as we had to fly from Tel Aviv to Munich and Frankfurt, and then back over the Middle East via Karachi, so it became rather tedious. Really felt like kissing the earth when we got out of the plane, but bad luck for Pauline Lockman – her suitcase, and that of Mrs. Slopak, didn't arrive! So much for German efficiency!

We walked out a little in the afternoon and were happy that we recognized some landmarks from our last trip about six years ago. Had quite forgotten how crowded and noisy and "markety" Hong Kong is. In the evening we had a birthday dinner, together with our friend Zipora Kessel, at the Jade Garden Restaurant, which was most enjoyable after the endless air flight meals. Sylvia and Harry Feller, fellow travelers from Jerusalem whom I only knew by sight, were also dining there. We ate fresh lychee nuts to celebrate.

I must have a good night's sleep. It is now 10:30 p.m. and tomorrow we are off by train to Canton, or rather Guangzhou, and Red China. I have decided to keep a diary of this trip, because I think it's going to be something quite different. In any case, we are all excited, and facing the fact that our planning is now becoming a reality, we are actually on our way.

Tuesday, May 31

First night in Canton (Guangzhou), yet it seems we've been here longer than a few hours. We left our Hong Kong hotel, the Holiday Inn, just before noon for the Kowloon Station, passing very imposing modern structures.

Several hundred others, mostly Chinese, were heading in the same direction, and the queues were very long. Those returning to the People's Republic were easily recognized by the packages and electric appliances they were carrying: ventilators, radios, tape recorders and more. Rivka claimed she could recognize them by their lean and hungry look!

Soon our leaders shepherded us quite quickly through passport control and down to our train. There must have been ten to twelve coaches, and first thing we noticed were the lace curtains at the windows! The restaurant car looked very inviting, with white tablecloths, miniature bonsai trees in pots on each table, and waitresses in white cotton jackets, dark trousers and caps. In fact, all the railway attendants wore white shirts, with a red star over the pockets and on their berets.

The train proved to be very comfortable with two armchair-style seats on each side of the aisle and plenty of leg room. They were covered with white slipcovers and lace antimacassars, and were fixed on swivels so that they could be turned in all directions, but everyone chose to sit facing the same direction.

The train rode very smoothly and soon we were passing through the Territories with its enormous housing blocks, well decorated with laundry, and land reclamation projects. The color TV over the door kept us entertained with music, advertisements and much talk on unidentified subjects.

We had looked forward with great expectation to the actual crossing of the border, yet we hardly noticed when we did so. There was a rather long stop, but no customs or passport inspection, just a large sign, if you caught it, announcing the People's Republic of China, and a red flag. The sun was shining, though the sky was rather cloudy, and the countryside was very, very green and well cultivated, mostly with rice and vegetables. Here and there were some brickyards, producing red or gray-brown bricks, and other unidentified factories. In the distance there were rounded hills. Alongside the railway tracks were dirt paths for pedestrians and cyclists and we saw many water reservoirs, all a muddy yellow color, as was the Pearl River when we later crossed it. In three hours we saw only two mechanized farm vehicles, and some bicycles.

There were many ugly buffalo wandering along, plenty of ducks, and surprisingly few people. The villages we passed were dilapidated and haphazard, of red brick, and usually built in a compound surrounded by a wall, or in rows of six to eight tiny rooms. I had the immediate impression of poverty and neglect.

This impression was strongly reinforced in Canton, where even the handsomest buildings were unpainted, dirty and neglected. The older sections were even worse; tiny shops and dwelling places, laundry hanging out everywhere, but on the other hand, every balcony was covered with greenery. There were hordes of cycles on the roads. Our hotel has sixteen storeys, but is shabby and simple; although built in 1979, it is still unfinished. We have private bathrooms with very hot water, as well as air conditioning and color TV.

The Canton restaurant, where we went for dinner, seemed capable of serving several hundred dinners at once, at various price levels. We were met by an explosive burst of firecrackers; it seems they were not in our honor, but for a bridal party, which we unfortunately couldn't see. Our vegetarian diet was a bit disappointing, especially after Hong Kong, but everything was tasty. Each dish was served separately, and there were at least three variations of mushrooms. Most interesting were fried hard-boiled eggs in sweet and sour sauce, and fresh pineapple. Not even the tea was served in traditional dishes, but I did manage the whole meal with chopsticks, to my own surprise. There seems to be a shortage of vegetables, since mushrooms, young broccoli and bamboo shoots were all we had.

After dinner we visited the Culture Park, but there were not more than a couple of hundred people watching the entertainment groups and folk dancing. We saw an "aquarium" with dead fish in formaldehyde; a photography exhibition, with romantic portraits and nature; scenes and travel shots, which were good but quite conventional. There were also amusement mirrors, a movie, and book stalls with an impressive array of children's books, very attractively illustrated. The event was in honor of Children's Day. but there were not many children. It was a rather dreary evening.

Back at the hotel, we found two channels on TV, one showing a traditional Chinese opera in colorful costumes, and the other an art show about jade carving and pottery.

Wednesday, June 1

A long day, starting with breakfast at seven and leaving at eight for Foshan, a town about an hour away, where we visited the Shiwan Pottery Factory, and I finally bought a Tang horse! Then the Taoist temple set in fine gardens but mainly an historical sight now. There was an interesting museum as well, but all the archaeological explanations were in Chinese. We also saw paper cut-out and lantern-making workshops.

On the way back we had a good lunch. Almost half of the group is eating vegetarian, for a variety of reasons, and although this is supposed to be a great gastronomic town, they have little imagination in this respect. We finished up visiting the imposing Sun Yat Sen Memorial. This is a large building with a pagoda-style roof, which contains a hall capable of seating five thousand people. No supports are visible inside the hall. The memorial is set in a large park, and a statue of Dr. Sun Yat Sen stands in front. It was an inviting spot for photographs.

A long day, literally crammed with new and disturbing impressions and questionings. In the morning the roads were already crowded with bicycle riders, going to work or school. No private cars, and the trucks and pickups we saw all belong to government factories or co-operatives. Nevertheless, the traffic was heavy, especially into town. Cyclists also use bikes for business and portering. We saw many ingenious varieties of baskets for transporting vegetables, pigs and birds, and only one motorcycle during the whole day, carrying two adults with a child sandwiched between them. The speed limit is thirty kilometres per hour!

There was terrible humidity, which got worse during the day. Again we were appalled by the tenements and seemingly terrible poverty, though we drove through a finer part of town and saw some new buildings, including a special hotel for overseas Chinese, and the World Trade Fair Centre. In fact, one can see that Canton was once a handsome town with well laid out, wide avenues, plenty of trees, large parks and handsome old buildings. This was especially noted on Shamian Island, which used to be the international concession of the foreign powers during the nineteenth and twentieth centuries.

Everything is so run-down and dilapidated, the pavements broken. Glimpses into the little side alleys showed appalling conditions. Shocking to see young women working on the roads and in construction, yet they are probably happy to have the work, since we were told there is much unemployment. On the other hand, most building sites seem deserted, and there were few people in the bright green rice fields. Lots of people were just sitting about or squatting.

For one moment I had the feeling that I was in Egypt again, which we visited two years earlier, but a greener, more fertile version. The dirt roads, the noise and constant horn-blowing, the crowds were strangely familiar. Yet interestingly, I noted in the raggedy crowds many young people and children who were very well dressed – the women in pretty dresses, stockings and shoes, girls and boys in school uniforms, little ones in bright dresses and gay hair ribbons.

Several groups of children were out celebrating Children's Day. And always the men's white shirts, very white, and the large white sunhat worn by men and women alike. Grannies were much in evidence, usually wearing the old style Mao clothes, and they seem to be kept busy caring for the little ones, even though since 1980 only one child is allowed per family. There is much carrying of young and even older babies, because there seem to be no baby carriages.

It was sad to see people on the pavement trying to sell a few wares, plastic dishes, a handful of greens or glasses of cold tea. Roadside cafés and kiosks are springing up in response to the government's permission to start private business as a means to overcoming unemployment. The kiosks didn't look too inviting to us, but were well patronized. We also saw many street markets.

At the factories we visited, people sat and ate at their place of work, and people walked about the street with their rice bowls in hand.

I couldn't help wondering what tales some of the older people could tell of the violent events they have witnessed or experienced during their lifetime, especially in recent years. Yet again, perhaps they are better off today than in days when "dogs and Chinese" were not allowed to enter into the international zones, or during the feudal times. "Everything is for the ordinary people today," the guide told us. "The grand old houses and the tennis courts are all for the ordinary people."

He also told us that the cost of a bike was equal to three months' salary, about ninety dollars. He himself had recently married and was allotted living quarters of thirty-two square metres by his work unit. This contains three rooms, and the rent is negligible. He also explained how each town is divided into seven districts, and each one has a different day off. There is no official day of rest.

We would be very curious to hear what they think about their living conditions.

Tonight, TV showed *Heidi of the Alps* with Chinese subtitles, children's fashions, sports, youth bands and other activities in honor of Children's Day. Afterwards, an American medical film demonstrating a cataract operation followed.

Thursday, June 2

We traveled by train to Changsha, a trip which took some fifteen hours! We had sleepers, four to a cabin, but it was not as comfortable as the express from Hong Kong and certainly not air-conditioned; but there were electric fans, and we got accustomed to the thermos of hot water, the covered teacups, and Chinese tea (leaves, not bags). Towards six o'clock p.m. it got cooler, but when we got in at three o'clock a.m., it was like a steam bath. The temperature was thirty-five degrees centigrade.

The countryside is very green and well-cultivated, becoming hillier, and quite mountainous in the background. The villages look quite prosperous, but we saw people coming to the wells with large buckets on shoulder poles to take water.

We were near the restaurant car, so there was much traffic in the corridor! In addition to our own group, there were lots of Chinese with their food bowls going back and forth. We crossed a large body of water, but I don't know whether it was a lake or a river.

In the morning we had visited a boarding kindergarten in the suburbs of Canton. There are about a hundred such places in Canton and about six thousand regular kindergartens. These were obviously "special" kids, well-dressed, well-fed, and they treated us to a lovely concert, with singing and dancing. "Jingle Bells" was part of the repertoire. They had a variety of flower and animal costumes.

Other classes were doing exercises, and still another group was swimming and splashing in the pool. There was plenty of equipment and space to play. There were about one hundred and sixty children, and they sleep over from Monday to Saturday in the upstairs dormitory full of little beds. The cost is ten yuan (five dollars) for half a year, plus twenty yuan for food. We wondered how many other children had five meals a day! These are mostly children of cadres (top officials), whose parents work or are out of town, children of academics and also some neighborhood children. We saw two white children of American families serving here. This is obviously a "show-piece," but they say it has existed since 1956, and the present headmistress has been here for eighteen years.

Then we drove up the mountain to the Canton Museum, an interesting old building, but it was closed. We drove on to Orchid Park, which was beautiful. The orchids were not in bloom but we were served cups of tea. We had a good lunch at the Bai Yun Restaurant, which had beautiful blue and white patterned glass screens and windows, and then it was back to the train.

Friday, June 3

What a pleasure to arrive in Changsha in Hunan Province. The light at the end of the long tunnel of night travel. Canton looked like Dante's Inferno in comparison. First of all, it is less humid and we were not perspiring all the time. The town was smaller and much cleaner, and although the living conditions are still crowded, there are no tenements. It is an educational centre rather than an industrial town, and it was here that Mao Zedong (Tse-tung) studied and began his political activities.

Blooming magnolia trees lined the wide avenues. After the hot and crowded night on the train, a ride that took sixteen hours and could have taken only eight by express, it was a pleasure to arrive at the state-owned Ruon Yuang Guest House, which is set in a beautiful estate. An ornamental lake containing carp and decorated with large pottery animals, fronted the main entrance. We entered a beautiful hall with an inside pool, rockery and a circular staircase, which led to comfortable rooms with en suite bathrooms. There were the usual thermos of hot water and covered teacups. We were privileged to be here since it is used mainly for VIP government guests, and we are absolutely delighted. Our anxieties about the accommodations had been alleviated.

Friday morning, June 3

We visited the hospital, founded as a pilot project by Yale University and said to be the best in the area. There was a special emphasis on acupuncture and some of the group even tried the treatment. It's primarily a teaching hospital, but as the doctors themselves admitted, still primitive and backward. The doctors traveling in our group were quite astonished at the conditions: eight hundred beds, and they treat twenty-five hundred outpatients daily. The three-story building had no elevators. There were many women doctors, all of whom wore white caps and coats.

Our guide told us that there is a need for a change with regard to salaries. Young doctors earn about fifty yuan (twenty-five dollars) a month, while senior physicians and professors can earn from one hundred and fifty to three hundred. The young doctors are going to get a raise but all has yet to be done slowly and carefully, so as not to upset the wage scale. In view of the doctors' strike when we left Israel, these remarks were very apropos and provoked some laughter, much to the guide's puzzlement.

We then visited an embroidery factory, where all the girls were doing traditional work and following traditional patterns. I wondered if there's any modern art and how it looks. People crowded around us at the bus stop, as they did at the hospital, and eyed us curiously. They looked a rather different type from Cantonese, more provincial, slightly Mongolian. It was difficult for us to gauge what they were thinking, but they were friendly. Apparently, they didn't get many tourists here. We were also stopped by students who wanted to practice English.

Our new guide, Mr. Wan, was much better than the previous one. He was a licensed guide, pleasant, informative and knew how to manage a crowd, although he was still quite young and couldn't have had that much experience. His black hair stood straight up, a style I have noticed on many men. I couldn't clarify if it's an ethnic feature or simply a matter of cut.

In the afternoon we visited the museum at Mawangdui, which houses artifacts and a female corpse from the Han Dynasty tombs dating back some two thousand years. The method of burial was similar to that which we had seen in Egypt, three coffins inside each other and the tomb dug into the mountainside. This was well reproduced in the annex nearby. It was amazing how well the body of the woman, still wearing her black wig, was preserved. The colors of the silk paintings and the lacquerware, the musical instruments, the variety of dishes, etc, were fascinating. Old silk books in scripts, which can be read today, were also part of the exhibit. It was really an extraordinary sensation to see the woman, and also her innards, on display! This also reminded us of the Cairo Museum. Pity they have no English explanatory material. The guide was a young woman, with a most pleasant, melodious voice, but she couldn't speak English and Mr. Wan translated.

Unexpected shopping in the museum shop which had some good reproductions of the exhibits, and also scroll paintings. There was also an official antique shop on the grounds, but I couldn't decide on anything, neither jade, porcelain or opium pipe, because of the pressure of time.

Friday evening, June 3

Since we had a semi-private dining room, we were able to have Kiddush with wine and *matzot* provided by observant members of the group, and after dinner we sang *zemirot* – perhaps the first time such observances were conducted in this city? We couldn't help feeling it was an occasion.

Later in our visit, we saw that the dining room next to ours was beautifully furnished in the Chinese style with dark bamboo furniture and lanterns. It must be for Chinese guests only.

There were many large houses on the estate, but most were empty. The guest house had been recently built and was really delightful; we could happily have spent more time here!

Saturday, June 4

Part of the group went to the porcelain factory and free market, and the Shabbat observers went for a walk. I joined them, thinking that a short walk would be very pleasant, but in fact we walked more than an hour and a half, and reached the Martyrs' Memorial, a museum of revolutionary history. This building, also set in a beautiful park, seemed to be similar in nature to Yad Vashem, our memorial to the victims of the Holocaust. The various rooms contained documents and photos of important people and high officers who had been involved in revolutionary activities, while many books contained the names of those who had been killed in the various uprisings. Large paper floral wreaths stood in the main hall.

During the walk we passed a school and saw kids doing their PT (physical training). There was one very white albino boy in the distance. The children and teachers were as intrigued by us as we by them, and it was impossible not to take pictures of them. One family insisted that their little boy shake hands. Others stared and gawked and all were happy to be photographed.

We were intrigued by the babies and little children wearing split pants, so that their little bottoms are exposed. Efficiency model! And economical! They can sit down anywhere and do their business with minimum fuss, and also save on laundry.

In the afternoon we made an official visit to a primary school. Not everyone in the group was enthusiastic about spending three hours at a school, but it was really interesting and enjoyable. We had our usual "briefing" from the principal (they love that word) then walked around classrooms and saw extracurricular activities. Paper cutting, clay modeling, games, and drawing, which was mostly copying from a book, but there were also two gifted boys in the class practicing calligraphy with brush and ink. But again

I felt that there was no creativity or self-expression; everything was copying and repetition. A group of gymnasts also gave us a little performance. Five girls and five boys about seven to nine years old, in leotards, performed on the beam and horse. They were very good and obviously being nurtured for higher things.

There were only about five hundred children in the school, and forty-nine teachers. Perhaps, it was a special school, since so many wore red scarves and were members of the Young Pioneers, which is a political youth movement open to all. The atmosphere was pleasant and all the children were well dressed. When the bell rang for recess, they rushed out into the yard, and quickly got organized into play groups, and made quite a noise. Many played ping-pong, or enjoyed singing and dancing games, or skipped rope. The boys and girls played happily together.

In the older school we were given a special reception, which was a bit embarrassing. The children were assembled in the yard and when we appeared, they divided into two groups and clapped rhythmically as we walked through to the entrance of the building. We were received in the visitors' room and a girl and a boy pupil served tea, very courteously and very pleasantly. They were about eleven or twelve years old. This was followed by a short performance of song and dance, including "Hello everybody, how are you?" and "Do re mi" from *The Sound of Music*. The children were very poised and pretty and performed like real little troupers, to a groaning old gramophone, in a space of about two by three metres – a real delight and unexpected aspect of Chinese life and education.

Walking through the streets later, we caught glimpses into "houses" of the old style. How can people live like that and retain their poise and good humor? Often the door opens directly into the bedroom, where the bed is the main piece of furniture, together with some small wooden chairs. Perhaps there is another room beyond. Everything looks dirty and grimy. We saw a little old lady with tiny feet, walking along with great difficulty; others were sitting in the street reading or just looking at us. At one tiny place, a dressmaker was sewing for a waiting client, and she also had a second machine in the corner.

It was rather touching to see little library nooks in the streets, where people borrowed books, mostly paperbacks, and sat and read, oblivious to what was going on around them. This scene repeated itself quite often during our trip.

We stopped at the market stalls to look for a skirt for Pauline, whose suitcase had not yet arrived. What a commotion. Everyone crowded around and when Dita took out a fifty-yuan note, what an exclamation! It was probably a month's earnings for most of them. But the skirt was not in good condition and we didn't buy it. Poor stall owner! She must have been disappointed, but we found something at our next stop and got a plastic bag into the bargain. White shirts seem to be the most popular attire for men.

The hat-maker also had good day, because we all decided to buy the Mao cap with the red star. I bet he prays for tourists every day. In that little shop we met a deaf man who introduced himself with notes written in English. Nearby was a funeral parlor where a wake was being prepared, mostly by letting off strings of firecrackers. There were large paper wreaths similar to those we had seen at the Martyrs' Memorial. Three hours later, when we left the opera, a large crowd was still there and the guide told us they were probably well-off people who could provide much food. "Such ceremonies used to be held at home but that is no longer possible due to shortage of space. Cremation is now the order of the day and often Buddhist priests are called into say the prayers. The government doesn't like these old customs," said the guide, lowering his voice, and adding, "but can't do anything about it."

We were a little late arriving at the opera and created quite a sensation as the word went around and everyone craned and strained to see us. The theater was full, and the audience consisted of young and old, not especially dressed for the occasion. I was surprised how the actors were able to maintain their equilibrium during the unexpected hubbub. The costumes were very colorful, but after an hour of traditional Chinese music and slow action, most of us felt we had had enough. It was not quite opera in the European tradition.

Sunday, June 5

We had a short morning visit to the Lovely Dusk Pavilion near the Lushan Temple in the mountainous forest area. At 9:15 a.m., there were already hundreds of families on outings, but after having seen the living conditions we could easily understand this. We rushed madly up the stone steps to the top to see at least the outside of the pavilion, and managed to get back to the bus on time. The guide quoted a lovely poem, written by the eminent poet Du Fu, who lived in the eighth century during the Tang dynasty, and in whose memory this and many other pavilions were later erected.

A TOUR TO A HILL

A stony path winds up to cool mountains
Towards cottages hid deeply among white clouds;
Loving maple woods at dusk.
I stop my cart to sit and watch the frosty leaves
Rather than February flowers.

Mr. Wan talked quite a lot about Comrade Mao because of his connection with the town, and when someone ventured to ask him about the Cultural Revolution, he replied, "We are not quite clear about what happened. Perhaps we should let the next generation talk about it. We do not know that criticism was overdone, and that the intellectuals suffered the most." The other targets of attack were mainly the landlords and landowners.

The morning traffic was interesting and we saw that many men still work as beasts of burden, pulling very heavy loads with the help of a yoke on their backs. Even girls could be seen occasionally at this work.

We went on to Orange Island, so-called because of the orange groves situated there, and saw "perfume carts" for the first time. This is the euphemistic name for containers of "night soil," the human excrement that is collected for use as fertilizer. Nothing is wasted in China.

We were sorry to take leave of our guides in Changsha. Mr. Wan was a delightful young man, very bright and personable. Miss Zhou was also very capable and anxious to please, and keen to practice her English. There was a long train journey ahead. We had a couchette for four and it was clean and comfortable, with the inevitable covered tea cups and thermos of hot water.

Now we were on the train to Zhen Zhou. Another twelve-hour trip, but we're really getting to see the countryside. It's all very green, very lush rice fields, some of which were already being planted for the second harvest. We passed many villages (or communes?) which looked well ordered and slightly more roomy, but still with dirt paths. Not many people were seen in fields. Many thatched roofs, and red-brick buildings were most prevalent. There was quite a lot of building going on.

One doesn't get as strong an impression of the aesthetic in China as in Japan, yet even in the poorest tenements, there are plants in the windows and balconies and often a platform arrangement extends out of a window to hold plants, as well as the laundry hung on hangers. At factories we visited, we also saw the use of ornamental lakes and attractive arrangements of flowering pot plants, to beautify surroundings. We have often been surprised upon entering an unprepossessing building to find attractive restaurants inside, with inner courtyards, gardens, pools, lovely glass windows and bamboo screens. The blue and white color scheme is popular for dishes and decoration.

It is really hard to understand how they produce such quiet, well-mannered children under such difficult living conditions. Most people looked clean and tidy, even smart, in their spotless white shirts. Only the older people seemed to cling to the bygone drab blue clothes, while the younger folk and the children have burst out into color. Mr. Wan told us that people are much happier today.

We have had some interesting conversations with our national guide, Mr. Wang, during the long train rides. He spent eight and a half years in exile away in the mountains because he was a teacher, an academic. He worked at physical labor for four years until the commune discovered that he was a teacher, and then they allowed him to take charge of educating children for the remainder of the time.

Another chat with Mr. Wang was about minorities. He talked so much about the equality of the minority groups, which constitute about four percent of the population, that I asked him what he felt about intermarriage. Would he mind if his son married a girl from a minority group? Mr. Wang thought it would not be a good idea, not because he was in any way religious, but because of the differences in customs and appearances. "If he marries a Muslim girl and has to go to the mosque on Friday, he will feel uncomfortable. And if he marries a Cossack with yellow hair and a big nose like you, she will feel uncomfortable amongst us!" We had a good laugh, because my nose is really not especially large, but it was a more objectionable feature than my blue eyes! We have realized that although Mr. Wang has heard of the kibbutz, he doesn't know just what and where Israel is.

I think I am most bothered by the way people walk about with their rice bowls in hand. In hotels and in the streets, people carry their bowls with them to their take-away stores or their work-place kitchens, and then often eat while walking or sitting in the street, or at their work-benches. Food seemed to be cheap, though not plentiful, but no one looks hungry. Does a family ever sit down to eat together? Perhaps we were really seeing a very limited aspect of life without having a chance to see more of the middle class. One saw people going home with a bunch of spring onions or greens, or a cabbage or a handful of cucumbers. One woman was carrying a few slices of ham on top of her cabbage, all unwrapped.

After a long but quite pleasant train journey, we arrived at Zhen Zhou after midnight and were taken to the Henan Guest House, which was in fact a twelve-storey hotel built in 1979. It was very comfortable, with plenty of towels, toilet paper and, as always, very hot water. We have found slippers in all hotel rooms, and the inevitable hot water thermos. These were seen everywhere, not only in hotels, so no wonder the Chinese product is the best! The summer blankets in this hotel were of toweling with attractive floral designs and colors. Looking out of the twelfth-floor window at 7 a.m., we saw mostly green treetops and parks. The early morning gymnasts and joggers were just dispersing.

Monday evening, June 6

We covered a lot of territory today with our local guide, Mr. Mao. In the morning we visited the White Village Brigade (Bai Dong), about a half-hour ride from Zhen Zhou. It was a lovely ride along a tree-lined road, with wheat harvesting going on on both sides of the way. Everything was done by hand. The country was quite flat, and we saw lots of lotus ponds. Apparently, the lotus root is a popular dish. We have already eaten the seeds, which look rather like round gooseberries but have no special flavor. For the first time we saw two horse-drawn drays with four horses each for transporting the wheat, and during the whole morning we saw only two tractors and threshers.

We arrived at the commune, which consisted of a large red-brick compound containing new and old buildings, and we were led to the usual reception room. This time we sat at one long table covered with plastic table cloths and jade-green mugs. Paintings and various banners hung on the walls, including one from the Australian-Chinese Friendship League.

The leader of the women workers spoke to us and explained the history and workings of the commune. She was twenty-eight years old and has worked at this job for about nine years; although she seemed to be very bright, she spoke no English. Afterwards we toured the commune. It was certainly rich and prosperous, with pigs, cows, apple orchards, night-soil processing, and a soya bean-curd (tofu) factory. It was interesting to discover at last that this pasta-like product, which is served to us quite often, is made by skimming off huge vats of heated bean-milk liquid and hanging the curd up to dry. This year the wheat harvest was so bountiful they had to call in soldiers to help out. It was all most impressive.

The People's Commune, we were told, is not only a production organization but also an economic and cultural framework. The first one was founded in 1956 and followed earlier co-operative and mutual aid schemes. The first commune was set up in Henan Province, which is the one we were now visiting, and then other provinces followed suit. Each county has twelve to fifteen communes, consisting of two to three villages, with about fifty thousand members. These are divided into ten Production Brigades, which are subdivided into Production Teams. They work collectively in the fields, but there is no communal living as on the kibbutz. The members get their grain, vegetables, money, and fireworks from the commune, and they have private bank accounts and use their money as they see fit.

Bai Dong used to be a poor village, due to the many sand dunes, its unproductive land and recurrent flooding by the Yellow River. The major effort in the early years was to level the dunes and cover them with one million cubic metres of mud. "Thus, under good party leadership, Bai Dong has become an extremely prosperous commune," said the guide. The average workday is eight hours – less in winter, more in summer.

The present philosophy is to reward for observing regulations and exceeding quotas. This gets good results, we were told. However, there are punishments for not following the rules or achieving the quota, but this statement was not amplified. Alex even had a conversation in Yiddish with a passing workman. The man had spent some years studying and working in California. He had picked up Yiddish and knew all about Israel.

The Brigade comprises five production teams, which work in five spheres – agriculture, afforestation, animal husbandry, industry, commerce and transportation. They have six tractors and one hundred and twenty machines for sowing, threshing, spraying and transport. We saw only two or three during our visit. There is a machine repair shop, and a small local store which caters to the members' daily needs. They sell wooden farm implements, cloth, shoes, rubber boots, stationery items, etc., but the shop, though quite large, was poorly lit. This dimness seems to be characteristic of Chinese housing.

Last, but not least, adjacent to the reception room, there was an art gallery, which exhibited paintings done by the members. These included traditional designs, portraits and semi-nudes.

In 1978, the total production value of the Brigade was 360,000 yuan, about $180,000, and this year they expected to increase this to 1.7 million yuan. Their income last year was 2,000 yuan per capita, and 310 kilos of grain was distributed per person. Other free services include kindergarten and schooling, water and electricity; flour processing, housing, medicine and haircutting. Ninety-five percent of the population has moved into the new housing units, consisting of two-storey red-brick buildings with large individual yards. They were allocated on the basis of twenty-five square metres per person. If a commune owns a brickyard, the members can buy the bricks for about 1–1.5 cents per piece.

We actually visited a home in the new housing section, which consisted of six rooms for six people. There was little furniture, but several bikes, and an old-style kitchen. In the yard were geese, a pig, chickens, night-soil containers, a cat tied by a red ribbon to a tree and flowering shrubs. It was very spacious.

We visited the clinic/pharmacy and heard about the paramedics or "barefoot doctors," who work in the villages after receiving from six to twelve months of medical training.

We asked Mr. Lee, our assistant guide, about courtships. It seems that here it is the girl who indicates her interest in the young man by sending him a handkerchief. If he is interested, he takes the hint; if not, he returns the handkerchief. This sounds better than a blind date.

Returning to town, we visited a beautiful antique shop, government owned, opposite the hotel, but found it hard to make any decisions. The sales girls actually giggled when I approached them, so my blue eyes and "yellow" hair must have been too much for them.

We had an afternoon visit to the Yellow River Diversion Project, a couple of hours' drive away. We had a crazy bus driver who thought constant honking at high speed was essential. There were crowds of bikes, and we saw many coolies, including girls, dragging loads. We held our breath nearly all the way because we have noticed that people are not very traffic-conscious. They walk or ride their bicycles in the middle of the road; they cut across in front of the buses without warning, and apparently are not required to use lamps at night.

The Mangshan Pumping Station is a tremendous pioneering job. It is an attempt to control the Yellow River by raising and diverting the waters into a forty–kilometre-long canal, which brings irrigation to dry areas.

There are also several pavilions leading to the top of Mt. Mangshan, from which there is a marvelous view of the Yellow River. During our visit to the pumping station we were served "white tea," a euphemistic name for plain hot water. I found it a poignant reminder of the hardships this country has suffered and the attempts to preserve the forms of hospitality in spite of them.

In the evening we went to the Martial Arts national competition, which was interesting because of our visit the next day to the Shaolin Monastery. But although it was an important event with big press and TV coverage, we found the shadowboxing (for men) and sword thrusting (for women) rather repetitive. We didn't have enough expertise to understand the finer points or the judging. However, we did see that Zhen Zhou has a very large and comprehensive sports centre, which was very well patronized.

Zhen Zhou is a really beautifully laid out town with parks and tree-lined avenues. Our hotel is situated on Golden Water Boulevard, which is seven kilometres long and forty-two metres wide, and has two rows of plane trees on each side. These provide wonderful shade for pedestrians and cyclists, who have special lanes at the sides of the road.

Though so many aspects of Chinese life are primitive, the emphasis on tree cultivation is remarkable. There seems to be conscious planning for shade-provision in towns and along the highways, not to mention the beauty that the trees — mostly poplar, acacia, willows and plane — add to the landscape. There are always trees along the rail tracks and roads that provide shade and mark out fields, thus providing practical and aesthetic functions. We felt that our own Jewish National Fund could emulate the Chinese method, rather than concentrate only on forests.

Tuesday, June 7

It was a long day, so it is difficult in the evening to remember everything. Our main destination was the Shaolin Monastery, four hours drive away, with its forest of stelae and stupas, and the ancient Buddhist temples, which were the birthplace of the martial arts. The founder of the monastery,

Sakyamuni, was a disciple of Buddha who walked three years from India to bring Buddhism to China. He taught that the monks should learn to defend themselves against enemies and opponents and that daily physical training would help keep the monks healthy, being a counteraction to the long hours of meditation that they practiced.

Our first stop in the morning was the Han Palace Tombs in Mixian County. It was most interesting to compare the stone carvings and wall paintings with Egyptian tombs. No artifacts were found here; they were stolen long ago. They are called Palace Tombs because they consist of several rooms whose purpose was illustrated by the wall carvings. For example, kitchen, dining room, stable, etc., as if they were still serving their normal functions. They are eight metres underground.

Then we stopped at the Zhongyue Taoist Temple, which was very picturesque and which consisted of a long promenade containing ten pavilions. Just as interesting as the historic stelae and giant cast-metal figures were the many ancient cypress trees growing in the courtyards. Some were over a thousand years old, with completely twisted trunks. Some of the calligraphy on the stelae was quite ancient and rare, and one stele described the five basic elements of the Chinese world – gold, wood, water, fire, and earth – of which all things are composed.

Although it has been open to tourism only since 1978, there are already signs of commercialism. There were many little restaurants and stands selling breads, postcards, and drinks, and all offering the same wares. How can they all be making money? We met one American and one Japanese group. The others were all Chinese, perhaps some from overseas.

Prior to that we had an excellent lunch in the local guest house, ten courses, with a greater variety of vegetables than in any other place – string beans, cooked tomatoes, lovely bean sprouts, cabbage, fresh cucumbers, seaweed, baked sweet potatoes, and good sponge cake. It seems that there are better and worse cooks in China, too, and they don't all know how to cook rice so that each grain is separate.

The landscape was very interesting, though not so rich and verdant as before. There are cultivated fields everywhere, mainly of wheat, but also some of vegetables, lotus and apples. Every centimetre is being exploited, right up to the roads, and even including dry river beds. Every little scrap of space is growing something. It is mainly a flat area, but cut up into terraces, which adds interesting effects. There are few stones, but the earth looks very heavy and clayey, so that the terraces need no retaining walls. Throughout the day we saw only two mechanical threshers. There were mostly ox-drawn ploughs, and a few mules, despite the fact that the harvest seemed to be at its peak.

We passed some old villages with tiny brick houses, over-painted white, and with thatched roofs. There were also some new villages, with good looking two-storey housing, enclosed by a wall. We saw some adobe villages, and some cave dwellings, which were nicely faced with stone and had adjoining gardens. One village had single houses in an unusual style, with large front verandas, two pillars and a colored geometric design across the whole façade. Others had pagoda-shaped roofs and animal decorations similar to those seen in the temples. There were many village markets at roadsides, and generally much activity and pavement living, except there are no pavements.

Breakfast is at 6:30 tomorrow morning and then we are off to Anyang. We skipped dinner tonight and tried to get to bed early.

Wednesday, June 8

A two and half hour train journey now to Anyang. Very flat country, miles of beautiful ripe wheat in fields, harvesting and threshing in full swing.

Anyang is a small town, but it also has tree-lined streets and several lanes for cycles. The drivers also honk like mad, and for the first time we saw pedicabs and mechanized rickshaws. Checked in at the local guest house and then went out to walk around. In the big street market where they were selling clothes and cloth, our group created a sensation; we attracted crowds, but whenever we tried to take photos, they melted away.

Zipora and I continued to walk through the residential area, and it made the most pleasant impression of any place we'd seen. The brick houses were whitewashed, with decorations and pictures painted on the walls. There were numbered entrances into courtyards, which seemed to house several families and lots of bicycles. Facing the entrance were more large paintings on the wall, and we had glimpses of little gardens, trees, tiny dwellings, some tidier than others. There was a water tap and a gutter in the street, where two women were washing clothes and vegetables, but we also saw one woman doing her washing under running water in her own courtyard. People continued to stare at us. Only much later did we realize that Anyang is not even mentioned in our guidebook, so the reactions of the population were more understandable.

The second street was a conventional one with several grocery shops and restaurants. We discovered a noodle shop, about two metres square, run by two women. It seemed that people brought their own flour. One of the women weighed it and returned equal weight in noodles, which were made on a hand machine by the second woman. Half a dozen people stood in the doorway, with their bowls of flour. Further on, we saw a shirt factory, a shop with four sewing machines and two cutting and pressing tables. There was heavy traffic because of the lunch hour and the many children coming home from school.

People carried cabbages and cucumbers, some unattractive apricots and rather poor tomatoes. The atmosphere seemed more normal than any other place. We finally found our way back to the main market street, where Zipora succeeded in buying some baby shirts and got rid of her local money.

I should mention that tourists get different currency than that generally in use and the notes are called Foreign Exchange Certificates. One can use them at the Friendship Stores, but small vendors don't always accept them. However, those Chinese who want to get to the Friendship Stores try to get hold of this money. Both kinds of notes have the same value.

We had lunch at the guest house, where we had some interesting new foods and other vegetables. We sat in a large dining room, part of which was screened off to give us some privacy from other diners. This was quite customary in many places.

At one o'clock we boarded the bus to drive out to the scenic area of Linxiang for an overnight stay. I had imagined we were going to some beautiful scenic spot to see waterfalls, forests, etc. and to relax. We were warned that the accommodation would be quite simple, and, in fact, when we arrived, there were the usual white slipcovers, hot thermos, slippers, etc., but no water in the taps or toilet! However, we were promised water for the evening.

We left Linxiang at 3 p.m. to look at the Red Flag Canal and the Youth Tunnel. This turned out to be another 45-kolometre ride up into the mountains and it was quite magnificent, although not the relaxation we had expected.

The Red Flag Canal is a water diversion project, designed to bring water from the Changho River to the barren land of Linxiang County, which has always suffered from drought.

From 1960 to 1970, the people of this county worked at cutting the canal through innumerable mountains. They also built many bridges and aqueducts to link up the various sections of this fifteen–hundred-kilometre waterway. We visited the last section, called the Youth Tunnel, named for the volunteer youth groups who worked for six months to cut through the last mountain. It was a most dramatic sight, especially coming down the 463 stairs! Even here at the top of the mountain, we had a "briefing" by one of the "model" workers and drank our "white tea" in the open under the trees.

The landscape during the drive was similar to that of the morning except that the mountains were closer, and it was harvest time here as well. I have found it quite thrilling to see such vast stretches of wheat fields, and all stages of the harvesting being carried out right there by the roadside – reaping, threshing, winnowing and binding. Even the road itself was made use of as an additional threshing floor, the buses and trucks driving over the wheat helping to crush and separate the grain from the stalk. I think that the number of tractors and threshing machines we saw could have been counted on one hand. There were also many donkeys and mules pulling carts. The kids were home from school to help.

I had never seen such scenes, and found it beautiful and moving to see how a people works its land. It was almost primeval, literally *ha-motzi lehem min ha-aretz* … "Who bringeth bread out of the land" – from the blessing over bread. A brilliant sunshine heightened the impression. And the people! They had a different appearance from the town folk we have seen so far, and were obviously peasants born and bred. Wherever we stopped they gawked in amazement, but fled at the sight of our cameras. Some of the smaller children even cried! There seem to be more old people here than in the towns, and they wore the old Mao uniforms. There were also more children and a few women with bound feet.

The villages all looked more or less the same, in varying stages of ruin. All had dirt lanes and many trees. Some houses were built in compound style, some in long rows, some had thatched roofs and some had pagoda-shaped roofs with decorations. We noticed small alcoves set into some of the walls next to the front door, but the guide couldn't explain it, so we did not know if they served as household shrines, or some other practical purpose such as niches for lanterns. But many villages have new housing sections, with larger or smaller units built of red brick in two-storey fashion. I think I finally discovered why the houses generally look dark – it's because there are windows only at the front. The back walls had no windows, and if they had been planned, they have been bricked up. Even the kitchen we saw at the commune had only one tiny window and it was quite dark in the middle of the day. Of course, the fact that they cook with small round briquettes of coal probably contributes to the blackening of the walls.

It was really a fabulous day and we returned to Linxiang just before seven. We had a new dish at dinner, peanuts and onions, and a horrible sweet pink soup, but good rice, a large fried fish, green beans, champignons, etc. I still cannot forget the wheat fields, surely one of the most entrancing sights I've ever seen, and those scenes remain fixed in my mind.

So far, our fears about the hotels have not been substantiated. We have seen various standards by now, and there have always been clean sheets and towels, though not changed every day, good toilet paper and soap, very hot water, sandals to wear in the room, and, of course, the hot thermos, cups and tea. There are very few mirrors, and a small one in the bathroom has to serve all purposes. Public toilets, on the other hand, are sometimes unpleasant.

We are disappointed that everything seems standardized. All the markets in all places sell the same clothes, blouses, skirts, pants and pretty children's clothes. Often the same material sold by the metre reappears in different towns. All craft shops sell the same scrolls, pictures, jewelry, embroideries, lacquerware and ceramics, with larger or smaller selections. Art is supposed to be "traditional," so one wonders what the new artists are doing. We did see some artists painting nature scenes at the Lovely Dusk Pavilion in Changsha, but otherwise we are offered the usual flower scenes, horses, etc.

Thursday, June 9

We left the Linxiang Guest House at 7:30 after a very nice breakfast. The specialty of the area seems to be very long, sausage-shaped fritters, and we also had a variety of sweet cookies. Very feeble coffee, but a big soup bowl of hot milk was very welcome.

Just before reaching Anyang we turned off to visit the ruins of the Ying Dynasty, as the latter half of the Shang Dynasty is called. They date to about 1,300 bce. We saw a small exhibition of artifacts, which included lots of ceramic cooking pots, bronze wine vessels and their heating containers, stone chimes, seashells, which seem to have been used for currency, and many skeletons of animals and humans. The most unusual items were the "oracle bones," the shoulder blades of animals inscribed with characters, which were used for reading the future or for solving problems. The Chinese considered these findings extremely important.

This was a slave period during which human sacrifice was practiced. The slaves were killed and buried, or even buried alive with their masters when they died. Miniature arrays of pottery figures were retrieved from tombs, rather like the Egyptian *ushupti*. There were very small sling stones, a rather large bronze cauldron, lovely jade ornaments and sculptures. We also saw an ancient chariot in the process of restoration. We did not see the excavations themselves. It seems that the Chinese cover them up after completing their research so that the ground can be re-cultivated.

We had a very poor lunch at the guest house in Anyang, and then went for a walk to the Chinese department store. When we passed a hairdresser, I was very tempted to have my hair done but there wasn't enough time. We saw another little reading library on the steps of a building. In the store we caused a sensation and were followed about by the crowd. Suddenly one young woman stepped up to me and delivered a harangue, which was decidedly unfriendly. The people around tried to quiet her down. I apologized that I only spoke English but she continued for another minute or two, then smiled and turned away. I would love to have known what was bothering her.

Soon we were on the train for another five-hour trip to Luoyang, where we finally arrived at our hotel at midnight. The guide book says that it was the most run-down hotel in China until it was renovated in 1980, but that it has an excellent kitchen.

The entrance hall indeed looked very elegant and spacious, with many shops, but we hurried upstairs to shower and bed. To our surprise, we had a suite – bedroom, sitting-room and very small toilet and shower. The furniture, very old-fashioned, included high beds, a wardrobe with a long mirror, sofa and chairs in white slipcovers as usual, but also a color TV and radio. We even managed to hear the BBC at last, and were glad to hear no news of Israel. Though there were hot water and towels, the plumbing didn't seem very efficient, and the toilet ran all the time. The Chinese carpets would have been lovely if they had been cleaned, but I guess that symbolizes the many contradictions we see in this country. Several others of the group also have suites, while some have enormous bathrooms with small bedrooms.

Our local guide is Mr. Chin, a very handsome young man, tall for a Chinese and very athletic-looking.

The train journey today was a bit unusual. Our long walk to the dining car – we are always in the last carriage, hooked on after the baggage car – seemed even longer than usual, which meant this was a particularly long train. All the carriages were third-class and filled with men, with an occasional family here and there. It was quite something to be inspected by all those eyes as we filed through the open corridor. Then suddenly we came to an air-conditioned car. We gasped in amazement. We thought we had the most comfortable car of all, but here was an even more superior class. Even the slipcovers looked cleaner, and the car was full of Chinese who made a sharp contrast to those traveling in the "hard" class, which had only six thinly padded bunks in each section. We were very curious as to who would be traveling in such comfort, but of course that also remained a secret.

In the luggage car there was a whole consignment of day-old chicks traveling in open cartons. They looked cute and indicated that somewhere chickens were being raised and eaten.

Dinner on the train was excellent and pleasantly served, but too plentiful. Beer and orangeade, of local manufacture, were provided as usual. Some of us are beginning to skip meals or eat less, since ten courses twice a day is really too much. Today, we had sugared tomatoes to start, stewed apples for dessert, good vegetables, fresh beans, tinned champignon and fried fish. Soup always comes in the middle of the meal, and the rice sometimes at the end, sometimes in the middle.

The train journeys are becoming a bit trying, largely because we always have to walk so far with our hand luggage. Several hundred metres to and from the train, to and from the dining car. Still, it is interesting to see the "ordinary" people and get a glimpse of another facet of Chinese life.

The guide said it would be about 34°C tomorrow, but dry. Some guides have asked us for comments about the service. They say that they are new to tourism and want to learn. At one of the museums, too, Rivka was asked to write down her professional opinion. The guide always makes a sentimental little farewell speech at the end of our stay, especially if it has been a longer one than usual, and asks us to convey his greetings to our family and relatives. This must be Chinese custom. We sing "*Hevenu Shalom Aleichem.*" Actually, we've had some nice sing-alongs on our long journeys, and the guides are always happy to hear *Frère Jacques*, which they also sing in Chinese.

Friday, June 10

We drove out to Longmen, or the Dragon Gate Caves. This is a whole cliff face of Buddhist carvings and sculptures several kilometres in length, dating from the sixth century. Again, the art of Egypt's Abu Simbel came to mind. It was a very busy place with lots of visitors, foreign and local, and lots of workmen working on the river, using small carts, tiny trucks and hand carts. This is another big project to raise the riverbed and divert the waters. The Red Flag Canal passed nearby. Needless to say, we had our usual "briefing" here in the usual visitors' room and the usual tea.

Thank God for our present driver! He rarely honks and drives more carefully than the last one. It makes a big difference to our enjoyment and I didn't have a headache today. We visited the old section of town on the way back.

Sunday, June 12

We were woken before five by the alarm clock and the noise of jogging and gymnastics outside. We were at the station by 6:15. It was deserted except for women sweepers in blue uniforms carrying big Chinese brooms. In fact, we were so early we found the sweepers lined up for inspection before starting work. Chinese music blared from the loudspeaker.

The train from Shanghai came in a few minutes later, and again we had the last carriage. Another long walk to breakfast. This time the baggage car really smelled. There were about five third-class cars, and this time there were many families, some even taking their pot-plants with them. Many were still sleeping and the blinds are down, so it seemed they had come a long way, perhaps even from Shanghai. There was laundry hanging up to dry, everyone had food supplies and thermoses. They didn't go to the dining car. Now we understand why there is a separate room across from the toilet; it was a laundry room with two basins where passengers can wash on long journeys. There was also a large furnace for heating water, where travelers could refill their thermos flasks. Later in the day, they even washed down the floor. They were amazingly quiet and composed.

We wondered where these people were going, in view of all the stories we had heard about lack of freedom of movement. On other trains the men had looked like work brigades, but perhaps these families were going to a new town. When we asked Mr. Wang, he said they had been visiting their families in Shanghai and were now returning to their own town on the Sino-Russian border. That is certainly another couple of days' travel.

The countryside was very beautiful as we climbed into a hilly region with mountains in the background. The wheat harvest was just beginning here, so the scenes were familiar, but still lovely. We saw many haystacks, also many vegetable gardens. The mountains and wadis were completely terraced, and the heavy soil needed no retaining wall. The whole landscape looked as if it was actually sculpted and every centimetre was cultivated. There were many trees, even small forests here and there. The main attraction was the large cave dwellings, looking very elegant with stone facades, doors and windows, often with a fenced-off garden. The entrances were arched, and at one spot we passed a row of caves with blue doors, so perhaps a familiar Muslim tradition from the Middle East was expressing itself in this largely Muslim area. I found the landscape most attractive.

Now we were moving toward the foothills of steep mountains, not cultivated but quite green, while plains stretched away to the right. Villages and factories, large housing developments, trees and more trees dotted the countryside. Young cypress saplings had been planted on the mountainsides and brilliant sunshine accentuated the colors. Marvelous craggy peaks were silhouetted against the skyline.

I am writing this on the train to Xian. Last Friday evening, since the hotel was quite full with Japanese, French and Australian tourists, we decided to have our Kabbalat Shabbat in the Bittermans' suite and most of us gathered there for Kiddush. Everyone was very conscious of the fact that Kiddush was probably being made in Luoyang for the first time ever, but Rivka says there were probably Jews here in other periods. After dinner, we also had *zemirot* and *benchen* (grace after meals) in the room and it was very enjoyable. The dining room in this hotel is in a separate pavilion at the back, across a garden. The cook is quite a character and believes in the personal touch. He comes around during every meal to ask in broken English, if everything is satisfactory. He takes his profession very seriously.

Part of the group went off to the theatre, but unfortunately Sylvia Feller had a bad fall and had to be taken to hospital. Luckily, nothing was broken, but she had a beautiful black eye, a sprained ankle, and suffered from shock. She said that the hospital was very primitive, but the lady doctor was very kind and gentle and she didn't feel the tetanus shot.

We woke on Saturday morning to pouring rain, and for those who would have to walk to the museum, a great disappointment. However, it cleared in the afternoon, and they eventually all got there.

The museum is a fine newish building in Chinese style, which opened in 1953. Though not very large, there are five halls with relics from the primitive or Neolithic period up to the end of the Sung Dynasty in 1280 ce. There are a large number of artifacts from more than sixty village sites, and from research on about ten thousand graves. The early historical periods are called Primitive, Slave Society (2100–500 bce) and Feudal Society.

We looked mainly at the bronze vessels and stone chimes and at a visiting exhibition of imperial furniture from Beijing. The atmosphere was very pleasant, but there were no other visitors.

As in most other places, the guide was a young woman, who spoke no English, and again there were no English signs in the showcases. She complained that some of their best pieces had been taken to Beijing.

Then, in pouring rain, we went to the park to see two Han tombs, with many chambers, and stone carvings. The similarity to Egyptian tombs is amazing, but here the color has not kept well!

In the afternoon I went unwillingly to the Taoist White Horse Temple, while Alex stayed at the hotel. In fact, it was one of the nicer places, having been recently restored and repainted, and was very well kept. There was a large hall with red columns and side pavilions with many stelae and stone figures found in the area, some of them enormous.

Then we visited the arts and crafts centre, which seems to be the main centre for the production of the ceramic Tang horses in the traditional three-color glaze. It was interesting to see how they finish off the mass-produced horses by hand. I bought a bronze reproduction of a mounted guard.

We made *Havdalah* in the Bittermans' room at 8:15 p.m., packed, watched the Royal Ballet on TV performing *Sleeping Beauty* in Beijing, and then went wearily to bed.

Monday, June 13

This was a day which was ostensibly to be devoted to archaeology but turned into an orgy of shopping – not entirely our fault, but because the tour is so arranged that we ften have too much free time. Or are the people of Xian shrewder businesspeople?

The archaeological sites, interesting as they were, did not take up much time. The Quin Shi Huang excavations with the life-size pottery warriors and horses were fabulous, but such a small section is displayed that we finished in about half an hour. Another half hour was enough for the museum souvenir shop. We then had an hour or more for the free market, which was really a riot, firstly of color and types, and secondly of noisy bargaining. About twenty-five to thirty women and members of their families were congregated in an open square in front of the excavation site, selling brightly colored padded and embroidered vests, old clothes and embroideries, animal decorations and various bits of junk. All were vying for the customers. It was really the first place where we've seen any "local" color or folklore. The stall owners on the right-hand side, where we were told to shop, seemed more restrained and careful, while those on the left got quite out of hand if we approached them, and it was very difficult to extricate oneself. We were quite caught up in the excitement. A good time was had by us, and a good profit was made by them. The guide said that all this sewing and commerce is put in after the regular working day.

On the way home we stopped at the famous Mauquing Hot Springs where Chiang Kai-shek was kidnapped by his officers in 1936. He was forced to put an end to the civil war and mount a united front against the

Japanese. Now it is just an ornamental park with lakes and many pavilions, a lovely spot that may eventually be restored to its original purpose. Some of the group were disappointed in not being able to swim.

We visited a cloisonné factory in Xian where we saw just one part of the production process. I don't really like this ware, unless the patterns, coloring and shape are simple, so I didn't find anything especially attractive, and portable enough, in their showroom. Again, we were finished before the allotted time. Most interesting was to see how the forms of ancient vessels that we saw in museums are still being copied today. Once again, "tradition."

In the morning we visited the Banpo Neolithic Museum, which was most unusual and very impressive. Unusual in that such a large site has been exposed and maintained in an enclosed, roofed-over area, and impressive because of the clear and simple way the finds themselves are presented. This is the only place so far where we had English translations. The Quin Shi Huang excavations were also enclosed in a large structure.

I experienced a rather unpleasant incident here. On my way to the bus, while admiring a small palm tree, I bumped into a man who was watering flowers with a triangular-shaped wooden pail. He accidentally splashed water all over my skirt and legs. The people nearby laughed, but I didn't pay much attention. However, after a minute or two, I became aware of a terrible smell emanating from me, and so did the others on the bus. Remembering the perfume carts and the "night soil," I quickly came to the conclusion that I had been doused in horse urine, if not worse, and realized that I couldn't remain like that for the rest of the day. I asked Mr. Wang if we could stop wherever there was a tap nearby, and after about five minutes I saw one of the other Chinese come out of a pavilion with a basin of water which he placed on the ground.

I couldn't take off my skirt, as I wasn't wearing a slip, so I knelt down and rinsed it out as best as I could. Then I also washed my feet in the basin and everyone had a good laugh. We resumed our journey, with me sitting in a wet skirt! Suddenly Dita produced an extra skirt she was carrying with her, so I could wriggle into that, and take off my own, which I held out the window like a banner. It dried after a half hour, just in time to go to the pottery excavations, and then I reversed the exercise. I remained conscious of the smell for the rest of the day though no one else complained, but it was so good to get out of those clothes and into the shower when we got back to the hotel!

Xian has the largest Muslim community in China, and we visited the Great Mosque, which was built in the seventh century. In the briefing room we were told the history of the community and of the impending fast of Ramadan. We had to take off our shoes to enter the mosque, but mostly we were impressed with the minaret, which was in the shape of a pagoda. We felt strangely at home in this distant spot.

We stayed at the Renmin Mansion, which is a very large estate containing five buildings in a spacious garden. It was opened in 1953, having been built for the Soviet advisors of that period, and was turned into a hotel when they were expelled. It was a good example of bombastic Soviet architecture with decorative Chinese elements.

Our rooms had been newly renovated and were most comfortable, with air conditioning and lovely modern bathrooms. There is even a chime at the door, and of course the laundry service is excellent as it was everywhere. Good shops with a large selection of items, including pure silk dress material.

The large dining room has a decorative ceiling, copied from nearby Tang tombs, and we discovered a separate dining room for Muslims, kosher no doubt, but no one was there at the time.

Tuesday, June 14

We were out by 6:30 this morning to see the exercising in the streets. I had expected to see mass organized PT, but in fact it was more of what we saw yesterday. There were large and small groups practicing the traditional martial arts, *taijiguan*, mostly senior citizens of both sexes. Others individually or in pairs, were doing warming-up exercises, or using a set of bars. Many played shuttlecock/badminton (without a net) on the pavement; others were jogging, etc. All this took place in and around the big square, against the background of bicycle traffic and people going to work. A water truck driven by a girl was washing down the streets. Old men were taking caged birds for an airing, while others sat under the trees playing a kind of board game, on paper.

One car drove by with only two little boys in the back and we wondered how important their fathers could be.

The people in the streets have been very friendly, offering hellos and smiles. Even little children waved spontaneously. I suppose they know that tourism is good business. Xian is probably the most visited town in China because of its pottery army.

This morning we went to the Shanxi Provincial Museum where there are more than two thousand inscribed stelae, but Alex and I decided to forego the trip to Quianlung, the Tang Emperors' Tomb, which is some sixty kilometres away.

Tuesday evening, June 14

We had a leisurely day after the fascinating visit to the museum, shopping, walking, repacking, and we slept in the afternoon. During our walk, we saw a wide range of livelihoods being practiced on the pavements: barbers, basket weaving, dough-kneading, noodle-making, dressmaking, and so on.

There was excitement at dinner with Arthur, who'd lost his camera, or had it stolen while shopping. This entailed visits to the police station and much running around by Mr. Wang, but the camera was not found, and I don't know if Arthur ever got his police note for customs and the insurance.

There was even more bad news and aggravation. It seems our flight tomorrow has been moved from the morning to the afternoon, which means a half-day wasted here and precious time lost in Beijing (formerly Peking). It has been interesting to observe, although our schedule was planned in advance, that we never knew where we would stay or what we would do until we arrived at each place. On arrival, only then would our national guide and the group leaders get together with the local guides and settle the details. It meant at least that with Rivka's help we had some say in the selection of tours.

Wednesday, June 15

At breakfast we discovered that last night's grumblings had borne fruit. The Klines, our group leaders, informed us they had arranged a visit to the Xinjao Buddhist Temple, a two-hour drive to the mountains. All groaned at the thought of another temple, but in fact it was a lovely morning. The landscape was slightly hillier and very green, with grand mountains in the background. Once again we found ourselves in the midst of wheat harvesting, and at one stage drove for several miles along wheat-covered roads, where village after village was using the main road as a threshing floor, even though they had proper threshing floors inside the village. Perhaps the harvest has been especially good this year. It looked very abundant, with haystacks piled up, some round, some stacked between trees, some in the usual house-shaped style. Everyone seemed to be out at work – men and women, young and old. The village scenes, in slightly better conditions, were picturesque; the old people were more numerous than in the towns, and each one was a "type" to be photographed. The dirt roads were beautifully tree-lined.

The Xinjao Temple is one of the eight remaining monasteries of the Tang period, and important as the burial place of Xuangzang, a monk and pilgrim, traveler and scholar. A large stupa marks the tomb of the famous monk. He lived from 600–664 and was a friend of the third Tang emperor. He spent seventeen years in India studying Buddhism and devoted himself to translating Buddhist writings into Chinese. He also built the Great Wild Goose Pagoda to house these manuscripts, and the monastery also holds a large collection of Tibetan Buddhist writings. This temple seems to be very popular with the Japanese, since many Japanese banners decorate the walls. In the well-kept and obviously frequented temple, we also noticed a small, Jewish-looking seven-branched candelabrum on the altar, but we couldn't get any information about its meaning or origin. The Klines, leaders of the group, were excited about this visit because it was the first time it was permitted. It is not a usual tourist site.

We arrived at the airport after lunch, and our hand luggage was checked with a fine-toothed comb. Every little package had to be opened! We had a good flight and got to Beijing at five in the afternoon. The drive into town took about forty-five minutes along a beautiful road lined with poplars and pines, behind which we saw new orchards and groves of saplings. The guides told us that they planted about 150 million trees after the "liberation" (from Chairman Mao) and since then have planted about a million trees every year. The Chinese observe a tree festival on March 12, and much of the planting is done then. We couldn't help comparing this with our own Tu b'Shvat, the New Year of the Trees, which falls in January and is marked by mass plantings.

The main road leading to the hotel is typical of others we have seen. It is fifty or sixty metres wide, and remnants of old villages can be seen alongside enormous new apartment blocks. Again, the bulk of the traffic is bicycles, but there are many taxis, buses and trolley cars.

Hotel Beijing really took us by surprise, as we didn't expect to be staying here. It is the leading hotel, situated on the main road, close to the famous Tiananmen Square. It occupies a whole city block and is comprised of three wings of various origins: colonial, Soviet and modern. The connecting lobbies are filled with souvenir shops, cafés and bars, and myriad tourists from all over. The whole atmosphere is completely different, and we could almost be in New York, London or any big city. We have a huge bedroom with bath on the fourteenth floor, air-conditioning and color TV, but the same plastic slippers and hot water thermoses remind us that we are still in China. After three weeks of our travels, we are no longer used to such luxury and it comes as quite a shock, but I suppose we will readjust fairly quickly!

I wanted to call my brother in London but the time was not appropriate. Since there is no direct phone link with Israel, we will have to get our news in this roundabout way after three weeks without any contact.

Thursday, June 16

We called Alec and Aliza at 6 a.m. We had a wonderful connection, and asked them to call the kids and wish Varda a happy birthday, and then let us know by return call if everything is well at home.

Today, the Great Wall!

We left at 7:30 for The Great Wall, a two-hour trip by train, and then another ten minutes by bus. We saw fantastic mountain scenery, with glimpses of parts of the wall and towers here and there. The morning mists finally cleared away and we were able to enjoy warm sunshine and cool breezes. The mountains were very green with underbrush, but not actually cultivated.

This turned out to be a very entertaining journey. After the girl attendants on the train served tea, they reappeared with a trolley of postcards and other small souvenir items. After a suitable pause they came back with embroideries, and then again with scarves and T-shirts. It became quite hilarious, as we never knew whether the sales were over, or whether they had another surprise for us. The time passed very cheerfully, and we enjoyed socializing with a group of Australians who were sharing our carriage.

We had a short walk to the main entrance, passing many souvenir stalls, and then began to climb the Wall, together with thousands of other tourists. One could hear many different languages, but Europeans were very much in the minority. And I really mean "to climb," alternating with many breathing stops. Though it took great effort, we finally made it up the steep incline and the last, almost vertical flight of stairs. It was reminiscent of the climb up the Tower of Pisa. Everyone was huffing and puffing in their own language, but it really was an experience and the view was well worth it. Going down was even more difficult because the stones were very smooth and slippery, so the handrail proved to be a lifesaver.

Parts of the Wall are about two thousand years old, having been built with slave labor by the same Emperor Quin Shi Huang, who was buried at Xian with his pottery warriors. In later periods the early sections were joined up. At its best period it was ten thousand kilometres long, but like similar fortifications in our time, this "line" couldn't keep out the invaders. After the sixth century, China was often overrun and the Wall fell into disuse until the Ming emperors tried to restore it. Now the Chinese are restoring it as a national monument and tourist attraction. It is about three metres wide on the top, wider still at the base. The old city wall in Xian was even wider.

After we negotiated the descent, we felt entitled to buy the T-shirt inscribed, "I climbed the Great Wall," and we decided not to give them away as gifts. We felt that only those who had actually climbed the Wall should wear them!

We had a box lunch on the train during another long journey, by rail and road, to the Ming tombs. The guide made us get off the bus and walk along the Sacred Way to the entrance. This avenue is lined with enormous stone statues of horses, elephants and dignitaries, an excellent location for photographs. The tomb we visited, the only one of the thirteen tombs in the valley which has been opened, is really a vast underground palace, four flights down. It was extremely cold. We saw the three red-painted caskets, which had fitted one inside the other, large chunks of jade, and carved marble thrones, but the main exhibits, gold dishes, crowns and jewelry, in a style similar to Bukharian work, were exhibited in the pavilions on the grounds. Of course, there were also souvenir shops, where we were taken, ostensibly for a free drink of cold Coca Cola.

We returned by bus to Beijing just at the rush hour. There were literally thousands of bikes, trolley cars, buses and trucks, and many taxis and private cars belonging to government cadres or foreigners. Most people looked a little more citified but the markets were the same markets, and the traffic seemed only slightly more controlled.

We went out for a duck dinner with the Fellers, Zipora and Martin, but didn't get it because the guide had ordered something else! Zipora and I were very disappointed after being vegetarians for three weeks. At 8:30 p.m. we couldn't get a taxi, and had to walk back to the hotel, trusting to our own intuition, and help from an American girl we approached, who'd been studying in Peking already for a year. Many people were out on the streets, it being a hot night. The street lighting is brighter than we have seen in other towns but the side streets were dim.

After we managed to locate the hotel, we found a lovely antique shop close by, and although they were obviously preparing to close up, the proprietors allowed us to look around. It was a very large shop, with several rooms, and in one of them we saw some modern Chinese paintings which had been exhibited in Europe. They were mostly street scenes in realistic style, not abstracts, but still with traditional elements. The rest of the merchandise was similar to what we had seen in other places.

Then, toward the end of the evening, we walked along the brightly lit boulevard to Tiananmen Square. We noticed the double row of trees along the northern wall of the Forbidden City, where the Gate of Heavenly Peace is situated. The trees provided deep shade for the small benches placed there, all of which were occupied by young couples. Rivka says it's the official Lovers' Lane.

I still find it pathetic to see the one-child families, and I can't help wondering how this and the next generation will grow up, without any extended family. I haven't mentioned the large billboards we saw in other towns, showing happy one-child families. These billboards were also used to educate the public on road safety by showing a family crossing correctly at a pedestrian crossing, etc.

The Beijing hotel also differs from previous accommodations, in that the car park in front is full of Mercedes, and big black Russian-made limousines with lace-draped seats and waiting chauffeurs. Inside the hotel, scales and ironing facilities are found near the service desk on each floor. In addition to the color TV and air conditioning in the room, there is a digital clock, a small refrigerator, and to our amazement, electrically operated curtains. It is very comfortable, but not typically Chinese!

Friday, June 17

In the morning we first visited the zoo to see the famous pandas, and then drove out to the Summer Palace to see its many pavilions and the beautifully decorated covered promenade known as the Painted Gallery. We had lunch in the Listening to the Orioles Pavilion (nothing like the Chinese language for hyperbole), then went for a boat ride on the enormous artificial lake, and heard an anecdotal account of how the Empress Ci Xi had built the estate and of the lifestyle there until the emperor was deposed. The pomp and luxury then were certainly a far cry from the drabness and uniformity of life today, but in contrast now, the common man's lot seems to be much improved. Our assistant guide, Miss Pan, then took us to the Temple of Heaven, which is a very large compound of prayer halls and piazzas, dominated by the most exotic-looking, splendid circular building: the Hall of Prayer for Good Harvests. It is a breathtaking sight, from the enormous red pillars within to the brilliant blue-glazed tiles without. Not a single nail was used in the construction, we were told, which dates back to the sixteenth century.

It is time for shopping, of course. At Alex's urging we went in the evening to an acrobatic show, half of which turned out to be magicians' acts. It is very popular entertainment and very good, but also very hot, in spite of the electric fans.

Saturday, June 18

It was 6:30 in the morning and we were up again. This was actually our last day in Beijing. I felt utterly exhausted, and we hadn't even begun. We had to go to the Forbidden City in the morning, to the Historical Museum in the afternoon and to our farewell banquet in the evening. Touring is really very demanding here. The temples always consist of many courtyards and pavilions, and there is always a lot of walking. Not to mention the shops, which are on every corner. Everywhere you turn, there's a shop, and of course, one must go in to see if there isn't anything special that one might miss.

But we have *done* the trip to China. It has taken almost three weeks, and although we have learned a great deal of its history, and seen a great deal of the country, its urban and outlying areas, and many facets of Chinese life, we feel that there is still much to come back for. I would certainly like to come back and do a little more leisurely the things that we haven't had time to do on this trip.

This morning we have to visit the Forbidden City, which means a lot of walking. Let's hope we survive it. The Forbidden City wasn't very far from the hotel, and from our window we could see the roofs of the pavilions and the palaces, but the atmosphere was so hazy in the morning that it was difficult to take a sharp picture. It doesn't really clear until ten or eleven o'clock, when the sun comes out and the visibility is much better.

Saturday evening, June 18

[N.B. I had thought to reproduce here the exact words of our guide, transcribing from my tape recorder in order to recreate more tangibly the "tone" of our travels. However, the Chinese have a habit of repeating the last words of a sentence, or of a thought, which doesn't make good reading when put down on paper. I don't know if they do this when speaking Chinese or if it is a problem of coping with a foreign language. So I have condensed the descriptions of the Forbidden City into proper English, and foregone the authentic touch. – E.R.]

We started our two-and-a-half-hour tour at the South Gate working our way through to the North Gate, which is situated on Tiananmen Square. The south or Meridian Gate was also called The Five Phoenix Pavilion in former times, because there are five buildings on top of it. Each one symbolizes the phoenix. In earlier periods in China, the dragon symbolized the emperor and the phoenix symbolized the empress. Construction of the pavilion city began in 1406 during the third Ming Dynasty and was completed by 1420. Hundreds of thousands of slaves, artisans and craftsmen were forced to work on the construction of this new capital, which had been moved from its previous location in Nanking.

Actually, additions and improvements went on up to 1911, by which time there were more than 9,900 rooms and seventy-two palaces, and many courtyards. About twenty-four emperors lived in the Forbidden City until the last emperor was overthrown in 1911 by Dr. Sun Yat Sen during the Democratic Revolution. The emperor was only six years old at the time, and he continued to live in the inner court until 1924.

The Forbidden City consists of two main parts, the front court, which was used on state or ceremonial occasions, such as receiving foreign envoys or celebrating the emperor's birthday. The second part served as private residential quarters for the emperor, empress and concubines. One emperor had two empresses and seventy-two concubines, and they all lived in different courtyards. The last emperor was driven out in 1924, and the city was then converted into a museum. It is also called the Palace Meridian, or the Imperial Palace.

Restoration began in the early 1950s, after the liberation, but some pavilions have not been touched for more than one hundred years. Of course, we could not see everything in the time at our disposal, but the guide showed us the main features of the palace and the ceremonial and private areas and regaled us with many stories. He pointed out the Golden Water River, which runs from east to west through the palace, and which is spanned by five marble bridges. These bridges represent the five virtues: benevolence, righteousness, propriety, wisdom and fidelity, and they also symbolized five arrows on a bow. The emperor, who called himself "the son of god," would shoot these arrows into the air and the arrows would tell the god what the emperor was doing on earth.

As we walked along we were very impressed by the vast squares, which were devoted to the ceremonial aspects of imperial life, and equally impressed by the number of Chinese tourists, who were also "doing" this now accessible historical site. Several hundreds, if not more, local tourists were to be seen everywhere.

The Hall of Benevolence or Supreme Harmony is the largest palace in the compound, the next in importance being the Hall of Perfect Harmony and the Hall of Preserving Harmony. The Hall of Supreme Harmony was used for state occasions and for the coronation, which was always a grand occasion attended by the high officials and military officers. The emperor would sit on the throne inside looking out at the assembly which was arranged in the square according to rank, from the first to the seventh. White lines mark the traditional divisions between the ranks.

The military officers and high officials would kneel down, kowtow, and say "longevity" many times. The emperor sat on his throne, while all the musical instruments – bells, drums, etc. – were sounded. A great deal of incense was burned in the enormous incense burners standing in a row in front of the palace. There are eighteen of them altogether because at that time, China had eighteen provinces, and they were each represented by a burner. Sandalwood, which has a very pleasant smell, was used for the incense and created a very agreeable environment for the great ceremony.

In former times, Peking (or Beijing) consisted of four cities, the Outer City, the Inner City, the Imperial City and the Forbidden City, one within another. The Forbidden City was located in the centre. The whole city was heavily guarded, with a watchtower and a city wall more than ten metres high. There was also a moat. The emperor still didn't feel secure enough, and was afraid someone might tunnel his way inside. So he ordered this area to be paved in a special way, seven layers lengthwise, and eight layers crosswise. Thus, this square consists of fifteen layers of brick. The other squares of the Forbidden City have six or seven layers, but here there are fifteen.

Besides the incense burners, there are also two statues of dragons, which belched forth smoke and fire to impress the assembled public, a round sundial divided into twelve *devetas* (hours?), and two enormous water cauldrons for fighting fires. Since all the pavilions were made of wood, these cauldrons were always kept full of water. They date from the Ching Dynasty, which began in the middle of the seventeenth century and were originally gold-plated, but the invading forces of the nineteenth century scraped away the gold in their looting and destructive campaigns. These containers stand about a metre high and have a handle on each side in the shape of a lion's head with a ring in its mouth. We also saw this motif, which looks so Italian to us, on the doors of the Han tombs, dating back two thousand years.

The Hall of Perfect Harmony served as a kind of antechamber to the Hall of Supreme Harmony, and here the emperor performed minor ceremonies such as examining the seeds and implements before the planting. Here he also donned his ceremonial robes before entering the main hall, and the sedan chair used to carry him about in the Forbidden City is kept here. In China there were many very young emperors, who were only five or six years old when they ascended the throne. The high officials would tell them what to do and say during the coronation.

Next we visited the Hall of Preserving Harmony where the Imperial Examinations were held. These examinations, the most important in the country, being the springboard to high position at court or in administration, bestowed on the successful candidates the title of Scholar. The Palace Examinations were the final stage in the three-phase countrywide tests. The number of entrants and their ages varied from year to year as there were no age limits. Old men as well as young could apply. The exam lasted three days and three nights, the results being announced in this Hall. Sometimes those who failed committed suicide from shame.

Some of the side rooms of this palace display birthday gifts and household items of the imperial household – table services, wine bowls of jade and gold, jewelry, imperial robes. One of the most unusual items was a mat woven of tiny uniform slivers of ivory, alongside an enormous jade carving weighing five tons. Other jade carvings, featuring dragons in ocean waves and mountains, represent a Chinese saying: "May your happiness be as wide as the Eastern Sea and your age as high as South Mountain." Also many statues of Buddha are on display because the Ming and Ching emperors were Buddhists.

We were also impressed with the Dragon Pavement, an enormous marble carving in the middle of the staircase. We saw this form of decoration in many places, but this particular one was outstanding because of its size. It was sixteen metres long, three metres wide, and almost two metres thick, and weighed more than two hundred tons. The motif was nine dragons in many clouds. Nine is the highest odd single-digit number, and nine also symbolizes longevity, so the dragon not only symbolizes the emperor, but also his supreme power.

The single slab was transported from Fonshan County, about one hundred kilometres away, over ice. In the winter they dug a well and carried the water every five hundred metres. They spilt the water on the road and when it froze, they could slide the stone over the ice despite its weight.

In our walk through the grounds, we couldn't help noticing the beautiful pebble paths, which were laid out in intricate designs and a variety of colors – much finer than those we saw yesterday in the Summer Palace. We visited the private quarters of the Empress Dowager, and heard how this tyrannical empress, Ci Xi, rose from being a concubine of the fifth rank by virtue of bearing the emperor his only son. This son became the emperor but died quite young. Ci Xi shared imperial power with the emperor's wife but eventually poisoned her, thus becoming the sole, formidable ruler of the country for more than forty years. She died in 1908.

Finishing our tour at the residential palaces, we came out at the South Gate and returned to the hotel.

Well, we survived two and a half hours in the Forbidden City, sightseeing, listening, and looking. There's a great deal to look at. It must have been most splendid judging by everything that we saw. Back at the hotel, we stood at the window, looking across at the view again. The weather had cleared, the sun was shining and we could see the red roofs of the Forbidden City. Now we could say that we had indeed been there, and I thought: this brings our visit to China to its formal end. The rest of the day would be anti-climactic. Tomorrow at one, we will be off to Hong Kong. Everyone was quite exhausted.

Sunday evening, June 19

Just a few hours in Hong Kong and already our trip to China seems like a dream. It is incredible that we actually did it. Perfect timing, because I don't think the group could have held together much longer. Also, we were quite sated with sightseeing, museums and temples, not to mention shopping. And finally, the weather broke. Torrents of rain fell in Peking this morning, and we felt lucky that we didn't have to do any outdoor sightseeing as we had done yesterday. In fact, we only had two days of rain during the whole trip.

We spoke to the boys at home and were glad to hear that everything is okay. We instantly felt relieved.

To recall the rest of our last day in Beijing, on Saturday afternoon, we visited the Historical Museum, situated on the left-hand side of the great square, opposite the Great Hall of the People. The Mao Mausoleum stands between these buildings, opposite the red reviewing standard, and is flanked on each side by an enormous Soviet-style sculpture, a realistic portrayal of the Chinese struggle for freedom. A pillar monument in front of the mausoleum honors the Chinese martyrs of all wars and revolutions. We were not taken to the mausoleum in spite of our requests, which definitely gave us the impression that Mao is being downgraded. The presentation of modern history in the museum is slanted, of course, but even so, the exhibits from all periods, especially of ceramics and wooden machines of Chinese invention, were beautiful. The building is very grand and spacious, but again, Rivka said that the very finest pieces had been taken away to foreign museums by the invading powers of the last century, and to Taiwan by Chang Kai-shek.

In the evening, our last night in Beijing, we had our farewell banquet. It was a Peking duck dinner, but many other dishes were served as well, and everything was delicious. The service on this occasion, at the National Restaurant, was really excellent and the food most enjoyable, but the duck was definitely the *pièce de résistance*, and I couldn't resist it. I thought I could be forgiven for taking part just this once in a non-kosher meal.

The waiter brought in the tray of shiny glazed ducks for our approval before he began to carve, and we were soon busy wrapping the pieces of duck in little pancakes together with plum sauce and spring onions. There was much toasting and singing along with the eating, and we certainly did justice to that meal.

Although we shared the dining room with another group, divided by a screen, we had a very gay evening, with many speeches, much toasting and singing. Altogether, it was a very enjoyable conclusion to our Chinese adventure. We were only sorry that our assistant guide Miss Pan did not join us, which only proved to us that in modern China too, some people are less equal than others. We all felt very sympathetic toward Miss Pan, not only because she was a pleasant young lady, but also because we had discovered that she and her fiancé were not permitted to marry. Although they were the right age, twenty-six and twenty-seven, they were both still students and not yet independent.

One afternoon in Beijing during a free hour, my husband made a brief foray to the Foreign Bookshop, which was just around the corner from our hotel. We have found such shops, larger or smaller elsewhere, but (he told me) the one in Beijing is really impressive. He returned with a big grin on his face. "Look what I found!" he called, and waved a book at me. I looked up and had to join in his laughter. The book was *My First Sixty Years in China* by Sam Ginzburg, published in 1982.

So there were still Jews in China, in spite of the exodus in 1947–1948, and here was one telling his own story and the story of China in its most recent upheavals. How many more like him could there be?

It was some time before I actually had time to read the book. It is not great literature, but it is interesting because of the light it sheds on the life of Russian Jews in that part of the world at the turn of the century; because of the light it sheds on Europeans living in the international zones of China; because of its closeup view of daily life and historical events in China in the last forty years; and because it is the story of a Russian Jew who threw in his lot with the Chinese, married a Chinese woman and begat a Chinese family. But if Sam Ginzburg thinks he became completely assimilated, the title of his book belies this. A "first" sixty years portends a second sixty years, which together add up to 120, and that is the span of the life of Moses and the source of the traditional Jewish blessing, "until 120."

It takes a while to readjust to the "big city" life of Hong Kong. We treated ourselves to a long-anticipated cheese platter and fruit for lunch (fresh pineapple salad), and it tasted fantastic. We slept in the afternoon, and then gave films to be developed and wandered a bit. We had a fish supper and real ice cream, again in the hotel. I then had a long, hot, relaxing bath, phoned the kids, and headed to bed.

The luxury of the Holiday Inn was welcome, but we missed the hot water thermos and tea of China. Who said Israelis are the world's greatest tea drinkers? They can still learn from the Chinese. We also got used to seeing the people there up at 5:30 a.m. doing their gymnastics, and cycling to work at seven. Here nothing opens before nine and sometimes even ten. It was good that we started in Canton and left Beijing to the last. We could have used another day or two there so that we wouldn't have been under such pressure, but of what we saw and did before, there was really little that we could have given up. That day and a half we lost due to changed schedules of trains and planes would have been much appreciated.

Now that our trip to China is over, we have a feeling of satisfaction that we have seen all these wonderful places and that it all went so smoothly. We feel we have achieved something, something which seemed so problematical and difficult before we set out, and we're looking forward now to starting on our way back; we have a short break in Hong Kong, a visit to Katmandu, then Frankfurt and Jerusalem.

PART II

Thursday, June 23

We arrived in Katmandu, Nepal, yesterday lunchtime, after getting up at 4:45 a.m. Zipora traveled with us also, for this last week. We and many other people were astonished to find that Hong Kong Airport doesn't function before 7 a.m., and we barely had time for coffee before boarding. We'd stopped over at Dacca but were not permitted off the plane. In Katmandu, Ruth Kariv and her driver met us at the airport.

It was very hot, about 33°C, and there was a drought. We checked in at the Sheraton and drove on to the Israel Embassy where Shaul Kariv, our neighbor in Jerusalem, is serving now as ambassador. It was very odd to sit down to lunch with Shaul and Ruth in Katmandu, yet altogether the atmosphere was very homey and pleasant. They were very solicitous, and Ruth appointed herself our official guide. In the afternoon she took us to the Swayambut or Monkey Temple. What filth! There were monkeys, dogs, chickens and raggedy children all over the place. Even the temples were dirty and neglected; though from a distance the stupas looked picturesque and were already familiar to us from China. One difference here was the large eyes painted on the outside walls, which reminded us of the Eye of Horus in Egypt. We had dinner at the embassy and were early to bed.

This morning we woke up at about four but got up at 5:15 in order to make the Mountain Flight. The weather looked very dubious. It had rained during the night, and the sky was still overcast, but we had to go to the airport anyway, because of the regulations about cancellation. It was a very mixed crowd of mostly Indian, Chinese and Japanese. We hung around in the very simple waiting room until 7:30, when the powers-that-be finally decided that the skies were clearing up. When I saw the plane, I nearly changed my mind. It was an "Avro," a small two-propeller airliner for forty passengers. In fact, the hour-long flight was quite comfortable; a bit too cloudy for good viewing, but we did see the Himalayas and Mt. Everest, and marvelous cloud formations.

Ruth joined us for breakfast and then we drove to Bakhtapur, or Badgheon. This is a very old village being restored with German help. The main parts looked clean and very picturesque, but the side streets and people are very dirty. Little girls carrying babies on their backs wanted to be paid for being photographed, and they were quite persistent in their efforts. This came as quite a shock after the cleanliness of China, particularly as there was no begging there and we were never pestered in the streets.

The government is trying to develop and re-establish cottage industries. We saw woodcarving, which copies old patterns from the fantastic windows and screen decorations on old buildings. There was also clothing from local textiles, but only a few shops were pleasant to enter. I saw a nice ivory-colored horse, but the shopkeeper wouldn't give a reduction, and it was too expensive. Some bargaining is expected here, but it is not as bad as in Hong Kong.

There were many wells in the village squares, where laundry was being done, and people were washing themselves. One lady we saw was bare to the waist and quite oblivious of those around her. Suddenly we came into a crowded street, and heard music from a brass band. We found ourselves involved in a noisy wedding procession, in which the groom was going, in a highly decorated car, to fetch his bride to the ceremony.

There were Hindu carvings and brasses all over the place; Tantra art was different and new for us but so far we hadn't seen anything particularly attractive.

We visited the bead market in the old quarter of Katmandu, very colorful and attractive. There is also a special Indian section which catered particularly to tourists from Pakistan, and that seemed to constitute the major part of their trade.

By now, we were all feeling very tired, certainly not as fresh as we were three weeks ago.

Friday, June 24

We left early for Pashatpatur. Ruth said we must get there before they performed too many cremations and the stench became too strong. Indeed, when we arrived just after nine and walked down to the river, we found one cremation in full progress, and the ashes of another already being strewn on the water. The river is a tributary of the Ganges, and therefore holy.

Every twenty metres or so, there is a concrete platform or *ghat* jutting over the river, and this is where the cremations take place. It was a rather shocking sight, as we could see the body clearly in the fire, and it took quite a while before I could bring myself to look. We felt quite relieved that we didn't have to witness half a dozen or more such ceremonies. Not far from the burning pyre, children were swimming, women were doing laundry, and others were filling pitchers to take home.

Ruth explained that such cremations are not accompanied by religious rites, and indeed only one person, probably the closest relative, attended to each pyre. Altogether, death is not a very sad occasion because it is seen as a release of the spirit into another form of life.

Many stupas stood on the opposite bank, where we walked to get a view among the many monkeys, beggars, dogs, cows and crowds of people. Many were making a pilgrimage to the Hindu temple nearby, which we were forbidden to enter. Lots of family groups, very nicely dressed and in holiday spirit were carrying flower offerings to the temple. Altogether, it was quite an incredible sight.

We went on to visit the Tibetan refugee camp in Patan, which is well known for carpet making. They had a wide selection of rugs, traditional patterns worked in beautiful colors and designs, but strangely enough the workshop itself was in semi-darkness. We really wanted to buy, but we had too much overweight as it was to take anything more with us, and air freight was too expensive. The people we spoke to were very anxious to hear about China.

We bought some batik pictures in a nearby craft shop and returned to the hotel for a rest. I had an upset tummy after last night's Indian dinner and the heat was quite wearing.

We went out to see the old town centre, then on to Erev Shabbat dinner at the Karivs'.

Saturday morning, June 25

The old town, which we saw yesterday, is full of temples and historic buildings and markets. The narrow streets were crowded with shoppers and very noisy and colorful. Then we continued to the embassy, where we met other Israelis serving in Nepal and had a very pleasant dinner.

In answer to our surprise at seeing the swastika and the Star of David used here so frequently, in temples and on buildings, Ruth made inquiries and was told that for the Hindu the swastika is a symbol of prosperity. Financial reports carry the symbol on the front page, and accountants use it on their statements. Later in New Delhi, when we visited the Birla

Hindu Temple, we heard the same explanation and saw it also prominently displayed on a special pillar.

This six-pointed Star of David, or Magen David, symbolizes the goddess of learning, and is therefore used to denote schools and also as a decorative element in temples. The six points symbolize the points of contact man has with the world (through which he gains his knowledge), and some even see in the star a sexual symbol of perfect union. It would be interesting to know exactly how their star became the Jewish Star of David (which only dates back to the late seventeenth/early eighteenth century), but so far no one has succeeded in clarifying the connection.

This morning, Ruth took us out to Dhulikhel, about an hour's drive. I had thought I should stay in the room and rest, but began feeling better as the day progressed. It was a beautiful drive up into the mountains, very dramatic scenery, and very sparsely populated, and we saw several families by the roadside washing in mountain springs. The little resort was new, built in motel-style, with a commanding view of the mountains on the Chinese border. It would have been very soothing to stay a day or two.

We returned to have lunch with Avi and Maggie, who live in a very nice little house. They are both at the embassy. Maggie also happens to be the sister of our chief distributor, David Marciano, so we brought them special greetings. She prepared a very good meal but I was afraid to eat too much homemade pita, humus, fish and wonderful rice. After a long visit, I felt very weak and tired. We returned to the hotel and I slept three hours till 6:30 p.m. Then I discovered that Alex was sick, with very bad diarrhea and a temperature. Alex refused to let me call the doctor. I hoped he would feel better by tomorrow so we could continue as scheduled.

Frankfurt, June 28

We had thought that breaking up our return trip from Hong Kong would make for easier traveling. In fact, boarding planes in the middle of the night, and spending so much time and effort getting to and from airports was more tiresome than a long flight. Our visit to Nepal was marred by our tummy problems and similarly, in New Delhi, we suffered from insect bites and sleep deficit. In Frankfurt, we made the mistake of feeling that we had to exploit the opportunity to see the town, and we did not rest as much as we had planned. By then, we were also anxious to get home as soon as possible, so real relaxation was impossible. At the same time, I knew from past experience that there would be no chance to rest at home and one must pick up immediately where one left off – if no worse complications were waiting.

Nevertheless, it is with a feeling of great satisfaction that we look back on the travels and experiences of the last month, and wonder how long it will take before we will be ready to go off again! Even to China!

The Modest Genius, Reb Aisel Harif

Why the Book Was Written

NOT ALL MEMBERS OF A FAMILY ARE INTERESTED IN GENEALOGY or family history, but for those who are, the secret of success in finding material lies in talking to your elders, telling your children and grandchildren about relatives, past events, birthdates, and *yahrzeits*, etc. It is important to verify old photos with names, places and dates, and keep in touch with at least some of your relatives so that the story of your family can be kept alive for future generations. This, thanks to my father, is why and how my book came about.

The Hebrew edition of my biography of my great-great-grandfather, Rabbi Yehoshua Aisek (Isaac) ben Yehiel Shapira (1801–1873), fondly known as Aisel Harif, was a direct and unexpected outcome of *Rabbi Aisel Harif: His Life and His Sayings*, published in 1991. This book was conceived as a memorial to my father, Ze'ev (Wolf-Velvel) Shapiro, who passed away in November 1979. He had kept the memory of Rabbi Aisel alive for us.

Known as Aisel Harif for his sharp tongue and penetrating intellect, Rabbi Aisek was a descendent of the great sixteenth-century *posek* and Talmudist, the *Maharshal*, Rabbi Shlomo Luria of Lithuania. Though a genius and author of eleven original works, Reb Aisel is perhaps best remembered by less learned people also for his razor-sharp wit and his genuine modesty.

In 1852, Reb Aisel was invited by the Jews of the town of Slonim in Belarus to be their rabbi. Though he had no wish to be a Rosh Yeshiva, he placed great importance on upgrading the existing yeshiva so that it became as prestigious as other Lithuanian centres of learning. He placed equal importance on the need for charity to take care of the sick and poor. Much of his time was devoted also to the redemption of the *cantonistim*, those Jewish youths conscripted into the Tsar's army for twenty years or more. And despite his many duties, he continued his own studies and writing.

I knew about him already as a child although we hadn't a single *sefer* of his at home, and my father was always delighted when he found a reference or a quotation of his in the Hebrew or Yiddish press, even in Australia. My father was naturally proud of this illustrious ancestor, but I think this pride was strengthened and became more important to him because of the Holocaust, in which ninety-nine percent of his immediate family in Poland perished. He was the only surviving sibling out of seven. Some seventy men, women and children were murdered, as well as other branches of the family in Lithuania and Latvia of whom we knew nothing in the prewar period. In later years this also led my father to reprint all eleven works of Rabbi Aisel, because he was sure that only very few copies had survived the war, if at all.

So when my brother Alec and I undertook this project we did not have to start from scratch. We had a fair amount of information, but we discovered a great deal more. I had thought at first to translate *Rabbi Aisel Harif*, the biography written by Y. L. Levin, first published in Vilna in 1918, but I found the Hebrew archaic and cumbersome and decided to write my own version in English. Of course, the basic facts remained the same. When I had finished the main body of the story, I was asked by my editor what the experience meant to me and whether I knew anything of the descendants of Rabbi Aisel. Finding the answers to these questions enlarged the scope of the book, and led to the real genealogical quest – checking through historical books that had been written in earlier periods, searching through *Yizkor* books of various towns, and looking up earlier editions of Aisel's *seforim* for the information contained in the prefaces.

This aspect of the work, which took a long time – almost three years – was spent largely in the National Library in Jerusalem. Still, I must admit that luck or chance also played an important role in the discovery of our relatives. For example, in 1973, my father, *z"l*, arranged, through the auspices of the Culture Department of the Tel Aviv City Council, a memorial evening to mark the centenary of the death of Rabbi Aisel. The meeting was well-attended and after it was over, my father was approached by two sisters who identified themselves as great-granddaughters of Aisel's through his second son, Rabbi Moshe Shapira, Chief Rabbi of Riga. They had come to the public meeting out of curiosity to find out who had arranged the evening and thus discovered my father, a great-grandson through Aisel's first son, Issachar Ber, therefore a cousin. So a whole new page of family connections and their war experiences was opened to us.

In 1991, my brother Alec in London found another branch of the family in New York when he and Bruce Kahn of New York applied to the same genealogist for information about their families. On seeing the same names in both letters, the genealogist realized that Alec and Bruce must be related, and put them in touch with each other. A very creative relationship developed. Bruce was an early pioneer in finding basic sources of research in Lithuania and Latvia. Contacts discovered by him and by Alec's friend, Saul Isseroff, enabled further research, though the English translations left much to be desired. Soon, local people began offering their services in tackling the old records in the Russian or Latvian archives.

In 1992, after my book was published, I made contact with Mr. Zvi Shefet, the chairman of the Irgun Olei Slonim in Israel. In the summer of that year, he led a group of members on a trip to Slonim and to Vilna. In Vilna, he found a small Jewish museum in the community centre that was run by a gentleman and featured his own private collections. This man, a former captain in the Soviet army, introduced himself as Josefas Sapero (Yosef Shapira), an *einikel*, or grandson, of Aisel Harif. He was very surprised when Mr. Shefet told him that there was a branch of the family in Jerusalem and that a book about Aisel had recently been written.

Contact was quickly established between us, which has led to an ongoing relationship.

Today, Vilna is an important centre for Jewish tourism because of its pre-eminence in the Jewish world before 1939. Thus, Yosef is in a focal position and meets many visitors in his museum. One day in 1997, a man from Johannesburg wandered in, looking for stamps and first-day covers featuring the Vilna Gaon, Rabbi Eliyahu ben Shlomo Zalman. He confided to Josefas his disappointment in his visit to Slonim, where he had hoped to visit the grave of his ancestor, Aisel Harif, but had found an empty cemetery. His name was Isel Krinski, and he was greatly surprised to find a relative in Vilna, one who even knew of the existence of other branches of the family. Isel soon got in touch with us. My brother and I were very happy with this development because we had lost all knowledge of this family, descendants of Aisel's daughter Nehama. We believed them to be somewhere in the States – therefore the New York inquiries – but Isel informed us that they had in fact migrated to South Africa in the late 1920s. However, we were also in touch with another branch in the States whom my father remembered from Poland. Thanks to the fact that Avram, son of Mordechai, Aisel's third son, migrated to the States at the beginning of the twentieth century, the families of his children, Isaac Mayer and Pauline Stavisky, have grown into a veritable tribe.

These are just a few examples of how apparently random events contributed to the expansion of our knowledge of our family, which resulted eventually in the second English edition of my book in 2004.

However, I must admit I had actually little to do with the genealogical tabulation. My brother, already a confirmed genealogist when my father passed away, was experimenting with various genealogical computer programs. During the 1980s, he traveled extensively to meet with my mother's surviving brothers in Argentina, Brazil and Uruguay in order to gather first-hand information from them about that family, the Schultzes. In the end, he worked through all the associated "married-in" families of my parents' and our own family, and registered some thousand names in the Dorot Genealogy Department of Beit Hatfutsoth, the Museum of the Jewish People, in Tel Aviv.

Such was the result of a happy and fruitful collaboration between my brother Alec in London and myself in Jerusalem to honor the memory of our father.[1]

1 The four books that resulted from this collaboration were:

Rafaeli, Esther. *Rabbi Aisel Harif, His Life and His Sayings: A Family Memoir*. First edition. Jerusalem: Ahvah Press, 1991. The Hebrew translation of this book appeared in 1993.

Rafaeli, Esther. *The Modest Genius: Reb Aisel Harif*. Second edition. Jerusalem: Devorah Publishing, 2004.

Rafaeli, Esther. *Rabbi Aisel Harif: His Life and His Sayings*. Hebrew version of the second edition. Jerusalem: Urim Publications, 2010.

... and Weddings

ONE OF THE FEATURES OF THE NEW APARTMENT IN DISRAELI Street, which I loved at first sight, was the beautiful wide staircase leading up to the front door. Shaped like an inverted Y, it gave the house a gracious period-like air, and I immediately thought what beautiful weddings we would have here when the time came. Of course, like many dreams, this one did not fully materialize, because three of the weddings took place in winter, necessitating an indoor setting. Even so, we had three weddings at the house, and one in a hotel – that was of the firstborn, who liked more formal occasions. Each wedding, just like each bridal couple, had a character of its own.

The first to wed was Lonny, the younger son, in February 1981, a little over a year after my parents passed away. In fact, the first time I saw the bride-to-be, Yuli Tamir, was at my father's funeral, which she attended out of sympathy for Lonny, but we did not "meet." When she began coming to the house, we found her attractive and rather reserved. It was an interesting surprise to discover that she was a descendent of one of the leading Mapai families, that of Dov Hos, and had grown up in that highly political environment of Mapai activists and national leaders. She was also very interested in politics, and was one of the founders of the newly established Peace Now movement. My father had been a staunch Revisionist ever since I could remember, and my husband had devoted some fifteen years of his life to the IZL before I met him. An uneasy alliance!

Yuli's family agreed that it would be nice to have the wedding at our home, and we invited Rabbi Louis Rabinowitz, an old friend of my husband's, to conduct the ceremony. He had been Senior Chaplain to the Jewish members of the British army during World War II, and then Chief Rabbi of Johannesburg, the Transvaal and Orange Free State. He was also a Revisionist. When he came to meet the young couple, he explained how he conducted weddings: the ceremony would start three minutes after the appointed time and would last sixteen minutes. No waiting for stragglers. And so it was – to everyone's satisfaction.

Fortunately, both sides had wanted a small family ceremony, with the reception being held immediately after. Many were in for a surprise when they saw the assembled guests, and thought a social revolution had occurred – Mapainiks and capitalists, Etzelniks and Palmah veterans – all coming together to celebrate a politically "mixed marriage." In those days, the rifts between the political parties still held sway, and the old animosities had not yet completely faded away.

The apartment had been decorated with beautiful floral arrangements, and we had hired an eminent caterer from Tel Aviv. Jerusalem was still lagging behind in these niceties, and although the food was excellent and beautifully presented, it was still not of the standard we see today.

Any awkwardness between the guests was smoothed over by the musical program supplied by the bride's very musical family. We had a piano, and sang together in a wonderful sing-along of Zionist and Yiddish songs, which all the guests enjoyed. My husband, Alex, then aged seventy-one, topped off the happy atmosphere by dancing a lively *kazachok*. My brother Alec and his wife Aliza came from London, which added greatly to our enjoyment.

Rabbi Rabinowitz also officiated at the next marriage, which was that of our daughter Varda, who married a fellow archaeology and Egyptology student, Amihai Ophel. This wedding took place in December 1982, as she wanted to make a gesture in my father's memory, whose birthday was on the sixth Hanukkah light. This was how we always remembered it, without knowing the civil date. When the time came to order a tombstone for my father, we had to look up his birth date in a hundred-year calendar book to find it.

Amihai's family had come from Yemen many years before. His father's family had left Yemen at the turn of the twentieth century. After a long stay in Egypt, during which Amihai's father was born, they came to Israel in the late 1920s. Sarah, the girl he was eventually to marry, arrived in the early 1930s, quite alone. When we met, I was very surprised at the good English Amihai's father spoke, and he explained that he had served in the British army in World War II.

Amihai and his three sisters were born in Israel, and Amihai's aunt owned a complete traditional Yemenite wedding costume which had been in her family, and was herself a professional "dresser." As a wedding present, she offered the couple a genuine *hina* (henna) ceremony, which was held two nights before the actual wedding in the Beth ha-Am of Yehud, Amihai's home town. The *hina* tradition was then enjoying a revival amongst young Yemenite couples; it is not of purely Jewish origin but a result of acculturation, and can be seen in various forms throughout the Middle East and even in India. The henna plant, or *kofer* in Hebrew, which grows profusely in Israel, was highly valued already in biblical times for its beauty, aroma, practical and medical properties. It is mentioned in the Song of Songs as one of the valuable spices to which the Beloved is compared. The root and/or the leaves are ground to a powder which, when mixed with water, creates an excellent dye of a reddish-orange hue that is popular as a hair dye or beauty treatment and for dyeing textiles. It naturally became a symbol of fertility and good luck.

The "dresser" had inherited the costume, the jewelry and the tradition from her mother, and was also obliged to lend it to poor brides without charge. She brought the traditional "singer" as well, who led the ceremony and the singing. It took two hours to dress Varda, and she also had to change her costume during the evening, according to the custom. She then wore a green dress, the color being an important fertility symbol, and exchanged the tall floral headdress for the close-fitting, hood-like *gargoosh*, decorated with large coins, originally Austrian gold thalers. She looked great in both ensembles. Typical Yemenite music was performed on large tins and drums as it had been in the old country, where Jews had not been permitted to use real musical instruments.

It had promised to be a very different evening, a promise which was fulfilled, with much beauty and exciting music, not to forget the candle dance, in which a basket of flowers and lit candles were carried on the head and passed around amongst the guests. An older woman whom the family wished to honor performed the henna application. She mixed the henna powder with a special liquid solution and spread the henna paste on the palms of the bridal couple where it stayed until the skin took on the color. In the past, it used to be applied also to the soles of the feet, as a blessing or wish that the bride would be happy and successful wherever she went and in whatever work her hands undertook.

Wedding guests could later decorate their hands or fingers for good luck, and for several days the color would show that they had attended a wedding. The mostly Ashkenazi guests were fascinated. Food was simple and not an important element.

The white-dress wedding was held two days later at our home; the Hanukkah candles were lit, the songs sung, and my parents were remembered on this happy occasion, which they had not been privileged to enjoy. Singing and dancing, and food, rounded out the evening.

The third wedding was that of Asi, our firstborn son, to a very attractive young blonde woman named Nurit Marton, a graduate in Fine Arts. They met when they had a difference of opinion about a parking place, but Asi left an apologetic note on her car window, and a friendlier relationship quickly developed. Her parents and sister had come to Israel from Romania in 1961, after her father, Dr. Alex (Sandu) Marton, had served for ten years as a gynecologist in some isolated little village. This was a punishment for being a Zionist and requesting permission to leave the country. He was born in a remote, peaceful little town in Transylvania, but the year 1944 found the family, after many trials and tribulations, in the ghetto of the Romanian city of Cluj. They were sent in one of the first transports to Auschwitz, where his mother was taken from her family and never seen again. The father and two sons continued the journey to Mauthausen and from there to a subsidiary work camp, where they managed to remain together for quite some time.

Then the younger brother caught typhus and died, and the father was shot dead because his ability to work was decreased after an accident. Now seventeen years old and alone in the world, Sandu managed to survive the oppressive conditions and emerged from the camps with a strong belief that his mission in life was to help the sick and the suffering, of which he had already seen plenty. He studied medicine at the University of Cluj and became a gynecologist. As mentioned, after his enforced service in a remote village, he was allowed to leave Romania. Along the way, he married Clarissa, and they had their first daughter, Ronit. Many years later he wrote about his World War II camp experiences in a book called *186 Steps*. This was a reference to the murderous stone stairway of his work camp, which the prisoners had to ascend and descend daily on their way to and from work in the mines and tunnels they were building. This stairway took a tremendous toll in human life.

Nurit was born in Jerusalem at the Bikur Holim Hospital, where her father was a senior gynecologist for many years. My father had helped build the hospital in the 1920s, and both my daughters were born there.

Their wedding, a very formal affair, was held at the King David Hotel with the rabbi from our local synagogue, Rabbi Burstein, officiating. Alec and Aliza came again from London for the festivities. There was a lot of Romanian-Hungarian music and dancing and a very *heimish* atmosphere.

In August 1995, we finally had our garden wedding. Karni was a beautiful bride as she made her way down the stairs to marry Ophir Barak, a very Orthodox young man from a Romanian family, who was studying film. Karni had already adopted the more observant lifestyle, a result of her search for a more meaningful Jewish life experience.

While she was still in the army, she had begun attending Kabbalah classes. Later, during her BA studies at the Hebrew University, she became interested in yoga and decided to take time off to study the subject and become a teacher. We looked askance at this decision, but she explained that (a) it would give her a second profession, and (b) there were many ideas in yoga that she could apply to her job as a social worker. We were happy that she had not ended up in India.

For the garden wedding, we had a low wooden platform made for the *huppah* and covered with a carpet so that it would be more comfortable than standing on the lawn. When the *huppah* was put up, it all looked very attractive. Although we had placed chairs around for the guests, there were not enough for everyone. The stairs came in handy for latecomers who ranged themselves there and had a great view of the ceremony. When everyone joined in singing *"Im Eshkahech Yerushalayim"* ("If I forget, thee, O Jerusalem"), the words and music floated out on the air of a late Jerusalem afternoon to create a wonderful magical moment. Another nice surprise was the arrival of Yuli, Lonny's wife, who came unexpectedly from the States, where she was doing postdoctoral research.

The young rabbi who officiated was a friend of Karni's, and although very Orthodox, was known for his openness to modern ideas. For instance, he asked his wife to speak to the bridal couple on the role of marriage in one's life, which she compared to an orchestra that could make beautiful music when all were in harmony, but could be most discordant when not.

Dinner was served on the adjoining tennis court of the Touring Club to the music of a klezmer band. The children presented me with a decorated broom with which I symbolically swept the floor to the music of the old Yiddish song about marrying off the youngest daughter, *"Die Mazinka Ausgegeben."* It was a wonderful evening.

However, beautiful weddings do not necessarily make beautiful marriages. Two years later, Karni, realizing that her life was not going as she had expected, decided to opt out. It was a great shock to Alex and me as we had no inkling of trouble until the matter was over. Some years and several grandchildren later, all the marriages had broken up, not because of any scandal but because each person saw they were going in different, incompatible directions. We became parents of four divorced sons and daughters, each event coming like a thunderbolt and proving difficult to digest. There were many unhappy conversations and discussions in our usually tranquil blue kitchen during this period. I began to understand that not always do the parents educate the children, but sometimes the children educate the parents, especially in some of the more difficult lessons of life – such as the art of keeping quiet.

In August 1999, Karni married a young man by the name of Shuki Mitz. He was obviously also observant, from a Romanian Yiddish-speaking family, and had a young son from a previous marriage. Strangely enough, the family met him for the first time when he came to visit Karni during the *shivah* for Alex. He and Karni made a nice couple. We were still in mourning for Alex, but we knew he would be happy that Karni had found a suitable young man and would not want them to postpone the wedding for a year. Six months later, we arranged for a morning ceremony at Shuki's synagogue in Ra'anana, and my brother Alec came again with Aliza from London. Though it was a small affair, it was a happy occasion, and Karni went on to have three children in the next six years.

Some five years later Lonny, the father of two grown daughters, married Liora Ofer, a very pleasant and attractive businesswoman with two adult children, a son and a daughter. They had a small, elegant wedding in the bride's home, the officiating rabbi being Rabbi Shmuel Rabinowitch, a family friend and the administrator in charge of the Kotel. The two families get on very well, and as none of the children lives at home, Lonny and Liora are free to come and go as they please.

Though my adult children seem to be happy now with their lives, there is still room for worry about the grandchildren (how not?), who range in age from four to twenty-seven, each in a different stage of his or her life, and having to deal with the uncertain and changing world around them. But this is worry twice removed. I don't have to advise or take responsibility, and I have no influence over world affairs. From my own experience, I have learned that one must do one's best in meeting the challenges of life and make the most of every opportunity, and that, with a little bit of luck, things usually work out well without interference.

Many have said that life passes like a dream, but it is a dream that has to be lived day by day, somehow.

Varda and Amihai

Scene at the Hina ceremony

Alex and Varda relax
after wedding 1982.

Asi and Nurit wedding 1988.

Left: Alex, Netta, Aliza; Right: Alec, I and Itamar, 1985

Lonny – a helping hand

With cousin Jean Saltzman; photo by her husband Joe, 1997

Karni and Shuki

Myself, Alec and Aliza at Karni's wedding.

Lonny and Liora – honeymoon at Galapagos Islands 2004.

12 Disraeli St., with cousins Fremd from Uruguay.

The Turkish Bath – the Hamam

Summer, 1984

MANY YEARS AGO, IN THE SUMMER OF 1984, MY HUSBAND AND I went on a three-week trip to Turkey. It was our first experience of "organized travel," and introduced us to the luxury of having someone else worry about the arrangements, the transport, the lost luggage and the daily program. The trip was organized by the Israel Museum, and as most of the participants were museum volunteers who knew each other, they made a very congenial group of a comfortable size. We went overnight by ship from Ashdod to the small Turkish port of Kusha Dasi, where we began our bus tour.

Turkey was a revelation to those of us who knew little about the country, and had forgotten whatever history we had once learned. The size of the country, its wealth of historical and cultural sites, its geographic location, simply amazed us.

Our first visit was to the ancient, well-preserved Roman city of Ephesus, and from there we traveled northward by bus toward Anatolia. In three weeks we were able to cover a lot of territory. The countryside was varied and beautiful, the towns were clean, and the history of the vast Ottoman Empire unfolded itself in all its impressive aspects.

One element, however, eluded us – a visit to a Turkish bath, a genuine *hamam*. This idea was fixed in our minds as something we *had* to do while in Turkey in order to have a real Turkish experience. The guide kept telling us that it was "no problem," but whichever hotel we stayed at either had no *hamam*, or it was under repair and/or closed. Our goal seemed unobtainable.

When we passed the halfway point of our tour and began the approach to Istanbul, the guide started to get excited. "Soon we will arrive in Bursa. We stay there at a real luxury hotel and they have a beautiful *hamam*. You will really enjoy." But alas, the beautiful *hamam*, really beautiful, was not yet open for the season. We were very disappointed and the guide, wanting to keep his customers happy, promised us that he would "arrange" something. By now we were quite skeptical.

But lo and behold, the next day he announced that he had arranged for us to go to the local municipal bathhouse; we would get our Turkish experience. A time was fixed. Men and women had separate facilities; towels were provided, so we didn't have to take anything with us. Not everyone was keen to go, but nevertheless, we were about five or six women and an equal number of men. We boarded the bus and soon arrived at our destination.

There were separate entrances to the two separate sections, although both were situated in the one building. An old crone, completely covered from head to foot in layers of clothing, took the entrance fee. When we asked about a massage, she nodded her head, a sign she understood what we wanted. She ushered us in to a large changing room with rows of wooden benches, and after we undressed, pointed us into the direction we had to go.

We walked into a great hall where there was a large pool, and along each wall were little alcoves each with a tap, where mothers were washing innumerable numbers of children, of both sexes and all ages, before they went into the pool. Suddenly a great hush fell on the public. We looked at them and they stared at us. *They* were *all* wearing underpants; *we* were all stark naked, having been told that we didn't need to take bathing suits or anything, because of the separate facilities. It took a few minutes for us to grasp the situation, and then we had to laugh – it was so incongruous.

There was no going back, so we just continued on our way, showered briefly and entered the pleasantly warm pool.

Just as we were beginning to relax and enjoy, I saw a woman beckoning me out of the pool. "Massage, massage," she indicated to me, and only then I realized it was the previously bundled up woman who had taken the entrance money. Now she was wearing only panties. I got out of the water, and she gestured to me to lie down on my tummy at the edge of the pool. Real luxury! This threw my friends into paroxysms of laughter, and I must admit, though I felt rather ridiculous, I had to laugh at myself. The woman squatted beside me and began to massage my back with what felt to me like Scotchbrite, but perhaps that was just the texture of her hands.

Only one other lady was game for this treatment. The others begged off.

We had a few more minutes in the water and our time was up. We trooped back over wet floors to the dressing room for our towels and clothes, and began to appreciate why the Turkish ladies of old wore those high platform sandals in the *hamam*, as seen in Turkish ethnographic exhibits.

We rejoined the men on the bus, and exchanged stories about our adventures in the genuine Turkish *hamam*. We had certainly had our Turkish experience, but I couldn't help wondering about the reactions of the Turkish people on seeing the cultured, shameless European ladies appearing naked in public. What would *they* talk about tonight at the dinner table, and probably for many more nights as well?

Melbourne Revisited 1987
Part 1

WHAT A STRANGE DAY! AFTER ALL THE TENSION AND WORRIES OF the recent weeks and the excitement of last weekend when we celebrated the birthdays of Asi and Karni, and Asi announced his engagement to Nurit – a sudden stop! Here, in Cairo waiting for my connection to Australia, I had a hiatus in which I had nothing to do but kill a few hours. It was strange to find myself in Cairo, which was then the shortest way to fly to Australia. The mix of people at the airport was completely Middle Eastern, as different from Israel as night from day – dark and very dark complexions rather than fair; dark traditional Moslem dress rather than the casual colorful clothes of the West.

At last, I had time to digest the fact that I was actually on my way to Melbourne – after an interval of thirty years. My feelings were rather ambivalent and therefore I had great difficulty in making this decision. Did I really want to go? Were there still people who remembered me and really wanted to see me? I had seen my relatives and closest friends within the last six or seven years when they visited Jerusalem. What would I feel when I went back to the scenes of my adolescent years? Excitement?

Depression? Nostalgia? But as the song says, "Everybody's doing it," making the sentimental journey back to childhood.

In the end, my brother Alec finally persuaded me to join him in accepting our cousin Jean's invitation to the wedding of her son Mark, which in itself would enable me to see many of my old friends. I dreaded the journey, but everyone seemed to survive it, so I would too.

I also had the time to absorb the fact that Asya, now in his mid-thirties, is finally to marry – to make a commitment; he is so utterly happy and elated, and Nurit Marton appears to be a pleasant and attractive young lady. We were really quite touched at the depth of his feelings. It had been many years since we'd seen him so happy and relaxed and declaring that life is good. It was quite a revolution.

The Heliopolis Sheraton is a very comfortable and luxurious hotel, and I had a good rest between flights. Though it was only a one-hour flight from Tel Aviv, the accumulated stresses of the past weeks' events, plus getting up early in the morning to make the plane, had quite tired me out. At the airport, we were kept in the bus a half-hour without explanation until suddenly a whole convoy escorting President Mubarak drove by, which explained the delay. He waved, little knowing who or how angry we were, but I did get a good look at him. I slept a couple of hours in the afternoon, then called home, showered, ate and returned to the airport around 11 p.m. for my connecting flight. No other Israelis were bound for the same destination as I.

Cairo to Bombay (now called Mumbai) is about a five-hour flight. I had a double seat so could doze a little, but actually, after some three hours, breakfast was served and a movie shown. Singapore Airlines' service lived up to its reputation. There were many stewards and attractive stewardesses, all pleasant and smiling, anxious to please. Meals were served on white napkins with real crockery and there were orchids in the wc. It was nice to be traveling business class. The airline also invited business class passengers to use the special first-class lounge at Cairo Airport. In Bombay, we were not allowed off the plane. Maybe just as well, as the night temperature outside hit 28 degrees centigrade and was very humid. Many passengers debarked, but the steward said that the plane would be full again. Hordes of cleaners came on and one couldn't move about. It was 6:30 a.m. my time, 10 a.m. locally. From the air, one saw many tin hovels and shanty towns, but the city itself was certainly more handsome. Nevertheless, the first sight left a bad impression.

Bombay to Singapore

We had a two-hour wait and a delay because of security checks. I'd always thought El Al was tops in security, but other countries also take this matter very seriously. In Cairo and Singapore, passengers underwent additional checks before entering the plane. We had a three-and-a-half-hour wait in Singapore. It seemed there was more waiting around than actual flying. The journey time to Australia is about nineteen hours of actual flying and seven to eight hours of waits and stops. The Singapore airport is as attractive as I was told, very spacious with a two-storey waterfall. Many fine shops but I didn't see any bargains. Good use was made of the VIP lounge, which provides snacks, coffee and drinks.

The time drags. I kept wondering how it would be to arrive in Melbourne. Would I be pleased that I had come? I was apprehensive, but at the same time, I did not feel the degree of tension that I had felt in recent weeks.

Adelaide

We flew this leg on a "Big Top Boeing," a quiet aircraft, but there was much turbulence. The plane was full. My neighbor was a German fellow coming to check on some machinery of his that wasn't working as it should. He liked to drink and talk, and he snored. I did not sleep much because a little Indian girl nearby screamed nearly the whole time. There was another unnecessary delay – a security check, even of transit passengers coming into the lounge. I saw the new face of Australia: less blonde and blue-eyed, and more European and Asian – the results of the new immigration policy of recent years, which aimed at rapidly increasing the national population of eight million, which was the figure during World War II.

One more stop and I will have reached my destination. Pity we couldn't go directly to Melbourne and skip Adelaide.

Sunday night, November 29

Only late at night was I given my first chance to jot down the happenings and impressions of the first days. The plane finally arrived in Melbourne on Friday. I was quite agitated and very, very tired. Went smoothly through passport control and customs and came out looking for my friend Claire Cymons, but I found her husband Albert instead. She had been held up somewhere and sent him in her place.

As we drove along and familiar sites came by, I began to get excited, but also bewildered. The street names rang bells, but so many big new buildings had cropped up to change the old scenes. I felt completely disoriented. We finally got to the South Yarra Hills where I was to stay, but I had to wait for the accommodation to be prepared. So I went with Albert to have a bite in a little café, run, surprisingly, by young Israelis. When I came back, I found that the apartment we had reserved was quite comfortable but not luxurious. I began to answer phone messages left by friends, but didn't accept any invitations for the time being. It was twelve noon local time, but twenty-four hours since I had left Cairo. I went to bed and slept on and off. In the evening I called my husband Alex to report, unpacked, received a basket of fruit and cheese from Claire and Sonia Sicree, which served me as supper, and went back to bed. These friends, who are cousins, are part of the little nucleus of friends from my university years.

Next I knew, the phone was ringing. I jumped out of bed, not knowing where I was, and looked distractedly for the telephone. Then I remembered that it was in the living room, and rushed to reach it before the person hung up. It was my brother Alec calling from London, but I just couldn't make sense for at least ten minutes, and we had a good laugh at my expense. He is due to arrive on December 2, and gave me his flight number and arrival time.

As the morning wore on I began to feel better, and at 12:30 p.m. my cousin Jean came to fetch Uncle Herschel and me for lunch at her home. Jean looked well and full of energy. Her father Pinhas, Uncle Herschel and my mother were three siblings out of eight of the Schultz family, whose lives had taken them in completely different directions. Herschel, a survivor of the camps who had lost his wife and two children, looked well in spite of his medical problems. Unfortunately, his companion, Dolly, was in hospital for observation. The lunch dragged on as the family trickled in slowly – the sons, Mark and Darron, and daughter Ilana. There was much talk and I heard the problems about Mark's future in-laws, and saw that Jean and her husband Joe had much aggravation about this wedding. They had little in common with the bride's parents, and the bride herself had a doubtful reputation.

My friends Sonya and Ron Sicree took me for a ride. Ron looked rather haggard, having had a second heart operation just a couple of months before, but to my surprise, drove the car. We went to see Carlton, where I had lived as a child. After having a bite, we walked along Lygon Street, which was full of cars and people. Restaurants, cafés and ice cream parlors had sprung up around this modest shopping centre, where my mother used to shop on Sunday morning. It was an extraordinary sight. In the old days, nobody walked in the streets at night, yet here was a distinctly lively continental scene. Italian seems to have become the second language of the country. Sonya and Ron met some friends, some of whom remembered me from elementary school, Habonim, or University groups.

After a few days, there was a pre-wedding party for Mark, attended by many of my old friends. I couldn't sleep much that night because of the agitation the meetings engendered, so I got up to update my diary. During the party, there were constant discussions of illnesses, operations and deaths – not very cheerful. The next day, Jean and Joe took me for a ride to Carlton. Although Carlton and North Carlton are lower–middle-class suburbs, the basic plan of wide streets, parks and gardens, typical of Melbourne, made for attractive residential areas even for the lower-income groups. As we came into Carlton through Elgin Street, I immediately looked for number

92, my childhood home – one of a terrace of three small houses. There it was, quite a shock, and I almost cried. In my mind's eye, I could see on the veranda the packing cases, which we had used in 1935 to go to Palestine. My piano teacher had lived next door but one.

We noted the still-existing Jewish landmarks: Allan Markov, the chemist; Aleck Sacks, the lawyer, still near the courthouse; and Altschuler's Jewish bookstore. We turned down Rathdowne Street, past the Carlton Synagogue, past the small Stone Synagogue, the rabbi's home, my elementary school, the old centre of the Ivriah Club, on down to 94 Amess Street, where we lived after returning from Palestine in 1936. The little house was still there, but I didn't have the courage to knock on the door. Incredible to see how little things had changed, mainly that the hat factory, which was next to us, was no longer. The iron lace railings, a feature of Melbourne architecture, which I had forgotten, caught my attention. Apparently, the houses in this suburb, whose population now is mainly Italian, are in great demand, and worth fortunes because of their proximity to town and to Melbourne University. It is forbidden to alter the exteriors, but permitted to remodel the interiors according to one's taste and pocket.

Tuesday, December 1

Pouring with rain and very strong winds. A call from Arnold Rose woke me at 8:00 a.m. I spent the day with Sonia visiting a contemporary art gallery and the National Gallery, and unexpectedly met friends. An interesting exhibition had been mounted called "Hatches, Matches and Dispatches" (Birth, Marriage and Death) – exhibiting clothing and accessories of the last hundred years. Very beautiful items, beautifully displayed. We also visited the Museum of Modern Aboriginal Art, which was very interesting, featuring the use of traditional tribal patterns in their art. The early Australian art was very impressive, and I had never seen it before displayed on any large scale.

Sonia left me in town and I went to have a look at the old Myers Emporium, one of the oldest department stores, founded by a once-Jewish family, and the equivalent of Selfridges in London or Macy's in New York. Christmas decorations were not exciting, and I didn't find the toy kangaroos I wanted to buy for the grandchildren. I managed to buy a pair of walking shoes, as I had brought nothing for such rainy weather, and walked a little before I got on a tram to go to the hotel. I had dinner at the Sicrees, a very nice evening, and we sat around the table chatting until 11:30 p.m.

Wednesday, December 2

I spoke on the phone with Alex and with Alec in the morning. No rain, but still very windy. Because of the time difference with London, I had time to rush out to Sotheby's, the auction house, about selling a small painting by William Dobell that I had bought many years ago during a visit to his studio. Dobell, one of the leading Australian painters at that time, was famous for his portraits, but the painting I had was a New Guinea scene. It had not "grown" on us and we decided to sell it, preferably in its country of origin. My visit to Melbourne was the ideal opportunity. The estimate was not as high as I had thought it would be, but I left it to be auctioned anyway. Then I had trouble getting a taxi and, after twenty aggravating minutes, finally shared one with a woman who was going in the same direction. Just had time for a quick coffee and then Jean fetched me to go to the airport to meet Alec. She was very tense and is obviously deeply unhappy about the wedding. This is Mark's first serious love and the girl and her family are unsuitable. I think Jean and Joe wouldn't mind if it were canceled at the last minute.

We met Alec and I thought he looked well in spite of the long flight from London. We returned to the apartment and had a bite to eat. Alec went to sleep and in the evening we visited his friend Lionel Landman. I could not help but think it was an odd, déjà-vu situation, Alec and I here together in Melbourne after an absence of thirty years, seeing old friends as if nothing had happened in between. Life plays strange tricks that are sometimes unpleasant, but fortunately also pleasant at times.

Alec and I at Ayers
Rock, 1987

From left: Di, Arnold,
Albert, Ron, me,
Sonia Claire

Karni visits old home
at 94 Amess St.

Thursday, December 3

We went to visit Uncle Herschel and had to eat a second breakfast. He enjoys playing the host, and this became a ritual during our visit. We stayed a few hours and Alec gave all the news about his trip to Uruguay and Brazil, where he had visited two other brothers of Herschel and my mother. He made this trip because he was working on the family genealogy, and wanted to grasp the chance of still being able to talk to the older generation.

Later we went to the Jewish Museum and talked to the curator, Dr. Helen Light. I gave her regards from the curators of the Israel Museum (where I volunteer as a guide), with whom she keeps close contact. The Jewish Museum had some interesting tapes about the history of Australian Jewry and I would have bought copies, but due to copyright problems, they were not yet for sale.

This evening was spent with Arnold Rose and his family. I had known Arnold's first wife Norma in high school, but we only became close friends while studying at the University of Melbourne. She passed away at too early an age and I felt sad at her absence, but life had inevitably continued without her. Arnold and Norma had married when they were just twenty years old, and their little house became a popular meeting place for their single friends on Sunday afternoons and evenings.

(All my friends seemed to have classy new cars, newer and fancier than what we have at home. Jean's daughter Ilana drove a jeep, but that was strictly for youngsters because it had a very high step. I thought my old Fiat looked very shabby in comparison.)

Arnold and his companion, Di, offered us the use of their place in Surfers' Paradise in Queensland if we decide to make the trip north. This town, on the so-called Gold Coast, had become a popular refuge from Melbourne's winter, and it was now the thing to own an apartment there. It was a real temptation. After talking it over with Alec's friend Lionel, a travel agent, we decided to go. I hoped it would work out well and that it wouldn't be too hot.

Friday evening, December 4

We had Shabbat dinner at Jean's with a Kiddush but no *zemirot* or *benching*, all very casual. The whole family attended. We sat and talked and Alec reported again about the family he had met in Uruguay, Brazil and Buenos Aries. My Saltzman cousins are a balanced couple – Joe talks little and Jean talks a lot. She was taking everything very personally and easily got upset, but then it was the difficult pre-wedding period and not a happy one, and that had to be taken into consideration. Mark asked Alec jokingly if he knew what an *aufruf* was, and Alec assured him that indeed he had a good grounding in Jewish customs, and would not disgrace the event. They wouldn't allow us to order a taxi, and Ilana took us home in her jeep, even though it was a very long drive. She states her views very decidedly, has a great sense of humor, and did very well in her law studies.

Saturday, December 5

It was a very busy day. Ilana and Herschel picked us up about 9:30 and we drove to shul, as did most of the congregation. Nevertheless, there was separate seating for men and women in the Orthodox way. The women's gallery gradually filled up. But it was quite a shock when the *chazan* (cantor) began to sing! A "broken" voice! Apparently, he'd had an operation on his vocal cords some years ago, and he sounded terrible and very hard to follow. The *lainen* (the chanting aloud of the Torah portion) was very prolonged because they called up about fifteen people instead of the usual seven, with the *chazan* reading it all. The women chattered the whole time. It was appalling. O for Shabbat in Jerusalem, I thought. Alec was one of the few who could be heard, and Mark said the *berachot* (the blessings said before and after every section of the Torah reading) very nicely. The most surprising was Joe's nephew, who chanted the *haftarah* beautifully. That was the best part of the whole service.

There was a nice Kiddush for the whole congregation and again, we met many mutual friends. This was followed by lunch at Jean's. In the afternoon, I visited Mrs. Lachman, a friend of my mother's, and her whole family, whom I also knew, was there. Mrs. Lachman had difficulty walking, but mentally she was fine. She could see well and still spoke Hebrew, having come to Melbourne from Safed in the 1920s. She was the last one left of the old guard, she informed me, except for Tania Saks, who was in the Montefiore Home and had become senile. A world gone by, and yet most Jewish elements in Melbourne today – the Jewish schools, the cultural centres and Zionist activities – had grown out of that world and the motivated people who pioneered it.

We sat around talking for many hours and had to rush home to be ready for the party that Claire and Albert Cymons were giving for us. On the way up, I popped in to see Claire's mother, who lived on the ground floor of the same building. She was eighty-five, somewhat smaller and frailer than I remembered her, but still very perky. Claire's apartment on the sixth floor is most unusual, consisting mostly of glass walls and terraces covered with pots, trees, artificial grass, and a wonderful view of the city. Some of the old friends and acquaintances were present. A very pleasant evening, and while we women caught up on the gossip, Alec talked business and politics with the men – and also gossiped. Again, I had the weird experience of being my old self, young and eager, and then having to remind myself that in fact we were all grandparents.

Came home well after midnight, but I had difficulty sleeping. I woke up feeling very tired and decided not to go on the Carlton walk with Alec, so he made an appointment with a friend. Claire and I arranged to go and hear Miriam Margolyes, the Anglo-Jewish actress, reading from the works of Gertrude Stein. She is appearing in a two-woman show called "Gertrude Stein and Her Companion." Stein's style of writing without punctuation in order to create a "stream of consciousness" effect was difficult to follow.

Sunday, December 6

The following day was very busy, with a luncheon and a dinner with friends of Alec's. We had a heated discussion on Israeli affairs and sat until 11 p.m. I have noticed the custom here in Australia of sitting at the table to the end of the evening, no matter how long it goes on. My Alex would find that difficult.

Tuesday, December 8

It was a *really* crazy day. I didn't think I could keep it up much longer. In spite of my apprehensions before the trip, we were treated as minor "celebrities," with phone calls and invitations from the most unexpected people. There were many calls in the morning and a lot of dithering with Lionel about the trip to the North, which had yet to be finalized. It was all very hectic, and the onrush of memories and emotions prevents me from sleeping well. Keeping the diary seemed to have a calming effect, but I was tired.

It took me some time to find Corinne (Smith) Whitbread, a "soulmate" from high school days. She'd had a varied career, including being one of the first TV presenters in Australia, publishing slim volumes of poetry, mothering three children, and presently teaching English literature for a correspondence school. She told me she has a Jewish mother-in-law, and I realized that the good old English name Whitbread, which I used to see on English advertising billboards (for beer) is actually a translation of the Jewish name Weisbrot (white bread), or its variation, Visbord.

Wednesday, December 9

I awoke this morning with a croaky voice, but with so much socializing, how can I stop talking? Alex phoned me and we had a long conversation. "Everything is fine," he said, which I mentally queried; he was keeping busy and was invited out a lot. There were more visitors dropping by. In the afternoon, I went again with Sonia to the Art Centre, which is a very impressive building with three different theaters and a concert hall. The Great Hall has a stained glass ceiling and is available for public events.

We took the occasion to visit the Champagne Diamond Exhibition of

Colored Diamonds, which was most impressive, and for me something quite new as I did not know there were such things. The evening was spent with friends of Alec's. Again, we sat at the table until after 11 p.m. My voice was not good. I am getting laryngitis, taking aspirin and drinking hot drinks.

How wonderful that I didn't have much to say about our children – here, there were all kinds of problems, divorces, illnesses, arguments, etc., etc. – not a lot of *nachas*!

Sunday, December 13

In spite of the phone calls, Alec and I managed to do most of the packing for our trip north the next day. By 11:30 a.m. we were able to get away and take a taxi down to North Carlton, where we spent our adolescent years. We got out at the Post Office at Richardson Street and walked down to our old place at 94 Amess Street. The house looked rather neglected. While we were taking photos and debating whether to knock on the door, a couple drove up. They told us they were the next-door neighbors. We decided not to knock and went round to the back lane to see the garage, to which a second storey had been added. A chap was working on his car at 96 Amess Street, just as Alec used to do in the old days.

He told us there had been an explosion in the chimney of the hat factory and it had collapsed. A fire broke out and destroyed the whole place, but that happened before he had come to live there. This factory had provided an important "piece of equipment" for the children who played in the street. They had devised a game of bouncing a ball off the sloping window sills of the building, a game with variations that could be played singly or in teams, and which kept them very busy. Of course, my parents did not allow me to play outside.

Then the same couple we had talked to in the front came out. They had seen the neighbor and told him about us, and said he would be happy to show us the house. They did not offer to let us go through their house, so we had to walk all the way around again. Anyway, the tenant let us in, and we looked all around and inspected the changes. The dining room and kitchen had been opened up and the old kitchen wood-burning stove was now only a fireplace. The bathroom and toilet had been turned into a long kitchen, and one of the small bedrooms (mine) had been turned into a bathroom. The front door had been changed for a double-glazed model. Overall, the house was unfortunately in bad shape, cracked throughout and apparently sinking. It was hardly a house that would sell for a fortune.

I asked about the large stone that had been outside the kitchen door, where I used to sit sometimes to cool off after a hot day. The fellow showed me how he had moved it down into the garden; he said it was blue stone and too nice to throw away. He must have realized by now that we really had lived there. There were still tomatoes growing, but surely not those my mother had planted so many years ago? He said they were there when he moved in.

He was a nice young man who was interested in the history of the place and in our stories. For us, of course, we experienced many mixed feelings. Everything seemed much smaller, and little odd memories constantly were popping up: the excitement of changing dishes for Pesach; the sheets of dough hanging on the chairs to dry when my mother made *lockshen*; the sight of my father polishing the family's shoes in honour of Shabbat; undressing by the kitchen fire in winter and rushing to bed in the cold bedroom; my father bringing me an early morning cup of tea (a habit my brother continues for his wife); and the arrival of my cousin Jean as a ten-year-old evacuee from the London Blitz . . . .

We walked on down Canning Street, with its grassy road divider, passing the spot where, many years before, a young boy had snatched my coat from over my arm, but the police did nothing to help us get it back. We passed the Lee Street School, still with its little (grades 1–4) and big (grades 5–8) schools, and then down Rathdowne Street to Elgin Street, where we took more pictures of our previous home at number 92. It was a very fine day, but by then I was hot and tired, so we stopped at a little Italian café to eat and reminisce. I took a cab back to the hotel.

We were picked up in the late afternoon to go to the synagogue for the wedding ceremony. Most people seemed very casually dressed. The bride arrived fifteen minutes late. A fiddler played *klezmer* music in the foyer. Darron, the bridegroom's brother, was resplendent in a dinner suit, silver bow tie, silver cummerbund and silver *kippah*. When the bridal party finally came in, Mark looked most handsome in an outfit similar to the one that Darron was wearing. Jean was very imposing in a long gray patterned gown, with a handbag and shoes of the same material. Gigi, the bride, looked good in her dress, although she had used too much makeup. The bridesmaids wore white, off-the-shoulder dresses with big green sashes. Mark's sister, Ilana, looked really lovely. The bride's mother wore a long green backless dress. There was much giggling under the *huppah*, which was decorated with white carnations. Joe, in his quiet gray outfit, and Jean were much moved in spite of their misgivings. Soon the ceremony was over, but everyone was asking how long it would last, because the couple was so obviously mismatched.

We were a little late getting to the reception, which was held, in Australian fashion, separately in a wedding hall. In between, the couple went to the photographer for their wedding pictures and the guests waited for them, sometimes quite a long time. The festivities were in full swing. There was Israeli music and the *hora*, with men and women dancing separately. Jean and Uncle Herschel were agitated because we were late. Lots of people came to say hello. Herschel made the *motzi* (blessing over the bread), and Mark *benched* (said the grace after the meal) and did a beautiful job. Alec was a bit nervous about the *sheva brachot* (the seven marriage blessings), but did well. We left fairly early, as we had to make an early start the next day for our trip to the North, but we didn't get to bed until 1 a.m.

Trip to the North – Ayers Rock
Part II

Monday, December 14

I DIDN'T SLEEP MUCH AND WAS AWAKE BY 5:30 A.M. THE TAXI COM-pany had refused to take our order the night before and it was difficult to find one in the morning. We didn't leave until about 6:40 and the plane was scheduled for 7:25. We made it at the very last minute. We were served breakfast on the way to Adelaide, and then again during the second stage of the flight. As the clock was going back all the time, it turned out that we ate three breakfasts by 8:30 a.m.

The view of Central Australia from the air is rather forbidding and overwhelming, a vast red desert, mostly uninhabited. Our destination, Alice Springs in the Northern Territory, is almost at the very centre of Australia. It was founded in 1860, originally as a telegraph station. It's the only so-called "town" in an area that produces livestock and opals. It is also one of the regional headquarters of the legendary Flying Doctor service. Our first impression was of a very busy settlement; the people looked different, hardy, sun-burnt, wearing short pants, wide-brimmed sunhats and sandals. A mixed company, they could have been landowners, cattle drovers, field hands or professionals, for all one could tell. A pioneering society.

We waited a long time for a taxi. It was hot, but not terrible. We finally got to the Sheraton Hotel about 11:30 and booked for the city tour at 1:30 p.m.

The hotel is absolutely beautiful, spacious and decorated in pastel shades. There were two queen-size beds in my room, but the wall-to-wall carpeting seemed out of place in that heat. The hotel had a large swimming pool and a Jacuzzi. We had lunch in the coffee shop, which provided a salad buffet; it seemed the same food was being served all over the world, although here they did offer kangaroo meat.

The city tour showed us the historical sites of Alice Springs: the Post and Telegraph Office, inaugurated in the second half of the nineteenth century. The Flying Doctor service was established in 1927 after years of planning. Its aim was to bring medical services to the Outback's isolated settlers, who lived in difficult conditions on cattle stations, sometimes comprising thousands of acres, often hundreds of miles from their nearest neighbors. We saw the Aboriginal Museum with its large diorama depicting their version of the "Dreamtime," the period that preceded the Creation of Earth and of Man. They also believe that Man was created out of the earth, but in a manner slightly different from the biblical version.

Tourism is the second industry after cattle-raising, and young people are attracted by job possibilities. We had lots of shopping time, as is customary in any self-respecting tourist country. The afternoon was very hot and by the time we got back to the hotel, we were utterly exhausted. I had a bath and crawled into bed but couldn't sleep. We got up for dinner, but by 10 o'clock were in bed and fast asleep. I woke at 2:30 a.m., at 5:40 a.m., and at 6:30 a.m. I got up to drink and to bring my diary up to date. The plane for Ayers Rock leaves at 10:30 a.m. The heat does not agree with me. I ache all over and do not feel my usual self.

Tuesday, December 15

During dinner, we got completely confused about what day it was. We wondered when we had left Melbourne for Alice Springs and realized that, in fact, we had left only the previous morning and today had come from Alice Springs to Ayers Rock. We seemed to be living in a completely separate world, unrelated to any other, and "suspended in time." Actually, we have moved about a great deal, walking around the town, swimming and writing. No energy for more than that.

Because the driver came and went without announcing himself, we missed the airport bus and had to take a cab. We found the airport full of people, and commercial planes were leaving for Darwin, Sydney, Melbourne and Ayers Rock, while others were arriving with returning families and tourists. The local population is used to flying and we saw at least twelve small private Cessna planes standing in the field, an improvement on the horse, or horse-and-buggy means of transportation. I was worried about the flight because I'm nervous about small planes, especially as it was very windy, but in fact the flight was quite smooth except for the last few minutes. There were about thirty passengers on our local flight.

It is rather awe-inspiring to see the vast red expanse of the Australian Outback, and at times the scene from the plane looked like a large aboriginal painting, particularly around Lake Amadeus. Dark circular patterns are scored upon the ground and wide black and gray stripes run up and down on a red background, all filled in with dots and dashes, representing trees, shrubs and/or water channels. The Aborigines get the color pigmentations – mainly ochre, red, shades of beige, and black – for their paintings from the earth and, when required, they add animal blood.

The temperature was 34 degrees centigrade, but I felt much better than I had in Alice Springs. Called my cousin Jean to ask about the post-wedding mood – she is resting, Joe has a cold, and the young couple has left for Bangkok.

Wednesday, December 16

Ayers Rock is a tiny man-made resort, catering to visitors who want to see the startling rock formations of Ayers Rock and the Olgas. The aboriginal name for Ayers Rock is Uluru, and the tourist resort which has developed around the area is called Yulara. Aborigines have lived in this region for millennia, long before the invading white explorers built simple hostel accommodation for themselves. Today there are two beautiful five-star hotels, the Four Seasons and the Sheraton, and two or three camping sites, known as "lesser accommodation centres." The town can accommodate five thousand visitors, and there are five tour companies.

Because Ayers Rock is completely isolated and unconnected to any grid, electric generators are essential. There is a natural water supply, so even if it doesn't rain for many years, water is no problem. The town offers many swimming pools, and solar heaters are everywhere. An interesting architectural design of large "sails" stretched over buildings provides shade. The site attracts many adventurous young people who come to see their country, taste the pioneering life and make money in the subsidiary services and industry.

Ayers Rock is a fantastic scene and well worth the visit. A single giant rock, it is 3.5 miles (5.6 km.) long, six miles (9.7 km.) round and 1,140 feet (347 m.) high. If not for the heat, I would have tried to go up, as Alec did for a short distance, but the fact that many people have lost their lives in the attempt is a deterrent. A memorial tablet honoring their memory lies at the foot of the hewn steps.

There are many aboriginal stories about the place, and some of the caves are held to be sacred to the various tribes. The walls are covered with primitive drawings that seem to illustrate some of their legends. The drawings are difficult to decipher, but concentric circles and a leaf pattern are common motifs. There is no real information of what these symbols mean or how old they are. The surrounding area is not real desert because the ample underground water feeds the surrounding low vegetation (spinifex) and small gum trees. Some small pools are found inside the caves, but these are for washing, not for drinking.

When we went again at 6:30 to see the sunset, there must have been several hundred people standing around – Japanese, German, Dutch, Canadians, Americans – all speaking their native language. One couple we spoke to planned to get to Adelaide by train, which is a twenty–one-hour trip. Others drive or go by tour bus. Although the Rock itself changed color, from bright vermillion to a dark brownish red, the cloud formations around the Rock were a bit disappointing, but in other areas the cloud formations were beautiful. The temperature ranged between 36 and 38 degrees centigrade.

Our hotel is very large – a square, two and three stories high, built around a swimming pool. The rooms are very comfortable but less beautiful than in Alice Springs. The large, spacious rooms contain the biggest clothes closets I've ever seen, though people come for only two to three days. Each room has a well-stocked bar and fridge and an electric kettle with coffee and tea. As in Alice Springs, the hotel was completely carpeted, although the public rooms were tiled. Aboriginal motifs are used as decorative themes.

The Aborigines have won the rights to some of their land only since 1985, especially unoccupied land, and receive royalties in the uranium-mining area in the sum of thirteen million Australian dollars per annum. In Ayers Rock, they lease the land back to the government for a national reserve, which earns them one hundred thousand Australian dollars yearly and the right to participate in the management of the reserve. Since strong tribal traditions persist, only a few leave for the cities and get educated. They claim to have been in Australia for at least ten thousand years. Songs and legends of the Dreamtime are central to Aboriginal life and must be memorized and passed on by each generation, usually around the campfire. Every Aboriginal is related to one or more Dreamtime ancestors, and they learn to revere them and their teachings. They also learn how subsist in the inhospitable environment, living on insects, small animals, grubs and occasional kangaroo meat. During their traditional "walkabout," they take off for weeks to visit their ancestral lands. In recent years, their distinct art style has achieved great popularity and desirability, and has become an important profession and source of income.

Thursday, December 17

I wrote much of the above this morning after a good night's sleep. My throat is bothering me again. We decided to have an easy morning and take the tour of the Olgas in the afternoon. It was only 34 degrees, but with a pleasant breeze. We found the same tour leader as yesterday, a personable young man, but we checked the water supply as he had accidentally spilt it yesterday and left us with nothing to drink. Same mix of tourists, but the Japanese were in the majority. It seemed to be honeymoon season for them, and northern Australia is a popular destination, though few speak or understand English.

We drove about nineteen miles (thirty kilometres) on a bumpy dirt road to reach the Olgas. This group of rocks were as impressive as Ayers Rock but in a different way. There are actually sixteen separate hills, the highest rising to eighteen hundred feet (549 metres). Approaching the gorge, we could see that they were not solid rock but collections of stones and boulders of all sizes compressed somehow into a solid mass of varying colors, called conglomerate rock. How this phenomenon came about has evoked much conjecture, but it is believed that the area was once covered with water, and some mighty upheaval brought the sea bed to the surface.

We returned to the hotel, too tired to drive out again, and watched the sunset from the roof. The view was good and sundown was lovely, but the Rock did not light up to its famous brilliant red, so we were rather disappointed.

After supper, we packed in preparation for our flight to Sydney the next day.

Thursday–Friday, December 17–18

It was a long day with much aggravation. In spite of an early night, I was unable to sleep. We left the hotel at 8 a.m., a little sorry to leave, as I had become fond of that great magical rock. The little airport, with its homely atmosphere, didn't have a souvenir shop or cafeteria. Our flight left at 9:40, and we flew back to Alice Springs over the same desert as on the outward flight. Now that I knew that underneath all that sand and rock was a vast subterranean lake, I wondered why they didn't make more use of it.

We checked in for the flight to Sydney two hours later. Casually, the official mentioned that the flight was through Melbourne. We were aghast – we had booked a direct flight, yet here we were with several extra hours of unwanted flying time. We were traveling Ansett, but suddenly noticed that the other airline, Australian Airlines, had a direct flight to Sydney leaving at 11 a.m., and we asked if there was room on that flight. The attendant was rather perturbed as he had just given us our boarding cards; while we went to the Australian desk, he went to his superior to clarify. We held up the queue for quite a while; eventually all the arrangements were made, the baggage transferred, special vegetarian meals ordered, and our tempers cooled down. Now the only problem was a four-hour wait for the connection to Surfers' Paradise, but we thought that was preferable to flying the long way round.

Happily, we boarded the plane and had a pleasant flight to Sydney, special meals and all. Again, we were amazed at the vast emptiness of the Australian continent, and we didn't see any cultivated fields or forests until we were close to Sydney. After we landed, Alec checked to see if our bags had arrived. We had plenty of time for our connection, four hours, and decided to take the airport bus down to the harbor and have tea.

I had never been to Sydney before, and after the geometric elegance and parks of Melbourne, the city was a disappointment. The streets are narrow and crooked, and great skyscrapers tower over the older, smaller buildings, creating canyon-like effects. We saw much building round the harbor area, spanned by the single arch of the landmark Sydney Harbor Bridge and distinguished by the iconic Opera House, the city's pride and joy. We wandered round the Opera House for some time before we found a cafeteria, and sat outside and watched the traffic on the water. We just managed to catch the airport bus, by stopping it in the street, and so managed to arrive back at the airport in good time.

Dinner was served during the hour-long flight, and we arrived in Surfers' at 7:30 p.m. local time, but 9 p.m. by ours. We waited for the luggage, and lo and behold, my bag was not there. The attendant checked all over, but couldn't find it. Eventually I went to the Australian desk to report the missing bag, and the clerk said, "Oh, hello, Mrs. Rafaeli, I've been waiting for you. We've had word that your bag is in Sydney; they forgot to put it on the plane." It hadn't occurred to him to notify me before and save me ten minutes of aggravation! "The bag will arrive tomorrow at 10 a.m., and we'll send it to the apartment by midday." As a well-seasoned traveler, I usually take a change of clothing and toiletry articles in my hand luggage when flying, just for this eventuality. Now, the one time I thought it unnecessary, my case was mislaid. At least it hadn't disappeared.

We found a taxi and were soon at the Peninsular Hotel. It had taken us three aeroplanes and twelve hours of flying to travel from the centre of Australia to the Gold Coast in what was essentially a five-hour flight. In that time – twelve hours – I could have flown from Tel Aviv to New York, or from Tel Aviv to London *and back*.

Utterly exhausted and aggravated, we had to identify ourselves at the reception desk because the letter of introduction that Arnold had given me was in the delayed bag. There were some frustrating moments until we finally opened the door of the apartment, found the light switches and located the sheets and towels, etc. I began to get organized while Alec went out to buy milk, tea and bread, and he returned with a note from the receptionist that Alex had already phoned twice.

We had tea and watched some film with a Jewish theme, which made me cry, so I went to bed feeling very miserable. Alas, even on the nineteenth floor, one hears quite a bit of street noise. I couldn't fall asleep, though it didn't bother Alec. I got up and had some tea, and decided to write up this crazy day in the hope that it would help to make me feel drowsy. It was 1:00 a.m. local time.

Saturday, December 19

I woke very early yesterday morning, Friday, and in spite of having taken a tranquilizer, felt headachy and tired. We took it easy until about 11:00 a.m. I called Alex and got all the news. I don't think he has been able to follow our travels.

Alec and I went out to look around and get our films developed. There are millions of shops, eating places, souvenir stands, hotels and skyscrapers. We had lunch and picked up the photos, and managed not to look at them until we got home. We went to the supermarket to get some supplies and bumped into some Melbourne acquaintances. We made a date with them for the following evening. We came home and slept a bit. Alec went to shul in the evening for Kabbalat Shabbat. I stayed home and looked at the photos. Most of them were really good, and will make a very nice souvenir. We ate downstairs in a fish restaurant.

Arnold Rose's apartment is very pleasant, elegantly casual in beige/cream colors, with some unusual pieces of iron sculpture standing around. Arnold and Di not only have taste but also the means.

There are unpleasant stories about Israel in the papers and it's worrisome.

We woke early this morning, Saturday, and called Varda about 7 a.m. All is well and busy with Chanukah; she is expecting a visit from Alec's wife Aliza, who came to Israel for her sister's birthday. Varda has done well in her university exams. I also called Lonny to say Hag Same'ach. The toys I sent had arrived and his girls were very happy with them. He was accepted for the MA course in Business Administration and will have to work hard this year.

On Shabbat morning we went to synagogue. We counted about twenty men and ten women. A guest rabbi from Sydney (Rabbi Kummelman, Av Beit ha-Din) gave a long sermon on Joseph in Egypt, etc. Apparently, he came for eight conversions! It's a busy place.

We finished late and went to have lunch at the same place as yesterday. On the way we saw some lovely artificial roses and decided to get some for our hosts. I think they will look well in the apartment, and hope Di will like them.

We went out to meet our Melbourne acquaintances and a few others of the gang came round. A couple of the women said they remembered me from the past. Medical conversation topped the agenda. Later, we took a cab and went to visit Lionel Landman's ex-wife, who has made her home here. Not very cheerful.

We finished packing, sorting the photos, and writing postcards at 11:00 p.m. We watched an ancient film on TV and went to bed. We leave tomorrow for Melbourne.

Monday, December 20

This is really the last day of our visit to Melbourne. We arrived yesterday afternoon (Sunday) after a pleasant flight from Surfer's, except that Alec didn't get his meal and had a fruit platter from first class instead. We unpacked and answered phone calls. A scheduled dinner party had been cancelled because the hostess came down with the flu. This simplified the evening, and we had a Chinese dinner with the Sicrees and Cymons instead. The evening together with our friends was pleasant, and we said our goodbyes.

Early this morning I called Nita Bluthal, a friend whom I hadn't succeeded in contacting earlier, and we fixed a date for lunch with another high school/university friend, Jeanette Noye. We arrived at Uncle Herschel's by 9:30 a.m. for breakfast as usual, and showed him the photos and chatted. It was difficult to leave, but we managed to get away by 11:00 a.m. We had a Russian taxi driver and engaged in a rather unpleasant talk about Israel. I arrived for the luncheon date at the Lyceum Club and recognized Nita immediately, but Jeanette had changed completely, very proper with white gloves. We chatted about families, politics, friends, etc. Both had been widowed some years ago, and Jeanette went back to university to take a course in environmental studies, which led to a very good job as advisor to the Minister for the Environment. There was a pleasant, friendly atmosphere.

Over the years the two women had remained close friends and spent vacations together. As students at university, both had been communists.

Afterwards, I went to meet Alec, who had lunched with friends at the Southern Cross Hotel, so we could go home together. One, who had been a frequent visitor at our home, wanted to know how life had treated me. I was with him for an hour and a half and I didn't get a chance to answer him. He only spoke about himself and the book he had written on philosophy. I felt really exasperated. It was 4:00 p.m. when I got back and I much resented the wasted time. There were many phone calls and Lionel came to settle the account with Alec, and what a shock over the phone bill!

We had dinner with the Joe and Jean Saltzman and other friends, and at the end of the evening we said our goodbyes.

12:15 A.M. I finished packing and had to get some sleep before leaving tomorrow for Sydney and home. My historic visit to my old home town was over, and I was very satisfied that I had made it.

Melbourne Revisited with Karni, 1989 Part III

In 1989, I made another trip to Melbourne with Karni. She had asked, and I had promised, that I would take her to Australia after she graduated with her social work degree, and I had to keep my promise. She was making a round-the-world trip, starting in London and coming to Australia from the U.S. We met in Sydney and after a couple of days proceeded to Melbourne.

Things hadn't changed much except that Mark was divorced, Darron had married Melissa, a very pleasant and attractive girl, and Ilana was working with a reputable international law firm which she was hoping might bring her a transfer to their London office.

There was much repetition of my previous visit and I enjoyed showing Karni where I had spent my early years: the houses we lived in, the schools I went to, the University of Melbourne. We met with my friends, some of whom she had met previously in Jerusalem. We also made a trip to Queensland, but instead of going to Ayers Rock, we went to Cairns, which is an important town in the far north, and the headquarters of the Flying Doctors service. Karni was very impressed with this project, which added much to her knowledge of life in the Australian Outback, and also to her professional knowledge. We visited the Rain Forests, aboriginal sites, and the Great Barrier Reef, which stretches for hundreds of miles along the coast of Queensland.

It was nice to spend time together, and she learnt more than any of our other children about my early life and attachment to Australia. They all know the unofficial Australian anthem, "Waltzing Matilda," and we also use this tune to sing Shir ha-Ma'alot, the introductory Psalm to the *Birkat ha-mazon* (Grace after Meals) on Shabbat.

At the end of the trip, I returned to Israel and Karni stayed on a while longer to visit the island of Tasmania and Ayers Rock, and then went on to explore Singapore and see London before returning home.

I had truly closed the biggest circle in my life.

◄ From left: Amihai Ophel, Itamar, Varda, Karni, Naomi Segev-Shapiro and Netta, 1988.

▼ Standing: Karni, Sonya, Ron. Seated: me, Albert, Claire

Our Trip to Riga and Moscow

1991

Monday, July 15 (El Al Flight LY6365)

9 P.M. WELL, HERE WE ARE ACTUALLY ON THE PLANE TO MOSCOW. Alex is going to visit Riga after sixty years' absence. After the tension and rush of the last few days, a bit of an anti-climax. We are really on the way, so everything is set in motion. Plane is leaving almost on time.

We thought the plane would be full, but there are no more than sixty or seventy passengers. Some look like *olim* going back to visit, some with young children, some yeshiva boys, some Israelis and a few who don't look Jewish at all.

3:30 A.M. Finally, we got to our hotel! The plane landed on time, 1 a.m., luggage delivery was reasonable, but our small bag with the food was missing! Also big luggage of many other people. We waited another hour, nothing came – probably went to Nairobi instead with the safari group, with all the mess we had at Tel Aviv. We were too tired to make a formal complaint, especially as several others were ahead of us, and then we had to wait forty-five minutes for the Intourist car. The Intourist people spoke no English and were not helpful with the missing bag – the young man left after an hour, while the lady waited until we wanted to leave. Then we had a bumpy ride of forty-five minutes to this hotel, the Cosmos. First impression is terrible but the room seems clean and comfortable, even has a mini-fridge (empty) and a heated towel rail in the bathroom.

We had time to have a conversation with the Intourist driver, who asked how the immigrants are getting on in Israel – "everybody would like to leave if they could, but they don't have the possibility." First impression as we arrived at the hotel – blonde streetwalker, with a very short and very tight mini, haggling with a customer (3:30 a.m.).

Can't keep our eyes open. We are both exhausted and deflated. It is already dawning and we're just going to bed – probably too tired tomorrow to do anything. Good night! If only the kids could see us now!

Tuesday, July 16

Slept intermittently and got up about 8:30 a.m. Outside, it is raining and foggy, but not cold. I have a terrible headache and shoulder cramps.

Finally, we got to breakfast about 9:30. There are many tourists and at least a better impression than at 3:30 a.m., but the hotel has about 1,600 rooms, so we don't know if what we see is a good proportion or not. Breakfast table is set with jam, bread, butter, milk (powdered), some kind of watery juice, hard-boiled eggs, sandwich with red caviar, tea/coffee.

Crummy service. Phone calls after breakfast, mainly about the lost bag, took up lots of time. Alex refused to make the trip out to the airport in order to sign a paper. I realize that all of the second half of the food is in the lost bag, including the soap, Nivea cream, etc. I discover that the immersion heater is not usable because it has a three-point plug, and local use is a two-point plug. I thought the floor superintendent would surely have an adapter, but she shook her head. When I asked if I could find one in the shops, she gave a loud, cynical laugh and said, "There is nothing in the shops." I also spent time making enquiries unsuccessfully at the various shops in the hotel. We spoke with Sonia Berman's son (she lives in Jerusalem) and made an appointment for 3:30. By twelve, still raining and we feel a bit fed up. We decide to take a taxi ride and do a bit of sightseeing. Heavy traffic, but we get to the Kremlin, St. Basil's, then walk on the Arbat a few minutes. This is a nice residential street, now a mall, full of little stands, all trying to sell dolls, lacquerware, and amber. Having read *Children of the Arbat*, it has more meaning.

Back to the hotel for a light lunch (with caviar), which costs us $16.50, but terrible service. At one stage, after a twenty-minute wait, Alex goes back to look for the waiter, who pulls out tins of caviar from his pocket, offering at one for $10 or two for $15! Everyone's trying to make something on the side.

Dr. Berman appears, after having trouble getting into the hotel, but he has managed to persuade them to give him a pass. Locals are not allowed to enter. After chatting an hour or so, he offers to take us sightseeing, in spite of the rain. He is a very serious, nice-looking fellow and tells us he makes the equivalent of $10 a month, but of course, the cost of living is correspondingly low. Strangely enough to us, he belongs to a Latvian Society, and wears an identifying badge. He is very nationalistic for Latvia, although he has lived for more than twenty years in Moscow.

He takes us to a small synagogue, Marina Rosha (Maria-in-the-Forest), tucked away somewhere in a forest! Imagine a wooden synagogue still in use in Moscow, but it is not so old, and was built in 1927. They say it has always remained open; it is very dark, neglected and untidy inside, but apparently they have a very active program, and many charity boxes. We talk with the young Russian rabbi who sported a very bushy beard, and a few young yeshiva boys from the U.S. and Israel, affiliated with the Lubavitch movement. There are two *Aronot Kodesh*, one apparently quite old, from another town. A round stained glass window is situated over the *aron*.

The general impression of Moscow is of lovely wide avenues, some parks, and lots of trees, but the buildings look dilapidated and many are in need of rebuilding – is this still World War II damage? "There is no *ba'al bayit*," we are told. "People don't own their apartments, so they don't care for them. Everything belongs to the State, and the State is responsible."

Little queues here and there where some vegetables are for sale, but one fruit stall has no customers although it offers apricots, plums, tiny pears, etc. I suppose he's too expensive. Odd to see little booths or kiosks all over, selling ice cream, sausages, clothes, or newspapers. The big shops seem empty, but are also hard to identify. Saw one big shoe store; otherwise, many *producten*, or groceries, and pharmacies. Metro stations, circular pseudo-classic in style, but we haven't investigated that yet. People seem reasonably well-dressed and no one looks hungry.

Hotel Cosmos. The room is clean, towels are changed every day, but the carpet is very stained. Every time we explore we find another restaurant, another little bar, or shop, or lounge. There are lots of people in the lobby, many groups from all over. Music with dinner, a night club with floor show starting at 8–9:30 p.m. (didn't go in). Service is poor. Lots of people stand-ing around at the entrance. Although the locals are not supposed to come in except by invitation, the dining rooms seem full of Russians. The TV news is given with additional sign language for the deaf. But, in spite of its comforts, the hotel is too far away from the centre, and rather inconvenient.

Fortunately, this hotel has a bank and also a business service, so perhaps we'll send a fax to the office tomorrow, but we discovered we didn't have our number. Tomorrow we hope to see the Kremlin and arrange the flight to Riga, etc. Berman will pick us up in the morning.

9:45 P.M. Going to sleep, to make up for yesterday. Today has convinced me that organized tours are more efficient than going individually!

Wednesday, July 17

Alex Berman comes about 9:15 to pick us up. First, he fixes the cord of the immersion heater so we can use it. Then he insists we drive out to Sheremetyevo Airport to see about the lost bag. His older son Victor also comes along. We think it a waste of time, but need a piece of paper for the insurance, and he can't understand that we would allow a bag of food to get lost without making a fuss.

An hour's trip there and, of course, back, and an hour and a half there.

The officials are impossible. Either they don't know what it's all about, or they seem to be deaf. One girl complains (in Russian) that she is tired, please leave her alone. Eventually we're taken to two storerooms, but didn't find the bag. At least we get some piece of paper from Lost and Found. When we leave the parking lot, it takes five minutes to pay one ruble, and two people to write the receipt and car number.

Alex B. points out many sites – the Riga railway station (pale blue and white like Wedgwood china), the Border of Moscow, with a memorial to the defenders of Moscow (i.e., an old anti-tank fence). Sheremetyevo Kolkhoz used to be a village belonging to the Count Sheremetyevo.

Stopped for coffee at a most unlikely looking establishment. We invite them, but they insist on paying. Victor stands in one queue and gets sandwiches (I have red caviar, because the rest are only meat) and coffee and fruit drink, apple or grape. Alex stands in another queue and gets cakes (almond macaroons and éclairs) and some kind of mousse and fruit cocktail. We wait by a table until people finish eating (they hurried!); we have quite a spread, and the coffee wasn't bad (black). They insist on paying the bill, which amounted to fifty or sixty rubles ($2–2.50).

They drop us at Intourist, where we order a private guide for the Kremlin, as we just can't be on time for the public tour; Thursday it's closed and Friday we want to go to Zagorsk. Then we decide to change our hotel for the last couple of days on our return from Riga in order to be in town, but for that we have to go round the corner to the head office, which has a very modest sign and almost don't locate it. We walk through the door and are stopped by a big commissionaire who spoke only Russian. We have to wait for him to call someone out, and then she takes us inside to a nice office. Of course, she doesn't know what to do, and calls in another young man, who promises to arrange it and please come back tomorrow.

We go back to wait for our guide, and are well entertained when a fellow comes for the Diamond Tour and starts aggressively asking the clerk: where do diamonds come from in Russia? Are they still being mined? Etc., etc. Then the guide of that group comes and he begins to pester her – was she married? (yes) did she have children? (no) why not? (she didn't want), didn't her husband want? (no), did she like being in Moscow? (yes, it was the best place in the world and she wouldn't change for anything). She's very attractive, like a young blonde Ingrid Bergman, fortunately with a sense of humor. Finally, to rescue her, I begin asking about the shows and museums and we have a nice conversation. The fellow is from Wales and has hair dyed a coppery red. I ask him why the special interest in diamonds but he doesn't explain.

Our guide, Natasha, is very pleasant and speaks very good English. We walk over to the Kremlin, through the grounds and to the Armory for an exhibition of historical royal clothes, carriages, icons, vestments, Fabergé eggs, enormous silver serving dishes, incense burners shaped like castles, armor, etc., etc. It's really interesting, especially the internal views of the Kremlin, which we're unaware of. It's a beautiful sunny day, so I hope the photos come out. We see the largest imperial cannon, made in 1856, each ball weighing one ton, but it is purely ceremonial and has never been used. Then an enormous imperial bell, weighing a couple hundred tons, also never used, and partly broken. The Palace of Congresses is a beautiful building, simple and modern, built in 1960, and fits in very nicely; grayish-white in color, not the classical ochre.

It was a good idea to have a private guide, as we could select a convenient time and have a good conversation. For example, we asked who the Kremlin belongs to, and who pays the upkeep – municipality says government, and government says vice versa. Natasha thought the Communist Party had footed the bill till now. She also said that church weddings are coming back into vogue after we saw crowns used by Pushkin and his wife at their wedding. Their use symbolizes that the husband is a king to his wife and she a queen to him. About the custom of women covering their hair – Natasha said it was to keep evil spirits from infiltrating into the body, specially as the wife has to deal with the outside world and mundane matters. It is also a sign of the wife's submission to her husband.

Getting a good look at Moscow . . . it is really very shabby. The town is dirty. Automatic drink dispensers on the street corners are often leaking, and there is nowhere to throw the cups. The same applies to little snack bars tucked away here and there. Unfinished ice cream cones litter the street. I ask Alex if he would like to feel like a Muscovite and walk along the street eating three ice cream cones, but he refused. Many dilapidated buildings, but here and there a little jewel of a church or well-kept new building. Enormous housing estates, ten to twelve stories high. One can hardly distinguish one shop from another, especially if you can't read Russian – but mainly *producten* (food), *apothek* (pharmacy), and sport. Even a shop for curtaining has a queue outside it and the women are being let in one by one.

Back at the hotel, we go to the Intourist service department. Although there are four or five desks, one rarely sees anyone sitting there. Usually the clerks are inside, chatting. We want to confirm our flight to Riga, but it seems there is some confusion about the voucher. Come back tomorrow! We are spending a lot of time on *siddurim*.

There is nothing at the Bolshoi, so maybe we'll go to the circus one night.

Scene in restaurant – waiters suddenly offering caviar at $10 a tin, or two for $15. Alexander B. says he can get it for forty rubles, which equals $1.50; he gets it from connections or grateful patients. His wife is presently in Riga, so we haven't met her yet. He is very serious and old-fashioned, kisses my hand, and says things like "I am happy to be with someone who has seen my beloved mother/who has helped my mother, etc."

Hope we can just concentrate on sightseeing tomorrow.

Thursday, July 18

Today starts as a beautiful day and we decide to take the City Tour and visit the Pushkin Museum. By the time we get to the Intourist Office, I realize I will be in trouble with my tummy. Fortunately, the Intourist Hotel is right next to the tour office, so that saves me.

We go to town by taxi – Alex went to look at the Metro station in the morning and says it was a menace, and that there were not enough instructions. I don't know when I'll get to take at least one ride.

This taxi driver is quite pleasant, accepting $5 at the outset (actually 140 rubles at official rate; the metre usually shows only twenty-five to thirty rubles). He takes us more through side streets, so we get other views of the city, much older, smaller buildings, many in near ruins. He asks where we came from, and says he has friends who have gone to Israel. We ask why his taxi carries no sign. He says taxis were in real danger from robbers because of the cash, so he often took off his plastic sign. But I suspect he's a moonlighter, since other cabs have a light on the roof or a painted sign. When I tell Alex to fasten his seat belt (he sat in the front), the driver says it isn't necessary as he has a taxi license!

There are only about eight people on the tour – Red Square, a glance inside St. Basil's, views of the Kremlin (a perfect day for photos) – then a ride to Lenin Hills. This was the official name under the communists from 1935 to 1999; now it is called Sparrow Hills. Then to the University and a general view of town. Parts of the city begin to look familiar. Our guide refuses a tip at the end, and the bus driver accepts, after some hesitation. We go round to the Intourist Head office about changing the hotel; of course, the guy is not in. I sit down on the step, and there's much consternation at the sight of me. I'm invited to enter and sit in the little garden at the back, but we leave right away. We walk over to the new Metropol Hotel, next to the Bolshoi Theater, as our friend Sylvia Hassenfeld, who had recently been in Moscow, said they had a "coffee shop" style of restaurant. When we see it isn't so, we settle for tea and canapés and a beautiful lobby. Cost: 8.80 rubles, about $5 at old exchange. We look at the restaurant menu, and decide we will *not* have dinner there.

We try to call Intourist – Mr. Pankratin is still not in. We take a taxi to the Pushkin Museum. It is a lovely building with lots of ancient art and archeology, and with many copies of Roman and other sculptures, as it was originally a didactic museum. Mainly we want to see the Impressionists, and it is really a beautiful collection, most of which we are not familiar with.

I have to get to a toilet again, and am told that the toilets were being repaired and I would have to go outside to the street! I have no choice but to go. I discover a mobile WC truck parked in the street, one part for men, one for women, which has about six toilets and a wash basin. I expected a chemical toilet, but this has running water, and afterwards I see that it's connected to the sewage system. I am not the only one to use it.

The Museum was opened in 1912, but I am surprised to see a glass roof for natural light. I thought this was a modern concept. Entrance was 1.50 rubles each. The tour probably charges $10 to $15. The most amazing thing about the museum is that there is only a very simple catalogue for sale, no cards or posters or books. They really don't understand about making money here, and how President Bush and James Baker expect the Russians to adopt an American mentality and economy overnight is beyond me. I think it will take fifty years.

The guide in the morning asks Alex what he thinks of Moscow. He says that it's very interesting, but that he can't understand such neglect and dilapidation next to beautiful historical buildings. "You must understand we are going through difficult times and have no money, but in a few years it will be better." On another occasion, we're told, "Even if people want to work, they feel there is nothing to work for. They cannot aspire to a better apartment, cannot buy better food or clothes, so they just scrape along on whatever they have."

We take a taxi back and pay $5 instead of the $10 the driver asks for. I'm beginning to feel a bit weak, and anxious to take some Sedistal for my stomach. We went first to the bookstore to get some writing paper – none. Envelopes – fifty cents each, a dollar with the stamps. Saw a nice book on the Pushkin Museum – $45. I asked the girl if she would mail it for me – she looked shocked, and said she didn't know where the Post Office is. I said what about paper to wrap the book – she had no paper, but offered a plastic bag! For paper, I should go down to the other newsagent – two sheets of paper for fifty cents!

In the room Alex gets through to the boss of Mr. Pankratin, who looks up our file, and says it would be okay to change the hotel. He would give instructions to the Intourist guide at the hotel. Victory! But nothing in hand. The first time an official was polite and helpful. Then Alex goes down to the service office about the flight to Riga. The woman we talked to before wasn't there, but the matter was arranged. We had paid for the tickets in Jerusalem – come back on Saturday to pick them up. Alex also negotiates a few sheets of typing paper, after expressing surprise that such a hotel has no stationery.

Okay. Now we can write home and start sending postcards, which we bought in the street. It is a problem to telephone.

Now waiting for Alexander B. to come for dinner. I'm not planning to eat.

Friday, July 18

Last night ended quite dramatically. Alexander and Victor were supposed to come at 7:00, and so we went down to the lobby to wait for them. After twenty minutes, we went down to the lower entrance in case they couldn't get in. I was beginning to feel faint and began perspiring, but didn't want to go and drink something. Finally, after 8:00 they appeared, having had problems getting petrol because Alexander had forgotten to fill the car. We went into the Galaxie [sic] Restaurant, waited for a waiter for about fifteen minutes. Only after Alex B. went off to complain did a waiter appear. I was beginning to feel really awful. I ordered chicken soup and toast, while the others had a full meal. By 8:45, I felt nauseous and left the table, got to the toilet in time to throw up, sweating terribly. Alex B., being a doctor, came into the restroom and started applying acupressure on my thumbs, and after a few minutes I began to feel better. We returned to the table, but still no food. I drank some mineral water and then felt sick again, grabbed a glass and used that. I felt that I had better go to bed and left, taking that awful glass with me to the cloakroom. I was happy to get into bed, and after a few minutes both Alexes came up. B. brought tonic water and bitter lemon, which he said was the best drink for this condition. They came again after they had eaten and brought some soup, but I didn't eat it; I only wanted to sleep. Berman did some more acupressure. I said I thought he was an urologist, and he said, "When there are no medicines, one must try everything."

I wake up in the morning refreshed, but decide that it would be better not to go to Zagorsk. Instead, we go to the Soviet Art Museum, which has been recommended to us, and Alex B. comes to fetch us as he had to meet his wife at the nearby Riga Station, and the museum was on his way.

His wife, Ann, or Anya, is very pretty and petite, green eyes, a doctor. She makes a "bob" to me when we're introduced – also to Alex. I don't think I look old enough for such a sign of respect. I can't make it out. I have to speak German (my Yiddish) with her as she doesn't know English too well.

The Soviet Art Museum is an enormous three-storey building with vast halls. We had to go to the second floor, and the attendant offered to take us up in the lift. One section is Soviet Art of the 1920s and 1930s, the other part a selection from the Tetryakov Gallery, which is now closed. Lots of social realism, portraits, still lifes and street scenes. Many Jewish artists, and the Oriental (Armenian) or Eastern Russia is well represented. But eighty percent of the works are heavy and dark.

I remembered a conversation I had with Victor at the airport, when I complained that the terminal was so dark inside – a dark copper ceiling, dark grey floor, black chairs and dim electric light. I told him how cheerful Ben Gurion (Lod) Airport looked, but Victor said he felt very well in that atmosphere. I often had occasion to recall this conversation, and was happy at the end of the trip to see that the departure hall was more pleasant. Those painters who use more color seem not at ease in that medium.

Bonus. We found an English book on the Pushkin Museum – a small one, at $10. Funny that it is not stocked at the Pushkin.

After we leave the museum it begins to rain and then pour; there are no taxis and we don't know which bus to take. We wait for over an hour for a taxi (some are full, some don't stop) and get really wet. We finally get back to the hotel at about 3:30. We have tea and sandwiches in the room and a good sleep.

We send a birthday cable today to Varda and hope it arrives before Shabbat. Also write a letter, but who knows when that will arrive!

We have dinner in the hotel – terrible service. I ask for a cooked vegetable plate, and get a plate of cold rice, sauerkraut, sliced onion, a tomato, chopped parsley stalks. So I also ask for chicken broth – he says there's only chicken noodle soup. It is tasty, but they could have strained the soup. I am not eating meat, and according to Alex's experience, am not missing anything.

We discover that the little newspaper shop also sells stamps and envelopes for rubles – one envelope costs fifty kopeks. One has to take a good look around this hotel to find whatever amenities they have. Alex gets angry in the bookshop. He wants the *Herald Tribune*, and instead of change, the girl gives him a postcard – he refuses and doesn't take the paper.

Saturday night, July 19

Not a normal Shabbat for me, as it meant traveling, but couldn't resist the circumstances. Alex B. took us to the main synagogue in Archipova Street. Classical pillars outside, a main hall inside – very nice – a handsome, nicely carved wooden balcony and the front row is separated into "boxes" for three or four persons. Huge circular chandeliers, and the Ark is set into a semi-niche going the full height of the building, and ending in a dome painted blue with gold stars. Below that were two Trees of Life on a gold background. The marble *bimah* is set right in front of the Ark. However, the acoustics were bad, the sound was unclear and the service difficult to follow.

There were quite a number of men, between fifty and sixty, and about thirty women, mostly tourists. Everyone seemed to be carrying a plastic bag. One character, apparently from a kibbutz, and looking as if she had arrived with Aliyah Bet, kept going around telling everyone she was from Palestine. I don't know what she expected them to do, but as there were no *siddurim* (prayer books) upstairs, there was much chatter, making it even more difficult to hear the prayers.

They took out three *Sifrei Torah*, which they carried right around the synagogue, then there was "*leinen*" in three different spots. A real *balagan*.

The woman sitting next to me asked if I was a tourist. When I told her I was from Jerusalem, she got very emotional, and told me a long story in

French, of which I understood little. She said she was coming to Jerusalem in August, and had an introduction to Rabbi Pinkhas. She said she was alone, since her parents had died (no longer young herself) and apparently had some problem, coughing a lot – TB? Anyway, I gave her my phone number and advised her to go to a religious kibbutz, but that idea didn't appeal to her.

We next went to send a birthday cable to our daughter-in-law Nurit, and then looked for the house of Alex's aunt Sonia, which we eventually found. Strangely enough, Alex has remembered the address since childhood, not even having it written down.

Alex B. then took us to lunch at the Slaviansky Bazaar, the Slavic exotic restaurant that has existed for more than one hundred years. There were large portraits of famous people in the foyer who used to patronize it, such as Chaliapin and Chekhov. Again very dark, all curtains drawn. A.B. ordered in Russian style – many hors d'oeuvres, soup, then chicken for Alex, sturgeon for himself and blini for me. This was supposed to be a fish restaurant, but besides sturgeon there is no fish – anywhere. Red caviar okay, black caviar, herring very salty, as is the sturgeon, hard-boiled eggs, tomato, cucumber, etc! Soup (fish) okay – Alex's chicken very tough. I asked for some jam instead of caviar for the blini, but there wasn't any. Alex tried to eat the chicken with his hands as he couldn't cut it and at least they brought him a fingerbowl. There was live music, which cost an extra three rubles. The bill came to 150 rubles ($5). Crowded, mainly with Russians, and there was a large queue at the entrance as we left.

We went to the main Berioska shop, which sells local arts and crafts, to look around, but it was just closing for lunch. We went to another branch in the suburbs, but discovered they use the old exchange rate of 1.60 rubles to $1, which makes it very expensive. This rate they call the Golden Ruble. We went to the Arbat, which was very crowded. Dolls, dolls, dolls, dolls. Then we went to the cemetery near the Convent of the Virgins to see the grave of Khrushchev and other monuments. Very elaborate with photos set in tombstones, sculptures, etc. We came back exhausted at about 4:30 and slept for a couple of hours.

We go to the Galaxie Restaurant for dinner. It's very crowded, and no one to show us to our places. So we go down to the other restaurant where Vitaly, our very first waiter, receives us with great enthusiasm, but soon afterward the place fills up, mainly with young Russians, and what looks like a sports team. The service becomes very slow. Vitaly brought me some fish (I think a small perch) which is impossible to eat. Alex had a good steak, but the chips, though brown, were raw. It cost 165 rubles. Live music and dancing. All kinds of girls and clothes. Where do they get the money? All smoke incessantly. We get tired of waiting for the bill, so get up and walk out, trying to explain to the head waiter what's happened. Vitaly comes running and apologizes that he's very busy.

Sunday, July 20

Hopefully to Zagorsk with Bermans.

This morning at breakfast, we scarcely have sat down when the waitress whips out a doll (*matroshka*) and a scarf for sale. We protest that we haven't eaten yet, and she's very contrite and brings our food. Then she offers the caviar. We have realized that it is not each waiter trying to make something on the side, but the hotel is behind this business. The caviar is kept at the serving station, and everyone has a go selling it!

The Bermans pick us up at 10:30 and we have a lovely drive out through the country – miles of birch (*berioska*) forests, bad roads, garden allotments, dacha estates. It seems the modern dacha is a tiny cottage with a sloping roof and a couple of metres of land. They cost about two thousand to three thousand dollars and are used on weekends. Lush and very picturesque from the road and we see much building on new sites. The drive is about a seventy–five-kilometre journey.

Zagorsk, the seat of the Russian Orthodox Church, is very picturesque, especially in the summer weather when the gold domes shine against the blue sky. Thousands of visitors and pilgrims come here. We see little scenes of old ladies asking priests to bless them; picnics; queues in the chapel for buying tapers, kissing icons and effigies. There's beautiful singing, *a cappella*, in the chapel with people joining in; many are writing *pitkaot*, or notes, giving names of dead relatives to the priests, to be prayed for – there must have been thousands. I wonder if they really pray for them. There are magnificent chandeliers some with red and green lights, and two fountains with holy water and people queuing up to fill their kettles, plastic bottles, mugs, etc. Old peasant types. The postcards give a better description than I can do.

We spend a couple of hours there and then go for lunch. In the outer square of the monastery, there are about forty tables selling dolls, etc. – really incredible. We can't get a table for lunch, as we have not reserved and they tell us to come back at 4:00! So we eat some almonds and crackers I have brought, and drink water. It's Sunday, so all the kiosks are closed.

Drove to the Abramzevo Museum, which is in a big forest park. We find a log cabin café there which is open, and finally get some food and drinks – tomato and onion salad, red caviar, tea, juice; the men have awful *shashlik*. The kitchen is a sight and I want to photograph it but Alex won't let me. As one has to wait at the service window to take the food, it is possible to have a good look at the inner workings. It is enough to put you off the food. Even here, the restaurant is dark. Beautiful drapes and net curtains, quite out of character, cover the windows, instead of leaving them open to the view.

The museum is quite interesting: a wooden house, old furniture, church, etc. in a beautiful forest setting. This used to be the home of a well-known writer, Sergei Aksakov, during the years 1843–1859, although it was actually built in the 1770s. After his death, the home became a meeting place and refuge for artists and writers, and is now maintained as a museum.

There's a tremendous traffic jam on the way home and we finally get back to the hotel at about 6:30, happy the car didn't break down! We saw four accidents during the day.

A really nice and enjoyable outing. Ann asks a lot of questions about Israel, but he doesn't seem to be particularly interested. They apparently have good jobs, work five days a week and she is a laboratory doctor, her own boss. She has just been to the seaside in Riga for three weeks, where her mother, also a doctor, takes a summer job at a *beit havra'ah* (sanatorium).

Alex's eye is bothering him very much today. Perhaps we should go to an eye doctor in Riga.

Monday morning, July 21

I feel quite tense about our trip to Riga, but Alex seems to be okay. We've had a good breakfast, red caviar and boiled eggs, as on the menu, and I had porridge as well – really excellent porridge with a pat of butter on top! With this, I won't get too hungry during the day. Packed and attended to details, and while cleaning up the bits of papers I happen to read the pamphlet about the Business Centre; it says they have a line for direct international phone calls, a complete contradiction to what the overseas operator downstairs had told us. I send Alex down to investigate, and sure enough, he came back after an hour, all smiles. Within half an hour, he had gotten through to the office in Jerusalem and spoken to Asi and Lonny. They were excited to hear from us, as they've been trying unsuccessfully to call us for four days and were getting worried. They said all is well, and they have received our cables. Alex told them I was subsisting on porridge and caviar, so I can imagine how that story will get round! Anyway, I feel really happy about the call – even though I didn't speak to them directly – the best I've felt all week. All attempts to get through to Lost and Found about the food bag have been unsuccessful. It's such a shame that we'll have so little to bring as gifts to Riga.

Intourist took us out to the domestic airport, which at least is more cheerful and pleasant than the other one. About ten of us were taken by the bus to the plane, and we thought: a whole plane for ten people! But after we boarded, the plane filled up completely with some large group at the back. Some of the seats were broken and it was not very comfortable. The flight was delayed about twenty-five minutes because of the number of planes leaving, so we were sitting almost an hour before takeoff. Similarly, at the end, we got off last and had to go through passport control. The flight took one hour and fifteen minutes. No trolleys and few porters, but we finally managed to find one and went off to the hotel. Alex said he didn't need a tranquilizer, but I did. I was so tense and worried about him.

Riga. First impression is of an attractive, clean city in good condition. The Hotel Latvia looks and feels like a real hotel (e.g., fresh flowers in the lobby), but the room was not very comfortable. We try to change, but the hotel is full. Apparently, many Latvians are coming to declare solidarity with the country, together with other holidaymakers. So I suggest shifting the beds round and that makes more room, and we were more comfortable. We unpack and Alex makes phone calls.

I actually fell asleep and woke about 9:45 p.m. Alex wanted to go out and find his parents' home and feel the city. He obviously wanted to be alone, so I had a cup of tea (the immersion heater is a godsend) and a sandwich, and made this entry, while listening to an opera on TV. I don't know what it is, but Perlman is conducting, and I think it's Leontyne Price – it sounds very nice. I hope Alex will not get too upset revisiting his childhood.

Looking out from the window on the fifteenth floor, the city doesn't appear to be very well lit. I see two or three neon signs. Actually, the brochure says there are about six hundred thousand people in the city, and two and a half million in all Latvia, so it's not a large country or city, but others told us later that Riga is home to a million people.

Alex comes back after an hour, deeply moved. He went out to find the house where his parents lived just before the war, somewhere close by. Suddenly, purely by instinct, he found himself right in front of the house where he had grown up. It was a real shock for him. He got the impression that it was now an office with a locked entrance. On the way back to the hotel he passed the little synagogue where he used to go with his father, still intact, and that too brought back many memories.

I wanted to give him a sedative, but he refused and seemed to sleep well till about 6 a.m.

Tuesday morning, July 22

Sara, the daughter of our friends in Beer Sheba, has apparently just had an operation, so there is some doubt whether we'll see her, but her husband is coming this morning to take us to Rumboli, and the cemetery. Her parents, Professor Zelia Cerfass, a top cardiologist, and his wife Leah, a professor of classic languages, had been part of Alex's circle of friends at high school, and came to Israel in 1990 to be with their younger daughter, Ilana, who had made *aliyah* shortly before the 1973 Yom Kippur war. Ilana had settled in Beer Sheba and found a position at Ben Gurion University teaching German, while her husband, Dr. Nahum Yavetz, a dentist, went into the army and subsequently opened a clinic. Ilana had a cousin, Bluma, daughter of Leah's sister, Sonya Itkin, who had come with her engineer husband, Ben-Zion Sandler, and daughter early in 1973, and also settled in Beer Sheba. Her mother joined her in 1978. Sonya spoke excellent English, and teaching it was her profession. She brought me a copy of Galsworthy's *Man of Property*!

It's very chilly this morning, and looks like rain. Perhaps I'll even get to wear the sweater I brought!

Breakfast is on the table, sausage and cheese and butter, a small Danish pastry and blini with smetana as the hot dish. Nice glassware, same white dishes with the gold rims as we saw in Moscow. This hotel is really a bit strange. Although it was built in 1978 and gave a first impression of being very fresh and nice, it's rather uncomfortable. The four small elevators are barely big enough to accommodate the hotel's luggage trolleys. The room numbers are on a small metal triangle at the top corner of the door, almost invisible. All woodwork is painted black. A second glass door inside the room conflicts with the wardrobe, which has three sliding doors, and the bathroom door opens outwards. There's a little step also, and no shelf space for toiletries in the bathroom. Bathmats are unknown in Russia, it seems. Still there are fresh flowers and plants in the public rooms, and flowers for sale. We couldn't get an English paper; the *Wall Street Journal* that they had was over a week old.

Tuesday evening, July 23

Today has been the peak of our Russian/Riga experience, the main reason for this trip. Sara and her husband came to pick us up about 11 a.m. They came with beautiful large carnations for me, very long-stemmed, and a small bouquet of cornflowers for Alex. However, Sara did not join us on the trip as she is just two weeks after her operation and a month away from their emigration to the U.S. We dropped her off at home and continued to the Jewish cemetery at Shmerli, where Ettie, a cousin of Zelia Cerfass, was waiting for us. She has been looking after Alex's father's grave, putting flowers on it regularly. This is very important in Riga, as apparently those graves that remain long neglected and unvisited are replaced by new burials.

As you come in the gate, there is a very large dark building with a dome and a large yellow Magen David affixed to it. This is the *beit taharah* and/or synagogue. On the right-hand side is a monument to a Latvian family that rescued about fifty Jews. I think the person was invited to Jerusalem as a Righteous Gentile.

The immediate impression as one walks in is of a large beautiful forest with lots of fresh flowers amongst the graves. There are some elaborate tombstones, some in Hebrew, some in Russian, some with Jewish symbols and some with photos or sculptures, in the Russian tradition. Little benches for sitting near the graves, which is a beautiful thought, are very practical. The grave of Alex's father has a small simple stone in Hebrew. He died in June 1940 after a massive stroke, some months before the Germans arrived. On the grave were two roses, probably put there by Ettie, and Alex places a bunch of carnations. He is very moved, and I too shed a tear. Alex says a few words, *Kaddish*, then *El Maleh Rahamim*, and finally scatters some soil on the grave that he has brought from Jerusalem. It is really something, to come after fifty years to say *Kaddish* at one's father's grave. There is something cathartic about this culmination of years of guilt and anxiety and longing.

This applies also to our visit to Rumboli, which is even more affecting, since his mother was murdered or died during the infamous Death March in November 1941, and so did not die a natural death. At the entrance to the Rumboli forest is a large stone memorial, with a Magen David, to those who died there. But when you go into the woods, there isn't a single sign or direction. We park in a little clearing, and a worker there directs us into the forest. We go some thirty metres along this little path, then come out to an area where there is a large rectangular mound, about six by twelve metres.

Another stone with an inscription in Russian and Latvian pays tribute to those who were murdered in a "bestial way" by the Nazis. Alex places the roses (his mother's name was Rosa) and scatters the rest of the Jerusalem earth, and says *Kaddish* and *El Maleh Rahamim*. He is really terribly upset, recalling the possible circumstances of her death. Perhaps she was lucky and died early on in the march, and didn't have to walk fifteen kilometres in the snow in order to be shot. But we shall never know.

As he walks around the mound, Alex suddenly becomes aware of the words "יד ושם" – Yad Vashem, in the bare earth in the grass, right at the edge. Probably a stencil had been put down when the grass was planted, and so the letters showed up, but I'm sure that not everybody would see it. It is the only Hebrew inscription there.

After these two ceremonies, I really feel I could use a drink! And the professor agrees with me. He tells us that Jews have a memorial day each autumn when they visit the site, but our companion isn't sure whether the Latvians do so. As we left Rumboli, I recalled that I hadn't seen any water taps at the cemetery. Then I remember that I had a bottle of water in my handbag, so we use that to wash our hands.

We return to the hotel quite exhausted, and decide to try the buffet lunch, but there is no such thing, in spite of the announcements. We go to the breakfast room, and are given quite a comprehensive menu, but scarcely anything is available except pork and beef! For vegetarians, hardly anything. Finally, I got some tomato and cucumber salad, green onions, smoked fish, hard-boiled egg in mustard sauce, and caramel ice cream to follow. No fish, as in Russia (what do they do with it?) and no fruit. I do seem to eat more bread then usual!

We both sleep about two hours, and then go out to visit Alex's home, school, father's office, etc. The last turns out to be a peculiar experience. We find the building in Reines Street, one of the main streets quite easily. Alex has the urge to go upstairs, so we climb three high flights of dark stairs and ring at the door. After a few minutes, a young fellow comes out, eating an ice-cream cone.

Alex tells him about his father once having had an office there, etc., and the young man says it's now a communal apartment. In the meantime a young woman also comes to the door, and when Alex asks whether he could come in and look around they say, somewhat surprised, "Yes, come in." But it's absolutely pitch dark. We can't see a thing. Alex asks if there isn't any electricity, and the fellow says the bulb has burnt out. We say thank you and leave. I'm really astonished at Alex, as he is usually very cautious. After all, they could have been drug addicts or whatever. Afterwards, I wondered if the young fellow had been very clever in inviting us in such a way. Whatever, it was a very strange experience. All the buildings we have peeked into have these gloomy, miserable stairways; I'm beginning to think the *olim* in Israel must suffer some kind of shock at the exposure to our light!

We walk slowly back to the hotel. We see many old two-storey wooden buildings painted in various colors, but I have finished my film. We also visit Alex's Hebrew Gymnasia, which is now a technical college. It is obvious that the population is not Russian, but looks more Scandinavian, European. One also sees many oriental-looking people, probably from farther parts of Russia (at the airport there had been a young black man going to Murmansk – Alex thought he was perhaps a sailor). Also, the architecture has a more Gothic character, as well as a regular European style. There is a strong anti-Russian feeling now, so the Latvians speak their own language a great deal, and there is talk of a law, which will discriminate in employment against those who can't speak Russian. They will have to take a written exam.

Alex wants some laundry done today. The floor lady says she has a friend upstairs who'll do it in a day (four shirts, underwear, pressing a suit). We speculate how much it would be. I figure $10, but in the end it costs fifteen rubles, and when Alex gives her fifty rubles, she protests that it's too much but takes it. People here are not so dollar-conscious as in Moscow, and few taxi drivers demand foreign currency.

Many tourist groups coming and going; today a large group from Germany. No English paper anywhere.

Tomorrow, we see friends of the late Nina Thol, and visit the Old City. Nina had also been a school friend of Alex's and was one of the first to come to Israel with her daughter, Vered, about a year after the Six Day War. Nina's husband had been a victim of Stalin's purge of the doctors in 1953, and she told horrifying stories about the isolation she had endured. Everyone ignored her. Even her friends were afraid of being seen with her, such was the fear then of the authorities.

We have supper in the room. It is 10:30 p.m., but not yet quite dark.

Wednesday, July 24

Had a quiet morning today, while Alex had an appointment with a friend of Nina Thol's daughter, and I wrote many postcards. I had salad and sprats for lunch (Alex had chicken, which was tough), and fresh strawberries for dessert. First fresh fruit we've had since we left home.

About 3:30, Sara's daughter, Tamara, came with her husband to show us the Old Town. She doesn't know English too well yet, and seemed a bit ill at ease, so it wasn't too comfortable. She thought I wanted to go shopping for clothes, but we just walked about. At one stage, we found ourselves again at the apartment of Murra's family (Alex's cousin in N.Y.), but still no answer to the bell.

We wanted to see the synagogue, but when we got near, the road was taken up; Tamara's husband (another Alex) told us some story about the road work being a permanent feature, to make life more difficult for the Jews. He took us round the back, but there was no access. I thought I'd try to get round the front again to take a picture when I suddenly saw the synagogue in the side street, quite sound and undisturbed. On closer inspection, we saw the door was open and walked in.

There was one *gabbai* inside. The place is much nicer and better kept than the synagogue in Moscow, though not quite so large. Apparently, Rabbi Goren, head chaplain of the Israeli army, had visited here a couple of weeks ago. There is a *mikveh*, but no rabbi; the *shochet* acts as the rabbi and *ba'al tefillah* (cantor, prayer leader). It seems that fifty to sixty worshippers is a good attendance on festivals. This is the only active synagogue left out of sixty-three before the war. The front outside wall is to be renovated soon, with the help of a donation from Israel. I wondered if this was the synagogue of Rabbi Moshe Shapira (the son of my great-great-grandfather), who had been Chief Rabbi of Riga from 1882 until his death in 1911.

After a couple of hours of walking about, we took a taxi to Sara and Misha's place. Tamara was horrified at the extravagance of twenty-five rubles, but it seemed silly to phone her father to come and fetch us. They live in an old house with a decent stairway lit by windows, but no elevator and they are on the fourth floor. It is a spacious three-room apartment, but a big mess because they are leaving for New York City in about a month. Actually, they have already sent their stuff, but are not sending furniture because of the freight charges. Misha told us that an Odessa mafia has taken over the haulage at the docks and charges a fee of one dollar per 1.5 kilograms when half the weight is the container itself. Sara put on lovely food, gravlax, which she makes herself, red caviar, sprats, and Hungarian wine. Much later she served a cake covered with cream, tea and *varenya* (strawberry preserves). There was another lady, a cousin, and the in-laws of the daughter.

In the end, this afternoon tea turned out to be rather depressing, and I felt we were witnessing the second destruction of the Riga community. These families were going to the States, except for the cousin who remains alone, and hopes to get to Israel, where she also has no one. The in-laws have a son who's been in the U.S. about a year, and is more or less getting organized. Sara's family is going because her husband's brother has been there ten years and is taking them over.

Misha, Sara's husband, is not interested in Israel. Sara doesn't want to go to the States and is anxious about her parents in Israel, but she has no choice. At one stage, she got quite upset. There are about five thousand Jews now in Riga, although others give higher figures, perhaps with the mixed marriages. Everyone except the old is planning to leave. Who will look after them, who will look after the cemetery, the synagogue? In a few years, there won't be any Jews left.

On the other hand, there is a Jewish day school with an enrollment of five hundred. Tamara told me a strange story. She has been recently divorced (there is a little girl of six), but since their exit application was made in the name of her ex-husband, she must leave the country together with him.

I asked Misha what he plans to do in New York. He said he was fifty-six years old, a professor of gastro-whatever-it-is. He thought he could pass the American exams, but that no one would take him for a residency (three years) at his age, or that he was even physically capable of doing the job. Sara's knowledge of English is very poor, so there's no possibility of her getting a license. He said their prime aim is to see their son, a young doctor, settled, and then perhaps they could run a private clinic for the Russian community.

We sat around and chatted till 8 p.m. On the way back, Misha showed us the memorial, which had been placed in the park where the Gogol Street Synagogue once stood and which on July 4, 1940, was filled with Jews and set alight. Today, Latvians sit in the park in the company of this grey boulder with the Magen David. Withered flowers lay there, and I was sorry we had no fresh ones to add. There is an inscription in Yiddish, Latvian and Russian commemorating the victims of the Nazis, but no mention of the synagogue fire. Had this been Rabbi Moshe's synagogue? We then drove back to the old ghetto area, behind the railway station, and Ms. Feige, who was with us, pointed out the sites of the various Jewish institutions and hospitals which had once stood there. She had been a nurse and worked there. Much of this area is still full of small old wooden houses, run-down, but picturesque.

Got back to the hotel quite exhausted, after 9 p.m., and really sad and depressed about what's going on here. Many phone calls during the evening; Alex has gotten quite involved.

Thursday, July 25

Sarah's husband Misha came to take us to Jurmaleh (the "seaside") – a twenty-kilometre stretch of nice sandy beaches and *dacha* resorts, but the water looks brown and uninviting. Misha says people are warned not to swim, but they do anyway.

However, the little resorts are lovely – individual houses, some grand, some small, some big hotels and pensions for organized unions or professions – set among the trees, lawns and flowers. The apartments rent at about five hundred rubles a month and families come to stay for two or three months. The parents take turns, one works and the other takes time off. It is only about a twenty- to twenty–five-minute drive from town. School holidays last for three months.

We stopped for coffee at a café, which provided only coffee and ice cream served with chopped peanuts. Quite tasty. This place, Dzinare, has a long shopping mall, but there's hardly anything to buy.

Two culinary surprises today – for breakfast, white cheese with *smetana* (thick sour cream) and at lunch tomato, cucumber and dill salad, also with *smetana*. My vegetable plate consisted of boiled potatoes, more salad and sauerkraut. Dessert was a square of gelatin in a pink watery liquid, and there was a plate of lemon slices and granulated sugar, apparently for eating. First lemon we've seen. The weather was lovely, not too hot with a pleasant breeze. The elevators broke down twice today and we had to walk up fifteen floors.

Afternoon

Alex had an appointment, so I decided to go "shopping." We had seen one department store with very nice windows, real window dressing, and I wanted to see what was inside. It was very disappointing. I finished the store in ten minutes! There was only one floor, and all the departments were arranged like stalls, with one central aisle. There were men's shirts and sweaters, women's blouses and sweaters, scarves and gloves, men's socks, toiletries, household linens, some jewelry and very little amber. It was quite crowded but there were no interesting souvenirs.

Afterwards, I went with Alex to the old home on Strelnicku Street again. We tried to locate the *shtiebel*, but Alex couldn't identify it this time. Then with great difficulty, we got a taxi to the house in Matveyevskaya Street, which he finally found. Apparently, the Rafaelowitch family lived here just after arriving from Drissa (near Dvinsk) in 1919, which they left because of the Communist revolution. They first had a tiny apartment, and after a year or so took a larger one on the next floor. The house, in a second interior courtyard, has been renovated and looks very nice from the outside. Someone tinkering with his car asked if we had once lived there. In 1922, the Latvians declared independence, and with their improved economic situation, Alex' family moved to the house in Strelnicku Street, where Rafaelovitch lived for six or seven years until he left for Heidelberg. The Latvians seem to be used to people coming around with cameras, but are also a bit anxious about property claims.

In 1935, the parents and Asya moved to the office in Reines Street, and after the father's death in June 1940, the mother and Asi were moved to other living quarters, where they lived up to the time of the Death March in winter, and Asi's running away to join the partisans, after which both were murdered.

Supper. Actually fried fish – some large sardines, or perhaps rouget – with a mixed salad of tomato, cucumber and shallots with a sour cream dressing, then ice cream cake and coffee. Almost a normal meal.

P.M. Trying to call Varda tonight, but seems like an impossible undertaking.

Friday, July 26

The call to Varda came through about 11:50 p.m. last night, and it was nice talking to her and to Karni, who happened to be there. Everything seems to be okay, but her little boy Avishai hadn't had his medical tests yet. About fifteen minutes later, Karni called us back and we had a longer conversation. Only incidentally, she told us that she has had a good offer of a job in Tel Aviv, that she has cut her hair short, etc.

Didn't sleep well, for thinking about everything.

At 9:45 a.m. Ettie came to join us, and we finally persuaded her to take the package (dried fruit and coffee, soup and milk). We went to see Mr Westerman, whose office is in the building of the Jewish Club, previously the Yiddish Theater, which the Jewish community had built. He'd been recommended as the community historian, after I began making my enquiries about Rabbi Moshe Shapiro. Now everyone considers me at least partly a native of Riga. They are quite astonished that I do not eat meat and do not ride on Shabbat. They are sure I am starving.

He was not too helpful, but gave us some addresses, and told us the town archives were now closed, but that I should write. He seems more interested in the history of the present century, and not in Judaism. But he had a long conversation with Alex about partisan fighting and his wartime activities. He assured us there was a Riga phone book, but when we asked at the hotel, they only had one for organizations. We went again to Shmerli with Ettie. I thought I might be able to track down Rabbi Moshe's grave, but the office of the Hevra Kadisha was closed.

Many people were visiting the cemetery, but none of the men wore *kippot*.

Sara took us for lunch/dinner at 2:45. We went to a nice restaurant in a hotel called the Ridzene, a hotel for Party guests and other favored visitors, where there were still bullet holes from recent shooting. The hors d'oeuvres were two kinds of cold meat, gravlax, jellied eel, tomatoes, cucumbers and olives. For the main dish, I had a fried salmon steak with potatoes and cabbage, which was delicious. Then came ice cream with fruit, something that was supposed to be a peach but was about the size of a small plum. Coffee. It was very nice and we finished after 5:00 (we did have to wait quite a bit). Apparently, this is a normal eating pattern here. Then I managed to get my hair done (seven rubles), and we're having "an evening at home." Maybe the kids will phone. Varda and Lonny did; they got a big kick talking to us in Riga.

Alex was very upset this morning when he heard a driver ask our taxi driver where Rumboli was. Neither of them knew.

The approaching move to the U.S. weighs heavily on Sara and Misha. She regrets now that they didn't move to Israel ten years ago, and both see the end of their professional life, and any kind of a productive life. What can one say to them?

Saturday night, July 27

Another busy day. In the morning we went to the synagogue in Piltivas Street, which is not far away. About forty oldsters and two or three tourists. An excellent *chazzan*, whom we could hear already outside, and something of a choir, or at least vocal accompaniment. The man we spoke to a couple of days ago is actually the *ba'al koreh*, and offered Alex an *aliyah*. My stomach turned over from emotion, so I can imagine how Alex felt. He was third, and said the *brachot* in such a loud clear voice, everyone turned to see who it was. I could have kicked myself that I didn't have the tape recorder, but I decided at least to take pictures. However, I did so from outside the door, and it wasn't too far away because the *bimah* was large, as was the *amud* in front of the Ark. It was a moving moment for Alex. Hoped the photos would turn out well, as I definitely wanted a souvenir of this scene.

Someone asked me to photograph him, and was prepared that I should do so in the synagogue, but I took him outside. During the *leinen*, which was conducted in a quiet way (and they do all the *misheberach* blessings at the end), everyone chatted and walked about, paying little attention. A woman who saw me from the other side came over and started talking to me in Hebrew. She had learnt the language as a child and still remembered, but she is not planning to make *aliyah* because all her family is here and there are "problems," so I presume they've all married out. I had great difficulty getting in a few minutes of prayer. During all this, a group of tourists came in the side door and stayed about fifteen minutes. Some of them looked Japanese, but afterwards outside we heard the guide explaining in Russian, so they may have been visitors from Eastern Russia.

I must say that though the synagogue is done quite tastefully in classical décor, there is an awful green neon Magen David over the *aron*, which I found very disturbing.

We met Sara's son Isandre as planned, and he went with us to the town library, another grand building with fantastic flights of stairs (maybe thirty to forty steps in each flight) and the stairwell was about fifty metres high. Of course, we had to go to the third floor. To be brief, we looked at yearbooks of 1896, 1900 and 1907, and in all of them found M. Schapiro, Rabbi, at the same address, 141 Romanov Street, but no one could tell us what that street was called now. Also, we found Rabbi Shalom Avin, the son-in-law, listed at the same address. There was no listing of synagogues in order to identify Adath Yeshurun, since synagogues are known here mainly by the street name. It seems to me that best references must be at Hebrew University or Yad Vashem, since they say everything here was destroyed.

Isandre took us to a nice restaurant, behind an anonymous door (he was our guest of course), and I had "trout" – quite good, except it was fried like a schnitzel in egg and flour. He seems a nice young man and is prepared to work hard to pass his medical exams in the States in order to get started there. I think he's about twenty-eight or so, married with a child, with another on the way. His wife's sister and her husband have been there about two years, and he has passed his exams and is working in a N.Y. hospital. Isandre hopes he will be helpful in guiding him through the U.S. requirements.

Returned to the hotel for a rest. Afterwards, Alex went to look for the relative that Murra had mentioned to him. He found the address, but the man was not in, and according to the state of the letterbox, is out of town. We have not been lucky with that side of the family. Meantime, I went for a walk and saw the start of the First International Marathon. The atmosphere today, another beautiful day, was really *shabbasdik* – shops closed, little traffic, people out walking with babies and children. Apparently, they have a five-day working week here. I am surprised by little things – the popularity of spike-heeled shoes, the high proportion of tall girls, very strong Scandinavian types, the heavy smoking, no souvenirs worth buying, and quite a sprinkling of Orientals, or are they Eastern Russians?

In the evening, the Rosenthals (friends of Vered, the daughter of Nina Thol) came to visit and we had a pleasant chat. One son, a top kidney transplant man, has been invited twice this year to Israel. His two children are now there, a married daughter, and a son who is to marry an Israeli girl at the end of the year. The parents would like at least to visit, but say that the over-70s cannot get health insurance. They told us that Romanov Street is now Lachplesha Street, as Alex had thought, and in the course of the conversation they told us that they had been married by Rabbi Shalom Avin, Rabbi Moshe's son-in-law, in 1934! Apparently, he was a very good-looking and impressive personality, and much in demand for weddings and celebrations. On his way back from Murra's relative, Alex stopped at 141 Lachplesha Street and found a large handsome building in expansive grounds.

Sunday, July 28

Mr. Friedman took us out. We thought we were going to the seaside, but instead he took us to his laboratories (testing of hydroelectric valves) and then to the aircraft testing centre. Mostly over my understanding, and apparently involved in some kind of joint venture with Germany's aeronautical industry. He took us to lunch at a nice little restaurant (the first one, the Lido was full) where we had delicious pineapple juice and fresh, grilled salmon. Came back to hotel to rest, then Ettie came for an hour. Alex discussed with her the question of putting up a new tombstone with names of his mother and brother. Very hard to say goodbye.

In the evening, Sara and Misha came with Tamara and her husband. Again, they brought flowers. I wanted to put them in the room, but they said to have them on the table in the restaurant. Indeed, the waiters provided a vase, and other parties also had flowers on their tables. But what shall I do with the flowers tomorrow?

We had dinner upstairs on the twenty-sixth floor. A marvelous view.

I had gravlax and vegetables. There was no wine, only champagne – they all had meat and what I see is the usual hors d'oeurves selection, enough for a meal in Israel. Dinner for six cost us $16. When it was time to say goodbye, they insisted on taking us to the airport tomorrow, so another parting postponed.

I forgot to mention that on the way home, Mr Friedman took us to see 141 Lachplesha Street. A really great house on a big corner lot – about forty-five metres frontage by sixty metres. If this is the right place, the synagogue must have also been in this building and the family probably lived upstairs. However, we could see no obvious signs that this had once been a synagogue, although there are some arched windows on the second floor. Today it is a school. The area is called Moscow Forstadt because the road to Moscow passes through here, and it is the beginning of the Jewish suburbs.

So our trip to Riga draws to its close, but our friends and many others are just at the beginning of their great adventure to America!

Monday morning, 9:15 a.m., July 29

We have finished packing and are getting ready to leave. What seemed to be a "mission impossible" has been accomplished, and I think we leave with mixed feelings. Thankful that we have done what we've talked about for years – a bit sad to leave the nice and also sad people who are staying behind – concerned for our friends who are going unhappily to the New World – and above all, happy to be on the last lap of the journey and on the way home. I doubt if we shall come here again. Anything else for me personally, regarding Rabbi Moshe Shapira, could probably be done by mail. So, goodbye to Riga!

The flight, uneventful.

There was nothing like coming back to Moscow to break the spell of Riga. Loud, dirty, not charming. We stayed at the Intourist Hotel, which is very central but like a bazaar, and terrible service. This evening we couldn't find anywhere to eat in the neighborhood; people sent us from one place to another. Finally, we came back to the hotel to have a cup of soup in the room, but an Australian couple we met in the elevator told us they'd finally found something on the sixteenth floor. It was just a little snack bar, but at least we had a cheese sandwich and a Danish. Couldn't even have two cheese sandwiches because these were the last.

Street scene not very appealing – officials unpleasant, queues outside every café or ice cream parlor – crowds congregating around anyone who has something to sell (e.g., perfumes) – lots of men about and lots of girls available. Many nationalities. We saw a group of Tartars today, and other types from the East (Uzbekistan, I think, or similar). The runaround one gets (e.g., to change money today Alex had to go halfway across town) makes one tired and fed up. Moscow certainly has no glamour and is far from a world capital. No shows to see in summer.

Tuesday morning, July 30

Phoned Ann Berman and she invited us to dinner. We took a tour of the Metro. Although it was off-peak, still crowded. The stations are really very luxurious, each one in a different style – sculptures representing Russian types, stained glass panels, mosaic pictures of Russian history, colored marble and semi-precious stones, etc., etc. The trains are very fast, covering long distances, but at the last stop (we saw seven stations on different lines) the escalators had broken down and crowds of people backed up, so we had to go to another station to get to our destination. Our guide was not Jewish, but married to a Jew, and told us that many of their friends had gone to Israel. Soon, there will be tours to Israel and Egypt. Went to the children's department store – what a horror! Crowds outside selling odds and ends, and inside hardly a thing. Had lunch at the Slaviansky Bazaar, which we eventually found; again caviar and blini. Afternoon at the Arbat, where we managed to do most of our gift shopping.

At 7 p.m., Victor came to fetch us with Ann, and it was a forty–five-minute drive to their home. Later, she insisted on driving back with us. It transpired that as she is the official owner of the car, and the son's permission to drive it has lapsed, she has to accompany him on his drives. They would not allow us to go alone in a taxi at night, even if we could have found one. Small apartment (tiny bedroom and toilet, as at Sara's), building in poor state. She served the usual *zakuski* (appetizers): nice borsht, pancakes, watermelon and cake. We watched President Bush and James Baker on TV at the historic meeting in Moscow.

Drove back along the embankment, which gave us lovely views of Moscow. Good that I brought her some coffee, tissues, etc. as she had gifts for me and the grandchildren. One never knows on which occasions the Russians will give gifts.

Wednesday, July 30

Appointments with the art people and visits to their studios. Living accommodation impossible to describe! What dilapidation and what dirt! The only really interesting painting was not for sale (a girl combing her hair), and the second fellow had some interesting work (delicate colors, religious themes) but very expensive. The procedure of buying and getting a picture out of the country is incredible, and I'm sure not many bother with it.

One of the painters has a studio in the Imperial Barracks. This once handsome building has been re-adapted and is now made up of one-room apartments, with a communal kitchen and bathroom on each floor. These facilities have big padlocks on them, and when I asked if I could see the kitchen, the painter said he didn't have a key; because he did not actually live there, he had no kitchen rights. Although there were some renovations going on in one or two apartments, the building remains a tenement, and negotiating the staircase comprises a real risk.

We thought we might still get to the Crown Jewels, but it got too late, so instead we packed and rested in preparation for the night flight. Now there is no tension and anxiety as at the beginning. We have been away about two and a half weeks, and it seems like an age. We have been to another planet, and we are very happy to be going home!

Alex has aliya in Piltivas synagogue, 1991.

Alex brings Jerusalem earth for father's grave, 1991.

Return from Riga – we get an "immigrant's basket of iveleges" from the children.

Maastricht –
Fifty Years Later

September 1994

ON THE NIGHT OF SEPTEMBER 14, 1944, THE 30TH INFANTRY
Division of the American army liberated the town of Maastricht in its
drive through Holland into Nazi Germany. This Dutch–German border
town lay close to the German line of defense, the Siegfried Line, beyond
which was the Ruhr Valley with its heavily industrialized towns such as
Essen, home of the Krupp family industries, the leading manufacturers of
steel and armaments. Little did those soldiers dream that half a century
later, the mayor of Maastricht would invite them back to the city for the
celebration of the fiftieth anniversary of that event.

My husband, Alexander Rafaeli, then a corporal in the Old Hickory
Division, as the 30th Infantry outfit was called, and living since 1949
in Israel, was not aware of the official contacts between the Maastricht
municipality and the veterans organization of Old Hickory in the States.
However, he was brought to the attention of authorities by Mr. C. B.
Arriens, who had served as ambassador of the Netherlands to Jerusalem
from 1975 to 1980, and who knew of Alex's participation in the Maastricht
campaign.

And so we received an official invitation from Mayor Philip Houben to
attend the celebrations on September 13, 14 and 15. At first we were hesi-
tant because the main events were scheduled for the eve of Yom Kippur

From left: Robert Kahn, myself, Ambassador Arriens, Roberta Arriens, Alex. 1994

(Kol Nidre), but then we felt that this was a landmark occasion for Alex not to be missed, and that we would be able to arrange ourselves without desecrating the holy day. It also meant that we would be away from the family on this day for the first time in more than forty years.

We arrived in Maastricht on September 14, together with Krik (nickname) and Roberta Arriens, whom we had been visiting in The Hague, to encounter utter confusion with regard to our hotel reservation. It took a couple of hours of phone calls and hotel hopping until we finally managed to find a room where we could stay for the duration – almost. After all the aggravation, we were delighted to discover that the Hotel du Casque was located just around the corner from the synagogue. The Arriens were also booked there.

That evening, we had dinner in the hotel restaurant with Krik and Roberta, and with Robert Kahn, a recently discovered American relative who was working in Düsseldorf and drove in to meet us. Robert was the brother of Professor Bruce Kahn of Rochester, NY, who discovered my brother through a New York genealogist. They had both made enquiries about their respective families, and the genealogist noted that the same names appeared on both applications, and put them in touch. It turned out that we had a common great-great-grandfather, Reb Aisel Harif (1801–1873) of Slonim.

Suddenly, halfway through the meal, a young man who had been sitting nearby contemplating Alex and the ribbons on his jacket, approached, and taking Alex by the hand, thanked him profusely for having taken part in the liberation of the city. The quality of life which the young people of Maastricht were now enjoying was due, he said, to those American soldiers, who had devoted years of their lives to fight against Hitler, and who had come halfway across the world fifty years ago to liberate Europe. He stressed this element several times, as if it was an idea, or concept of behavior, which he couldn't quite comprehend. Perhaps he was a little tipsy. We were rather taken aback by this unexpected incident, but I recovered sufficiently to reach for my camera and record the moment.

Such spontaneous expressions of thanks and appreciation occurred several times during our stay and reflected the welcoming attitude of the population.

The following morning we walked across the square to the Spanish Government House for the mayor's reception. It is so called because it had indeed been the local seat of the Spanish government before the independence of Holland from Spain was achieved in 1648. The flags and banners gave the town a festive appearance, and the music of carousels and Ferris wheels in the square filled the air. At the reception we met the mayor and his wife, the governor of the province, leading citizens of Maastricht, the American ambassador and military attachés and their wives, and mayors from neighboring French and Dutch towns.

Colonel Towers, one of the former commanding officers representing the Old Hickory Division, was wearing a pale blue jacket and cap, with the appropriate emblems, and we later saw that the whole American contingent was wearing the same identifying jackets. Colonel Towers seemed a bit suspicious of Alex, who in his regular clothes was obviously not in the official American delegation, and yet had been invited to the reception. He queried Alex about his service and his postings during that campaign, and being satisfied that he had indeed been there on active service, accepted Alex as a genuine veteran and presented him with the badge of the Old Hickory Veterans Association.

Alex wished to present Mayor Houben with a letter and gift he had brought from Ehud Olmert, then the mayor of Jerusalem, but as the schedule was strictly planned we could not do so, and were given an appointment at another time.

After the reception, the whole group walked over to St. Servatus Cathedral for the commemorative mass. Unlike the previous day, which had been bright and sunny, a steady rain had set in and, as Alex had come to Europe without a coat, we had to wait for an appropriate opportunity to rush away and buy him a raincoat.

The cathedral is a grand Gothic building but painted white inside and not gloomy. It is about a thousand years old, and the original foundations, dating back to the fourth century, can be seen in the crypt. Beautiful cloisters lead into the cathedral, which was packed with local citizens and the contingent of veterans who had come, about a hundred strong, and with their families and grandchildren. The Mass was celebrated with all pomp by Bishop Wiertz, accompanied by a wonderful choir, and speeches were made in Dutch and English, honoring those who had fallen in battle, and thanking those survivors who had come from abroad to share in the celebrations. At the end of the mass, a young boy played the Last Post, and as the congregants filed out of the church, they were greeted by hundreds of small children waving American flags and singing, "For he's a jolly good fellow . . . ."

Large red and white umbrellas, the colors of Maastricht, were distributed to protect the participants from the heavy rain. The mayor placed a wreath at the memorial corner at the side of the cathedral, and the whole company embarked on buses to the site on the river where the monument to Old Hickory was to be unveiled – except for our minibus, which would not budge because the battery had gone dead. It took a good half hour before a replacement arrived and brought us to the site. Coffee and sandwiches were being served under a marquee, where everybody crowded into to escape the rain, except for the military band, which played on valiantly until the formal ceremony began. Old soldiers looked for buddies, all equally grey-haired, but Alex did not find a familiar face, except for Mr Arriens. However, this did not prevent spontaneous chats and reminiscences. Over all hovered the amazement, the sense of wonder that fifty years, half a century, had passed since the original events had taken place.

The gate-like monument and the pillar bearing the legend stand near the Provincial Government buildings by the River Maas, at the exact spot where the American army crossed into the town. The monument was created by the local Jewish sculptor Albert (Appie) Drielsma, and later he told us it was inspired by the verse "This is the gate of the Lord; the righteous shall enter through it" (*Zeh ha-shaar . . . zaddikim yavou bo*) (Psalms 118:20). The mayor, scorning an umbrella, made his speech and cut the ribbon. His secretary told us on a later occasion that he had to change his clothes three times that day after being soaked through.

The next scheduled event was a visit to the American military cemetery at Margraten where a torch that had been lit at Normandy was to be brought by a relay of runners. A set of chimes was also to be presented to the town by the Old Hickory veterans. This event was preceded by a parade of the veterans with their families through the town. In a variety of military vehicles, and loudly cheered by the crowds, the command cars and jeeps, one sporting a Union Jack, drove slowly through the town on their way out to the cemetery. However, the rain delayed everything and the cars which were supposed to take us to the cemetery were late. Alex and I began to worry whether we would get back to the hotel in time for our *seudah mafseket* (the last meal before the Yom Kippur fast) and whether we might not be delayed by some unforeseen mishap. At the last moment we decided not to take any chances and left the mini-bus, postponing our visit to the cemetery until after Yom Kippur. The Arriens joined us for our pre-fast dinner, as they were planning to return home next morning to The Hague.

The *Kol Nidre* service was scheduled to start at 8:15 p.m., summer time still being in force, and we arrived in good time at the synagogue, which we found to be of a medium size and rather austere. A plaque to mark the one hundred and fiftieth anniversary of the synagogue's founding had been placed in the entrance hall at the time of its restoration in 1989 by the Joint Distribution Committee (USA). Before the World War II, the Jewish population of Maastricht numbered seven hundred, and in September 1994, it numbered fifty. The total attendance that evening was about thirty-five, of whom ten were tourists, eight or nine were Russian émigrés, and the services were conducted by two young *yeshivah* men who had come specially from Amsterdam. The men and women sat separately on either side of the central aisle, with the *bimah* in the centre. The women's gallery upstairs was not used.

Although the service and the melodies were fairly familiar, there were some Sephardi elements and prayers we could not follow, and some traditional prayers were not said at all. During the *Yizkor* service the following day for example, the men came to the *bimah* and gave the names of their departed relatives to the *baal tefillah* who announced them out loud. Ben Wesley, the leader of the community, addressed the congregation and also noted Alex's presence at the services, and welcomed him as one of the liberators of the city. Alex was also called to stand by the *baal tefillah* as a "witness" during the *Kol Nidre* prayer.

On the whole Yom Kippur passed pleasantly enough, the temperature being about 16°C, with people coming and going for various periods of time, among them Appie Drielsma, the previously mentioned sculptor of the monument. At the end of the services, a young American woman, Renata Jackson, who was teaching at the Emerson University extension in Maastricht, invited us and the other English-speaking tourists to her nearby home to break the fast.

The following day, in spite of the heavy rain and cold, we took a taxi to the cemetery at Margraten to pay our respects to the first husband of a close friend. It is an extraordinary sight, an enormous park with beautifully kept lawns and over eighty-five hundred graves of American soldiers, marked with white marble crosses or Stars of David. The municipality had placed a spray of carnations at each grave, each in its own little plastic container, together with the flags of Maastricht and America. Bunches of flowers here and there showed that the boys had not been forgotten, and that relatives or friends had recently visited the cemetery.

If one wishes to visit a specific grave, as we did, one gets the directions and number of the grave from the Information Office. A high memorial tower houses a small chapel, where we discovered, to our surprise, preparations for a funeral. Although a large cross hangs on the wall, we saw a white sign near the coffin bearing a Magen David and inscribed with the Ten Commandments, giving the impression that this was to be a Jewish funeral.

We were puzzled that a soldier who had perhaps been killed in an accident would not be flown home to the States, but we heard later in the day that the soldier in question had been killed during the war and temporarily buried in a field. Now, fifty years later, a farmer had discovered the body, and it had been possible to identify the man because his dog tags were still there. It seems that the family had decided that he should be buried with his comrades close to the battle area; or perhaps there was no family left to bring him back home.

In the afternoon we went to our appointment with Mayor Houben at the town hall and presented him with Mayor Olmert's gift and letter, and also with a copy of Alex's autobiography in which he wrote about his participation in the liberation of Maastricht. In the ensuing conversation the mayor told us of his plans to visit Jerusalem next year, for the planting of a forest in honor of Queen Beatrix. We were happy to meet again with the mayor's secretary, Ms. Vissar, who had been so helpful to us during our stay.

On Saturday we explored the Old Town, and saw the Roman ruins under the Hotel Derlon, Less happily, our concierge informed us that we would have to vacate our rooms. If we did not want to look for another hotel, he could offer us two single rooms. We knew it would be hopeless to look for another hotel, so agreed for the remaining night to take the two rooms, which turned out to be in the attic at the top of a steep flight of stairs.

And so on Sunday we checked out of the Hotel du Casque and said fare-well to Maastricht, to which we now felt deeply attached. Time returned to its normal pace after fifty years had been brushed aside. The grey-haired men had been young again, the battle had been fought again, the victory won again. The wonder of it was that they were here once more bringing the past to life for a short moment, before it faded away into the history books. One day in the future, those flag-waving little children will say: Do you remember those Americans in the blue jackets who came here once, and we went to the church and sang for them?

We boarded the train to Paris, looking forward to our first visit there in more than twenty years. The experience of Maastricht was deep within us, and we were happy that we had taken up Mayor Houben's invitation.

Maria Therese: The Story of an Unusual Friendship

IN THE SPRING OF 1996 MY HUSBAND ALEX ANNOUNCED THAT HE wanted to go to the States one last time – to pay a goodbye visit to his cousin and friends. I was not too enthusiastic. I had had a lot of back trouble and did not relish the idea of long flights, short stays and carrying luggage. Also, Alex's failing sight meant more responsibility for me, but he was so set on the idea we made our itinerary, called on all the people involved, and decided that if we survived and were to be already in San Francisco, we would make our twice-cancelled trip to the Rockies. It was to be a five-week trip covering five states, nine or ten separate visits and the week in Canada. The highlight would be the reunion with Maria Therese.

Maria Therese. She belonged to the period of my husband's student days in Germany. They had had a short but meaningful friendship and he hadn't seen her or heard from her for more than sixty years. Yet she was as much a part of our family as if she had been living with us all those years, a woman of strong character and personality who, in absentia, had become woven into the fabric of our family tapestry and legend.

When Alex and I married in Tel Aviv on January 20, 1950, we probably seemed an unusual match. We had come from opposite sides of the world, from Riga and from Melbourne, and there was a difference in age. He was a European and had that special romantic aura which seems to surround speakers of Russian. He was a graduate of Heidelberg University, a veteran of the Second World War and an ex-Irgun activist – a man of the world. I was the product of an observant family, a British education, and of the provincial Australia of that time. I had graduated from Melbourne University and worked as a journalist with the local Jewish weekly, but my practical experience of politics was negligible.

Nevertheless, Alex and I also had much in common. My father was a staunch Zionist and had emigrated illegally from Poland to Palestine in 1921. My mother and brother Alec joined him about a year later. During this time they lived in Herzliya, and when I came into the world, I was the first girl, so I was told, to be born into that community. Because of the difficult economic conditions of this period, and with much inner conflict, my parents decided to join friends who were emigrating to Australia.

Because their families remained in Poland, our family life was very much orientated to the "old country" – as well as to Palestine – so I came to feel more European than Australian. We spoke Yiddish at home, and there was not that pressure to identify with the new country, as there seems to have been in America. My father was a Revisionist, a follower of the legendary Jabotinsky, so Alex's political opinions were not strange to me. In addition, Alex also had an uncle in Sydney who was a well-known philanthropist, so he was not entirely an unknown quantity.

We both had relatives in Israel, some who had come in the 1920s and early 1930s, and some who had come after the war. When it came to friends, however, the scene was different. I had come to Israel with my brother Alec and the few Australians I knew had gone to kibbutzim. Alex, on the other hand, knew a great many people from his political work with the Irgun in Palestine, Europe and America, and from his student days. I was intrigued by them as they were quite unlike the people I had known back in Australia. Some of them dated back to the Hebrew Gymnasia (high school) and to the very early days of Betar, the Revisionist youth movement, founded in Riga by Jabotinsky. Many of them had been at university together in Heidelberg and had belonged to the same Zionist fraternity. Each spoke several languages and they were on the whole successful and talented people. I was younger and not as sophisticated, so I was rather intimidated at first.

Many of those friendships lasted a lifetime, and I sometimes wondered what quirk of fate had brought such a gifted and varied group of people together in Heidelberg at that particular moment in Jewish history. One of this group was conspicuous by her absence. Maria Therese. She was the daughter of the German General Baron Kurt von Hammerstein-Equord, a career soldier who had been an officer during World War I, and eventually was promoted to chief of staff by Chancellor von Schleicher in 1929. Because of his military career, his wife and family of seven children had moved about all over Germany, eventually returning to Berlin.

In the early 1920s, this city was cosmopolitan and intellectually challenging, with young Jewish writers and artists playing a prominent part. Maria Therese was the second of the older three girls, the three boys and another girl coming after. Their mother, Maria von Luttwitz, who was half-Hungarian, was also from a military family, a nationalistic and anti-Semitic one, but far from being authoritarian. The von Hammersteins wanted their children to have the freedom to select their own careers and to develop their own personalities. The General regretted having been sent to a military academy at the age of eleven, while his wife wanted her girls to have every opportunity to study, an opportunity that had not been available to her. During the years of World War I and the early 1920s, the General was mostly away, and his wife was wholly in charge of the young family. They had a rather unorthodox and sporadic education because their mother would take them out of school for long summer vacations, which they spent in a variety of villages visiting family and friends. They reveled in the beauty of nature and also enjoyed fresh and healthy food, which was unobtainable in Berlin. Maria von Luttwitz was apparently a strong-willed woman, and Maria Therese was to follow in her footsteps.

Maria Therese attended high school in Berlin where, surprisingly, she gravitated to the Jewish pupils rather than to those of her own privileged circle. She developed a very close friendship with Vera Lewin, who was the daughter of a distinguished Berlin doctor, and with whom she kept in contact for many years. When Vera went on to study at Heidelberg University, Maria visited her there and became acquainted with that volatile and talented group of students already mentioned. Their awareness of the dangerous undercurrents of German politics and their Zionist idealism appealed to Maria, and she felt theirs was a cause she could identify with, even embrace. She would have liked to study in Heidelberg too, rather than at Berlin University, but the General did not agree, remembering his own unhappiness at being away from his family. Probably through Vera, Alex and Maria Therese became acquainted in 1932 and a close relationship developed, but always Alex felt that she could be endangering herself and her family by her open association with Jewish students. He describes the atmosphere of this period in his autobiography, *Dream and Action*.

When Hitler came to power in January 1933, his politics and personality were not to the General's liking. However, he remained in his position, hoping to influence the course of events, but he soon realized that that was impossible and resigned a year later. He was too liberal and decent to support Hitler's policies and methods, and the family was outraged by the political assassinations, which eliminated some of their own friends, such as General Kurt von Schleicher, Maria's godfather, and his wife. However, while the General was still serving, he was privy to official documents and used every opportunity to warn Jewish notables that they were "on the list." Maria, known in the family as Esi, would go on her motorcycle, which she had acquired with a legacy from her godmother, to bring the message of impending danger, and so some people were able to save themselves. The General was also able to have some members of the previous government posted abroad. Maria went several times to Prague to bring newspapers to a journalist who was not permitted to return to Germany, and sometimes she was able to take people over the border. However, her children knew nothing of these activities until many years later. The General had even been involved in one of the early plots to assassinate Hitler, but a last-minute change of schedule cancelled the plans.

After completing his studies in 1933, graduating with a doctorate in sociology, and having witnessed book-burning and other acts by the Nazis, Alex returned to his family in Riga, stopping off in Berlin to meet with Maria, who arrived at the hotel on her motorcycle. She wanted very much to join in the Zionist experiment. Alex had a hard time dissuading her and thought he had succeeded. A few months later, he immigrated to Palestine on a student visa and, after spending some time at the Hebrew University doing research under Professor Arthur Ruppin, set about organizing his life here. Some of the Heidelberg circle were already in the country or arrived soon after, and Alex soon found his niche as an insurance consultant with the newly-established insurance company, Migdal. At the same time, he was the economic editor at *Ha-doar ha-kalkali* (*The Economic Post*), published by Rafael Abulafia, but eventually became involved in activities of the Irgun. One day, early in 1934, he was surprised at the re-appearance of Maria Therese, who had come to see Palestine with her own eyes and to check whether she could fit into the picture, but again, Alex and her friends thought she would be placing herself and her family in danger and did not encourage her to stay.

I do not know what other reasons there were for her desire to remain in Palestine, since I never had a clear explanation of what the relationship between her and Alex really was, and in her journal, this visit is never mentioned. An excess of modesty on both sides? The desire of one not to embarrass the other? The realization that a future together was just not possible in light of the situation at that time? Whatever the right answer, she wrote a letter to him in July 1933, after the Berlin meeting, in which she said (and I translate freely from the German):

Dear Sasha, – I was very happy to get your letter .... Have you already been looking at books? A superfluous question. Anyway I find the program very good and I will make one for myself too. With what do you plan to start? ... It would be very nice of you if you were to write to me from time to time. I believe we created the basis for such a correspondence on that Wednesday evening. You know that everything that occupies your mind also occupies mine, more or less. I was very surprised indeed about how many concerns we share, and how similar our development has sometimes been . . . . You know that I don't get very close to people and because of that those I do get to know and those who get to understand me are valuable to me. Therefore, Sasha, even if we might not see each other for a long time, remain my friend and tell me sometimes about some of the things with which you are involved. I need you. Your Maria Theresa.

Later on, Alex heard from Vera Lewin that Maria had married a man of Jewish descent named Joachim Paasche, who also had an interesting background. He was the son of Hans Paasche, a former ranking naval officer who used to take his sailors on tours of the countryside rather than have them spend their leave in pubs. A great adventurer, Hans had traveled extensively in Africa and had exciting stories to tell his wife and children. He was also a writer but politically he was an active pacifist, decrying the horrors of war and the expansionist aggression of his government. In the summer of 1920, he was assassinated by extreme right-wing elements while on a picnic with his children. He was thirty-nine years old. Since his wife had died two years earlier during the flu epidemic, his son Joachim was taken in and cared for by his Jewish but non-observant grandfather. That family had originated in Poland, and after settling in Germany had in the course of time become devout conservative patriots.

Understanding that they would have to leave Germany, Maria and Joachim decided to immigrate to Palestine. Somehow, they had become acquainted with Enzo Sereni, a leading Italian Zionist activist, and traveled with him on the boat to Palestine, where they joined his kibbutz, Givat Brenner. Some years later, in 1943, Sereni was one of a group of Hagana members who parachuted into their countries of origin to try to alert the local Jews to the threat of deportation. Unfortunately, he landed in German territory. He was captured and sent to Dachau concentration camp, where he was shot.

It was the autumn of 1934. The Paasches spent almost a year on the kibbutz, but the climate did not agree with Jochen, as he was called in the family, and because of his ill-health, they returned to Germany. Maria had made extensive preparations for this venture and had enjoyed the agricultural work, even though they lived in a tent. Despite their hardships, there is not a word of disappointment in her diary. This was an expression of that fortitude which was to stand her in good stead in the future.

Since the Nuremberg Laws were now being more strictly enforced, Jochen was not permitted to resume his law studies, so he continued his study of Japanese and Chinese. The Paasches spent many sleepless nights waiting for the knock on the door, especially after the Gestapo had once summoned them for an interrogation. Maria Therese was pregnant and felt strongly that she did not want her child to be born in Nazi Germany. Their only option was to emigrate to Japan. Jochen, who had always been interested in the Far East, felt that they would be able to arrange themselves there. They took leave of their family, saying that they would be back in a couple of years, but the General thought it would take much longer to overthrow Hitler's regime, and he could see that a war was in the offing. Jochen and Maria remained in Japan for thirteen years, and all four of their children were born there. What happened to them during these years we only learned later, and I will return to that story later on.

By now, Alex had lost contact with Maria Therese. He was busy with his underground activities in Europe on behalf of the Irgun. World War II broke out in September 1939, and he succeeded in escaping to America. There he joined the Bergson Group, the Etzel delegation to the United States, which was conducting massive campaigns in order to win public support for the establishment of a Jewish army and for efforts to rescue the Jews of Europe. He enlisted in the American army in November 1943 and served in the European theatre. Because of his knowledge of languages, he was recruited into counter-intelligence, where he concentrated his efforts very successfully on finding Nazi leaders who had gone into hiding. But the tensions of his work, together with his great anxiety and guilt about the fate of his family, brought on a nervous breakdown, resulting in an honorable medical discharge at the end of the war. He returned to America, where once again he took up his work for the Irgun and the Bergson Group, which was then concentrating its efforts on winning public opinion in support of a Jewish state.

I came to Israel in February 1949 and eventually found work as a journalist in the offices of the World WIZO Organization. There I met Vera Lewin, who was the literary editor of their monthly journal, and also of the *Ha'aretz* newspaper. When Alex came to see her one day, he caught sight of me and asked Vera to introduce us. We married on January 20, 1950, his mother's birthday, and I began to hear about Alex's past life and to meet his friends, who formed the basis of our social life. Out of the mix of our two family histories and our individual experiences, we began to weave the family tapestry of stories and legends, upon which we reared our children. Needless to say, Maria Therese von Hammerstein, with her motorcycle, was one of the more colorful characters in this story.

During 1990, when Alex began preparing material for his memoirs, he asked my brother Alec in London to try to find more recent information about Maria Therese.

Alec checked with the German Embassy and various libraries. Though he found material about her family, there was no mention of Maria. Early in 1991, Alec attended his regular Rotary Club lunch. On hearing of the arrival of a guest, a German TV correspondent newly retired after many years of duty in India, he introduced himself to Mr. Hans Joachim Werbke and asked whether he happened to know of the von Hammerstein family. "Yes, indeed," he replied. Ludwig was a director of Berlin TV and a member of his own Rotary Club branch. He would ask him as to the whereabouts of his sister Maria.

One day in April we had an excited phone call from my brother. Maria Therese was alive and well in California, and if Alex would write to Ludwig in Berlin, he would send us the address. Within a matter of weeks, Alex had written. We soon received a reply from Maria, who seemed as astonished as we were at this renewed contact. She and Jochen were living again in San Francisco, where they had arrived from Japan in 1948 in order to be

Alex with Sara, left, and her sister Denise, 1994.

Alex with Prof. Gottfried Paasche, Sara's father, 1994

From left, myself, Vergilia, Maria T., Alex. San Francisco 1996

near their youngest daughter, Vergilia. The oldest daughter, Joan, had not been happy in the States and had returned to Germany. Another daughter, Michaela – a Hebrew name, incidentally – was a professor of Renaissance studies in Oregon. Their only son, Gottfried, was a professor of sociology in Toronto. We followed each letter with great excitement but it soon became clear that the Paasches were not in the best of health. Maria Therese suffered from rheumatoid arthritis, among other problems, and in November 1994 Joachim, now John, passed away at the age of eighty-three, having suffered a stroke some years before which had left him partially disabled.

Their early years in the States were actually spent in Washington, D.C., where John had a position at the Library of Congress in his specialty, and in the 1960s and 1970s they visited Germany several times. When his job at the library came to an end, they even made a prolonged stay in Marburg in the mid-1970s, and here Vera Lewin came to visit them on her first trip to Germany after the war. However, John decided that he could not live in Germany after all, and they returned to San Francisco to be near Vergilia and her husband, Henry Dakin, shortly after they had had their first child.

All Maria's siblings had re-established their lives in Berlin after the war. Both Kunrat and Ludwig were journalists, and the former specialized in exposing the evils and atrocities of the Nazi regime and all forms of political violence. The youngest brother, Franz, became an active theologian heading the Jewish-Christian dialogue organization, and was active in the World Council of Churches. Some of the siblings visited the Paasches in California after they settled there, and the families remain in close contact.

Following her husband's death, the family decided that Maria Therese should make her home with Vergilia, a decision that probably was not easy for her, but they continued to heap lots of attention and affection on her. Alex would phone her from time to time, as we could see that writing was becoming a problem. Sometimes there was just a line or two, and then gradually the notes came to be written by others to which she laboriously added her signature. She began to ask if it would be possible for us to come and visit her, but both Alex and I were having health problems at that time and it was just not possible. However, the idea did lodge somewhere in our minds.

In the early summer of 1994, she wrote us that her granddaughter Sara, together with her husband, was coming to Jerusalem for a year to study for the Conservative rabbinate. We couldn't make head or tail of that. When we eventually received notice of the date of their arrival and their address, we were happy to see that they would be staying nearby. At the first opportunity, Alex walked over to greet them even though it was getting dark and he needed a torch. He was very excited about the prospect of meeting Maria Therese's granddaughter. He found the apartment and knocked on the door. A young woman opened the door and on seeing him, exclaimed, "SASHA!" She knew him immediately. After a short visit, he invited them to tea the following Saturday. Our daughter Varda, unable to resist the temptation of such an historic meeting, joined us.

It was one of the strangest afternoons I have ever spent. Sara was blonde and blue-eyed and her husband, Michael Orlow, was quite the opposite. It was obvious that she was a convert, but how could it be that she was studying for the rabbinate? They were still honeymooners, having married just a short time before coming to Jerusalem, and very charming. Michael was a medical student who was taking time off so that Sara could do her compulsory year in Jerusalem. This fact alone impressed me greatly because I still had difficulty adapting to the new style of equality in marital relationships. Sara addressed Alex as Sasha, a sure sign that the friendship dated back to the prewar era, for this, of course, was how she had heard her grandmother talk about him. Varda and I sat as if mesmerized by this young woman – the granddaughter of the legendary Maria Therese was actually sitting in our living room!

I finally managed to ask her about her studies. What had moved a young convert to want to become a rabbi? "Oh," she said looking at me with a smile. "I'm not a convert. I'm Jewish. My father is Gottfried Paasche, but my mother's name is Carol Levine and she is the granddaughter of Rabbi David Levine, who graduated from the Jewish Theological Seminary in 1908 and was ordained by the illustrious Solomon Schechter. She grew up in Manhattan!" Wonders will never cease. "My mother married a non-Jew who never converted, yet she has everything a Jewish mother wants. She has a son who became a lawyer, a daughter who became a doctor, and another daughter who will be a rabbi." We had a good laugh at that, and she went on to say that although the family had not been particularly observant, they had been brought up with a strong national identity, and all three siblings had married Jews. Had Maria ever imagined that she would have a rabbi for a granddaughter? Would her father have accepted that even though he was anti-Nazi? I also asked her about the origin of the family name and she replied that it was derived from the Hebrew or Aramaic word *Pascha* (Pesach).

Sara and Michael became part of our family for that Jerusalem year, and came for festivals and many family occasions. They also had relatives in the country on Michael's side. We met her sister, Denise, and her brother-in-law when they passed through Jerusalem on their round-the-world-before-we-settle-down trip, and were impressed that they were doing this with the minimal luggage of a backpack. Later on, when I had learned more about Maria von Luttwitz, the Hungarian great-grandmother, I realized that this simplicity was a legacy from her. Her concentration on the important issues of life, her modest and unassuming attitude and her great love of nature, which she had shared with her husband, had molded the lifestyle and education of her family and the ensuing generations as well. By the time their year was up, Sara and Michael had walked across Israel from the Mediterranean to the Galilee, had traversed the country from north to south and, at our urging, had gone to Petra, but traveled through Jordan on the regular bus lines. Also during this year, our Varda and Sara found they had a lot in common, both being busy with questions of Jewish identity and education. Varda's work brings her occasionally to New York, and they always make a point of meeting.

Sara's parents also came to visit us, and the resemblance between Sara and her father was striking. Our meetings with him were fascinating for the family stories he told, partly about their lives in Japan and partly about the experiences of the von Hammerstein family in Berlin during the War. When the General died in 1943, the family arranged a hasty burial during the night so that they would not be embarrassed by an unwanted Nazi state funeral. In July 1944, two of his sons, Kunrat and Ludwig, took part in the failed plot to assassinate Hitler. Because they had once lived in the military headquarters where the attempt was to be made, they knew of secret exits from the building and were able to escape. Others, less lucky, were caught and executed. In revenge, the Nazis arrested the General's widow and her two youngest children, Hildur and Franz, and sent them to Dachau. Later on, they were moved to Buchenwald and then taken on long marches which brought them to Italy, where they were eventually freed. In the camps they were not placed with the Jewish prisoners but in an adjoining section separated only by a barbed wire fence. Probably Maria Therese only heard about this after the war, but in the meantime, in Japan, she knew that there was much to worry about besides their own problems of daily survival.

After hearing of all these stirring events, I began to feel that I should write down this unusual story of my husband's friendship with the German general's daughter; but a series of illnesses and unhappy events began to fill our lives. So it was not till long after Alex had passed away that I began to feel composed enough to attempt this task.

At first, the Paasches were happy in Japan. They were fascinated with the lifestyle and the local customs, and were happy that they could live very frugally since they had been unable to take money out of Germany. There was an interesting international community and they also met a previous acquaintance who had reached Japan through the General's help. But within the German community, they had to be careful to hide their political opinions. Jochen had some difficulty finding work because the embassy would not take people who were not members of the Nazi Party, but he found steady work in a legal firm exactly on the day that his first child, Joan, was born. This job, as a translator, lasted for four years. They found friends among the Christian community, both European and Japanese, who were very helpful in difficult times, such as caring for new babies and sick children, or looking for food and housing.

However, the charming, peaceful atmosphere did not last long. The population seemed to become more and more aggressive after the signing of the treaty with Germany and the preparations for war, first against the Chinese and then against America. Europeans who could began to leave the country, and those who stayed found themselves ostracized as foreigners. Education for the children became a problem because they had been attending Japanese schools. At one desperate moment, Maria even thought of returning to Germany, but their custom of opening the Bible or other important book at random and finding an appropriate message there, known as the *sors Vergiliana*, saved them from this step. This was also the reason that they selected the name Vergilia for their youngest daughter – it was classical and had emotional overtones for them, and it would also pass the scrutiny of the official when they had to register her at the German embassy. Faith gradually became more and more important.

Gottfried recalled seeing his mother standing at the window for long periods of time, staring out over the ocean as if trying to see what was happening in Berlin. There is a photo recording just such a pensive moment. I wonder whether she ever thought of how her life would have been had they remained in Palestine. However, the war finally ended and the American occupation brought easier times, though it was hard to explain their situation as Germans in an enemy country. Joan and Gottfried quickly learned to hang about the American camp, where they were given lunch every day, but it was difficult for them to understand they were the defeated and not the victors in the war, as they had previously felt. Jochen soon found work as a translator of Japanese and Chinese, and eventually in 1948 they came to the United States and settled in California.

While Jochen found work in his field, Maria worked at first as a cleaning lady because she was determined there should be enough money for her children to get a good education. Eventually, she found more congenial work during the time they spent in Washington.

Our trip to the States went well and as planned. We arrived in San Francisco a few hours late, but found Gottfried still waiting for us. We checked into the hotel, freshened up, and went to meet Maria. Vergilia lives in Pacific Heights on a typical picturesque San Francisco street. The living room we were shown into was a warm, comfortable room with a grand piano, plenty of books and a large picture window looking out over the Golden Gate Bridge. Maria had often mentioned this beautiful view in her letters. Vergilia welcomed us as if we were long-lost relatives, and said that her mother would be down shortly. The air was full of tense expectation and I felt that I could hardly breathe. Alex too was in anxious anticipation. Then Maria Therese came slowly down the stairs, assisted by Gottfried and using a walker. She stood in the open doorway and looked at us. The years had not dealt kindly with her and the vicissitudes of her life had left their mark. I remained where I was standing while Alex went to her, took her hand and kissed it. Sixty years vanished in that moment and it was a great effort for me not to cry. Alex helped her to the sofa and they sat down and began to talk in German, as in the old days. I gave her the gift I had brought from Jerusalem, a pretty silk shawl printed with an Anna Ticho flower painting, which she immediately put round her shoulders. I sat down to talk with Vergilia and Gottfried. I confess I felt a little like an intruder, but they were both so happy to meet with us, both for Maria's sake and out of their own interest in the friends of her youth.

The three days with them passed quickly with lots of talk, and sightseeing in and around the city. The morning after our arrival, we were scheduled to go with Gottfried and Maria to see the redwood forest. We arrived at the house to find that a friend who used to be an opera singer had come, as was his custom, to sing for her. She was reluctant to leave, but he assured her that he would return within a couple of days. Another day, Vergilia took us to see her husband's centre for computer services, which he had set up many years before, having quickly recognized the potential and need for such a facility.

Then she took us to her toy shop, The Ark, which only stocked toys made of natural materials. No plastics. It transpired that Vergilia was a firm believer in the teachings of Rudolph Steiner, an Austrian philosopher who lived from 1861 to 1925, and developed a "mystical" philosophy leading to a new system, which became known as Waldorf Education. He was the moving force in establishing a Waldorf School in San Francisco, where Vergilia's own three daughters were educated. She had probably heard these ideas from her mother. Maria Therese had had an anthroposophist friend in Japan who gave her Steiner's books, which greatly impressed her. His goal was to enable students to realize as fully as possible their individual paths through life, through the development of a harmonious relationship with nature and by feeling themselves an integral part of the universal design. Artistic forms of expression were an important element; basically, the ideas were close to those practiced by Maria Therese's mother.

But I think the most memorable evening was a family dinner we had at the large dining room table. There was another visitor from Berlin, and the date was fairly close to July 20, the anniversary of the plot to assassinate Hitler. That was the main topic of conversation. I don't recall the woman's name, but her father had been involved and was unfortunately one of those arrested and hanged. I felt transported back into another dimension of time and place. They talked as if this tragic event had occurred just recently, and every detail was still fresh in their minds. Then I remembered our own Jewish propensity for remembering past tragedies and not allowing them to be forgotten, and it was no longer so strange.

Saying goodbye was difficult, as we all knew that another meeting would be very unlikely, but it had been a beautiful visit and I could see that Alex was very content. He had the satisfaction of having seen some sort of logic emerge from his turbulent life, of seeing the closing of this particular meaningful circle. Surely, he was no longer the excitable young student with the ambitious plans, and she was not the strong-minded young woman dashing about the country on her motorcycle, but in their mind's eye they had not changed, and in memory they would be forever young.

Some months later, Alvin Grauer, a friend of Alex's, passed away in New York. Alex phoned to express his sympathy to his wife, Frieda, and to inquire about her situation. She told the following story: she had called the synagogue to ask the rabbi to officiate at the funeral, but he was already scheduled for another event and promised to send his assistant. The assistant came to talk to her and get some background information on the family, and to Frieda's surprise the replacement turned out to be a young woman. It was Sara. When she heard that Frieda and her husband had met in Japan in the U.S. army, she replied that her own father had been born in Japan and had grown up there, and this brought the two into a long conversation. When Frieda heard that Sara had spent a year in Jerusalem, she said that she had good friends there, the Rafaelis – perhaps Sara had met them . . . .

Early in 1997, we had a call from Gottfried. Maria had been hospitalized for a few days and it had been decided that she could no longer be cared for at home but should go to a nursing home. However, Maria did not like the place she was in and wanted very much to go to the Jewish Home for the Aged. For this, she would need a recommendation as she was not Jewish, and he asked Alex if he would agree to write such a letter. On the strength of the letter which he wrote, Maria Therese was accepted into the home as a Righteous Gentile, and Alex felt that he had repaid a debt which many Jews owed her. Alex continued to telephone her from time to time, not always successfully, and we came to rely more and more on Vergilia and Gottfried for news.

About a year later, we had a visit from a friend and colleague of Gottfried's, Professor Ya'akov Glickman, an Israeli who also worked at York University. Gottfried had been wondering what kind of tribute he could make to his mother in recognition of her unusual life and character. The family had come to the conclusion that they would make a documentary film that would tell of her background and the course of her life in that unhappy period of history. Professor Glickman had been so fascinated by the story that he wanted to help, and he had come to Israel to interview Alex and any other friends of Maria's that he could locate. He wanted to tape the interview right there but Alex said no, he was rather tired and had to collect his thoughts first. He preferred just to talk.

Alex did not live to see the film. He passed away on February 28, 1999, of a heart attack, following an operation for a broken hip. In the summer of that year, Professor Glickman arrived with the demonstration film that they had made, which had been given the title *Silent Courage*. We showed it to family and friends. In the photos included in the film, I was struck by the resemblance of both Gottfried and Sara to the General. On the cover of the cassette box was a picture of Maria Therese on her motorcycle. Now our children knew that Daddy's stories about her were quite true, and they were able to put her in her proper perspective. Professor Glickman had thought to find more material about Maria and her husband, in order to expand the film, but the archives of kibbutz Givat Brenner did not go back to the 1930s and most of the people he sought were no longer in this world.

Early in February 2000, I had a black-edged card from Vergilia informing us that Maria had passed away on January 21, peacefully in her sleep. The eulogy at the funeral was given by her granddaughter, Rabbi Sara Paasche-Orlow. (The date of Maria's passing was the day after our wedding anniversary, and the birthdays of both our mothers.)

On the night that Joachim met Maria Therese for the first time, he wrote in his diary,

> The door opened and a tall young woman came in, looking straight into my eyes across the table. Her face was self-possessed and she did not smile . . . I looked with curiosity into wide, grey and very strong eyes, thinking, 'My God, this is somebody.' But I was more or less aware that I could somehow measure up to her . . . . Her dress and makeup was of the utmost simplicity so that nothing artificial disturbed the human relationship. She seemed not concerned with outward appearance at all . . . . Her conversation was interesting, yet unemotional so that from the beginning there was a real conversation going on with no end in sight . . . . There was relaxation and ease.

On another occasion he found her "in a state of mournful meditation . . . . As if by a strange insight I suddenly realized that her life was a profoundly problematic one and that she needed help and sympathy." The friendship developed and Joachim was surprised at the number of Jewish friends Maria had, among them, the sister of his friend Ernst Lewin, Vera, who years later, in Tel Aviv, introduced Alex and me to each other. In a short few months, Maria and Joachim married, at Maria's initiative, in a very small civil ceremony.

So, such was the essence of Maria Therese von Hammerstein-Paasche, which captivated her friends and which inspired her husband, children and grandchildren with the basic values that they continue to treasure and practice. Such was the woman who made a lasting impression on my husband and who occupied a special little corner in our family because of the great affection they had for each other. Yet stronger still was the unseen affinity between them, because of shared values and ideals, because of their courage and steadfastness in a world gone mad.

Maria was the unusual product of an unusual family living in very unusual times, who, unknowingly, in spite of time and distance, had her little niche in the life of the Rafaeli family in Jerusalem.

A long and detailed obituary about Maria Therese, written by Douglas Martin, appeared in the *New York Times* on February 13, 2000.

From left, Sara, Maria T. and grandson Raziel, San Francisco 1997

That Morning in February

1999

It is almost a year now since Alex passed away, yet the events of that morning are deeply imprinted in my mind and keep repeating themselves, as if I were watching a movie. Perhaps I don't recall every little item because sometimes the children will mention something I don't remember, but certainly the main events are still very clear.

I remember that I phoned him at the hospital at eight in the morning. It was a Sunday, February 28, 1999. He told me he hadn't slept very well and was anxious for me to come to the hospital. I told him that I would be there in an hour and that he should do his exercises in the meantime. I reminded him that his cousin Alex Kahn from Australia would be calling him shortly, as Alex and I had agreed, and he sounded happy at the prospect.

We hung up, and I continued with my breakfast and the newspaper. I thought about our son Lonny, who was probably just getting on the plane with his two daughters for a skiing holiday in France. Our older son Asi had already left with his two boys the day before for the Dolomites. When I asked him why they were going so far away, he replied that his friends had made the arrangements and he had simply fallen in with their plans.

At about 8:45 the phone rang. A female voice announced it was the hospital calling, and where were my sons? She couldn't find them anywhere. I was immediately alert and asked what was wrong, adding that my sons were abroad. Dr. Rafaeli has had a severe heart attack, she said, and I should come immediately, and "bring someone with you." It's amazing how alert one becomes when danger is perceived. I understood the situation immediately. I put on my shoes and grabbed my coat. I asked Zilpa, our maid, to call our daughter Varda, as I didn't want to waste time with the phone, and hurried off to the hospital.

When I came into the ward I was horrified. Alex was lying flat on his back with some enormous pipe down his throat and a flashing machine by the bed. The room was a mess. The patient in the first bed had been taken away, but the third patient was still there, behind the curtain. I felt very sorry for him. The scene was familiar and reminded me of a recent hospital stay of my own. A woman in the ward, who had come in for a pacemaker, suddenly became very agitated in her sleep. As I called her name, the staff rushed in with their equipment, pulled the curtain round the bed, and began trying to resuscitate her, but without success. There was a lot of tumult until they gave up. I imagined a similar situation with Alex.

The nurse came in and began explaining that Alex had had a massive heart attack, even while the doctors had been there in the room on their rounds, and it was their duty therefore to put him on the respirator. The doctors were waiting for my agreement to an operation to implant a pacemaker in place of the external one they had given him.

At this moment Varda arrived and told me that Karni, our younger daughter, was on her way from Ramat Gan, and we went to speak to the doctors. As I said, they wanted to operate and put a pacemaker in Alex's chest, but Varda and I were adamantly opposed. This was the last thing Alex would have wanted. He had long been haunted by the fear that he would be incapacitated by a stroke, as his father had been, and he didn't want to end his life in long, drawn-out suffering. We told the doctors how depressed he had been by his increasing blindness and the subsequent inactivity, which had been torture for a man who had been as active and athletic as he had always been. We felt also that as he was nearing his ninetieth birthday, his age was a factor to be considered.

Varda's eloquence and my insistence finally persuaded the doctors. Still, they called in a neurologist who indeed established there had been severe brain damage. Therefore, nothing would be done to prolong his life, but at the same time they could not disconnect Alex from the temporary pacemaker and oxygen once it had been connected. We must simply wait for the end. How long could that be? I asked. They could not tell – perhaps hours, perhaps days.

We felt some slight relief that we had averted the operation, and now turned our minds to the problem of informing our sons. By then, Karni had arrived, and agreed fully with what we had done. The Filipino male nurse we had taken arrived for his shift, and was visibly shaken by the sudden turn of events. Both daughters-in-law arrived and set themselves to making contact with their husbands. How thankful we were that morning for mobile phones.

We had thought that we might still catch Lonny before he boarded the plane, but they had left on time. However, with the help of her connections, Yuli managed to get through to the cockpit of the plane, but they refused to call Lonny to the phone. They agreed to pass on a message that Alex was in a serious condition, and later Lonny told us that the minute he saw the captain coming towards him, he knew something was wrong. Nurit was having a more difficult time because we didn't actually have Asi's phone number and she had to work through our company office. It was also hardly likely that we would find Asi in his room in the middle of the morning. In any case, this was how the office of the pencil factory learned of the situation, and the staff continued to keep in touch throughout the morning.

And so the hours progressed. From time to time one or another of us went to sit by Alex and hold his hand. Could he possibly be aware of our presence? We hoped so even though it seemed doubtful. There was something Kafkaesque about the whole situation: Alex lying motionless on the hospital bed with that awful pipe down his throat; the five women of the family trying to cope with the unexpected situation; the frantic attempts to get in touch with Asi and Lonny; the Filipino nurse wanting to be of help but finding nothing to do; the hospital staff coming and going; and the office staff calling for more information. Yuli and Lonny were already living apart, having decided to divorce; but she stayed with us in spite of commitments of her own.

The minutes ticked by. Only after much persuasion, the male nurse finally left, accepting his wages for the day. Then it was two o'clock, and suddenly the doctor came to tell us it was all over. Yuli's phone rang and it was Lonny on the line; he had just landed in Geneva. She told him that Alex had just passed away and he said they would come straight back on the same plane. The doctor permitted us to see Alex. The pipe had already been removed and he looked like his old self, sleeping peacefully, at rest. We cried, trying to grasp the fact that he was really gone, and that we would no longer hear his voice or his sprightly step around the apartment.

We had a little time to sit with him, as a certain period had to elapse before he could be taken away, and as I stroked his forehead, I wondered at the unexpected turn of events. Just twelve days ago he had fallen in the bedroom, apparently a few moments after getting out of bed. I had been in the kitchen preparing breakfast when I heard a crash and a loud cry. Running to the room, I found him lying on the floor by the walking machine in great agony. He had obviously stumbled onto the metal base of the walker and injured himself. I soon realized I could not get him up, and that probably I shouldn't even try. I covered him with a blanket and phoned Lonny, who lived nearest to us. Within a few minutes he arrived and we immediately called an ambulance. Though we arrived quickly at the emergency room, it took many hours before the doctors diagnosed a broken hip and we concluded arrangements with a surgeon. They finally took Alex to the operating room in the evening. By that time the whole family had gathered.

I remember how he was after he came around from the anaesthetic – in a complete state of shock. He was in pain and he didn't stop talking, mainly in Russian. He didn't remember why he was in hospital and wanted to go home. We were very worried but the nurses assured us that this was a normal reaction to trauma, especially in older patients. We saw little improvement during the following days. He complained that the bed was uncomfortable and the sheets had to be smoothed out every few minutes;

every wrinkle in his pajamas bothered him and he didn't stop talking. He wanted to go home and asked for his clothes. He hardly slept at all – the drugs were either too weak to kill the pain and to induce a good sleep or so strong that he became over-stimulated. He was in a constant state of worry and anxiety and it was painful, and wearing, to be with him.

As the days passed, he gradually became more lucid and able to understand his situation, but he would suddenly go off again, back to his childhood, it seemed. Only the Russian nurses could understand him, but it was clear to me that he was fretting himself away. One day, when Karni was sitting with him, he told her he was afraid of missing the train. He couldn't find his bundle and was afraid he had lost his ticket. He was so agitated that she rolled up a blanket with some of his clothes, placed it on his lap, and put a "ticket," a piece of paper, in his hand. This calmed him down and he sat quietly in the armchair, waiting for the train. He was obviously reliving one of the episodes of his childhood when, during the 1918 Bolshevik upheaval, they had hastily left Drissa for Riga in the middle of the night. Karni, who was familiar with the story, could understand what was going through his mind. She had been moved to tears, as I was when she told me about it.

"The soul of a man is like a dark room," Alex used to say, quoting an old Russian saying, and I often thought of this during those days in the hospital, while trying to follow his train of thought.

Suddenly, Varda's phone rang, interrupting my reverie. It was Itamar, her son, our oldest grandson, wanting to know what room we were in. She had completely forgotten that he had planned to visit and bring his grandfather some chocolate. For a moment we were all dumbfounded, wondering how to cope with this situation, but Varda quickly recovered her presence of mind and told him to come up the stairs and she would meet him. I think I shall never forget the expression on Itamar's face as he came into the department. He didn't know where to look or what to do with himself and was fighting to control his tears. He had come, on his own birthday, to bring his grandfather some chocolate, and suddenly his grandfather was dead. Only after some time did he approach the door of the ward to look at him. It was heartbreaking. I recalled that his other grandfather had died the previous year, just two or three days after his *bar mitzvah*, which had coincided with the festival of Purim. At that moment, I wondered if he would ever be able to enjoy his birthday, or Purim, ever again for the rest of his life. Many weeks later he told me he threw the chocolate away as he could not bear to eat it.

Two veteran managers of the pencil factory, Yosef Salamon and David Marciano, arrived, also overwhelmed by the unexpected turn of events and by the immediate problems, but they were very helpful and knew what steps had to be taken. We speculated about what had brought on this heart attack. We knew Alex had been increasingly depressed because of his growing limitations over the last months, his feeling that life was no longer worth living. I thought that he had simply worn himself out since the operation with lack of sleep, the constant pain, the restless talking and his inability to accept his situation. Even though he had made it to rehabilitation and seemed to be making progress, the future did not look too inviting to him. I wondered also whether the fact that his sons and their children had come the day before to take leave of him had not had some symbolic implication for him. I was told he had cried when they left.

But this was all conjecture coming from our need to understand. In the end I felt that although all these elements played a part, his time had simply come and I was grateful that his wish for a quick end had been fulfilled. He had lived a turbulent life, and had experienced the major events of the century: World War I, the Communist Revolution, early Zionism and the impact of Jabotinsky on his visit to Riga, the rise of Nazism while he was studying at the University of Heidelberg, where he made many life-long friends. Then came his period in Palestine, where he started graduate studies at the Hebrew University in 1933 and began his career in insurance. He came into contact with members of the Etzel, the underground organization of the Revisionist Movement to which he then devoted many years of life, in both Europe and the U.S. He served in the American army in World War II in Europe, first as an infantryman and later in counter-intelligence.

He knew that his father had died in June 1940 before the German invasion of Latvia, but he was deeply troubled about the fate of his mother and brother, feeling guilty that he had not succeeded in getting his family out of the country. He learnt only later that his mother had died in the terrible winter Death March to the Rumboli forest on the outskirts of Riga, and that his brother had been killed in action with the partisans in the Riga forests. The cumulative strain of his work and of his personal anxieties led to a medical discharge in 1945, and repatriation to the States. Alex then tried his hand at business in the States, while at the same time continuing his political work on behalf of the Etzel. With the establishment of the State of Israel, he decided to come and help develop industry in Israel. He had decided not to continue with politics but rather to establish himself and build his life anew. We met in Tel Aviv towards the end of 1949 and married in January 1950, gradually bringing our four children into the world.

All these memories rushed through my mind while we sat and waited. I thought that my husband had really lived his life to the full, a twentieth-century Jewish life, full of trial and tribulation, balanced by some satisfaction with his achievements and with his growing family. He deserved the peace that was now his lot.

The orderlies came to take him away and that was a very difficult moment for us all. I did not realize then that Varda, of her own volition, accompanied Alex to the morgue. As we gathered up his belongings, the nurse came by and told us quietly that we had made the right decision about not operating. They had many comatose patients, she said, whose families had tried to prolong the lives of their loved ones in a similar situation.

We returned home to face the organizational problems of a funeral. At 11 o'clock in the evening, Lonny and the girls rang at the door, exhausted but all wound up from the events of the day. Asi and his sons did not get back until the following night. Thanks to uncooperative taxi drivers and airline clerks, it took them thirty hours to return from Italy, and the funeral took place only on the following day, Tuesday, March 2.

The funeral was attended by a very large crowd, which included people he had known in his various careers. During the *shivah*, the house was similarly full as we all sat at home together, in various rooms, and friends and relatives came to condole. John Hassenfeld, the son of our friends and partners in Nashville, Tennessee, came to be with us. He and my niece, Naomi Shapiro, were very helpful, seeing to the shopping and meals and answering the telephone. Then, on the eve of Purim, someone came from the synagogue to read the Megillah for us. There could not have been a more Jewish, soul-touching moment. I think Alex would have enjoyed it.

Alex at mass grave in the notorious Rumboli forest where his mother, Rosa, was murdered. 1991.

Harvard

THE YEAR 2000–2001 WAS AN OUT-OF-THE-ORDINARY YEAR FOR the Rafaeli family. We were getting used to the reality of life without Alex, who had passed away in February 1999. I began to appreciate the expression that "life is stronger," which I had always regarded as a meaningless cliché, offered in times of bereavement. Now I began to realize that it was true, that life continues on its way, forcing us to get back into the routine of work, school and festivals, forcing us to deal with problems that need our attention.

Essentially, this was Varda's year, a turning point in her life and in the lives of her children Itamar, then aged fifteen, Inbar, thirteen, and Avishai, eleven. She was now living apart from her husband, waiting for a divorce, which was a long time coming. Back then, Varda was the Assistant Director for American Jewish-Israel Affairs in the Israel Office of the American Jewish Committee. She decided to apply for, and received, a Wexner scholarship to study at Harvard's Kennedy School of Government, family expenses included. In the summer of 2000, she packed up the necessities for a year away, and with her children was off to Boston for a challenging year.

The Wexner Israel Fellowship Program is part of the Wexner Foundation's activities. It was inaugurated by Mr. Leslie Wexner, who is dedicated to educating and training public leaders in Israel, as well as professional and volunteer leaders serving Jewish communities in North America, thus making closer contact between them more possible. Wexner strongly believes that Israel benefits by exposing directors and high-ranking officials of various government ministries and non-profit organizations to the experience of an Ivy League university. Candidates must bring recommendations and meet the academic requirements of Harvard University as well as the Foundation itself. They are subjected to a long period of evaluation and a final interview before being accepted. Approximately ten candidates are accepted into the program each year.

The project, which has been running since 1989, enables Israelis from various spheres of activity and from different areas of the country to study in a mid-career program of Public Administration with more than two hundred students from around the world. The Israeli group Varda belonged to was very congenial, which proved to be an important element in the success of the year's stay in a foreign country. Though strangers at first, they gradually became like a family. There were many children of similar ages, and they began to celebrate Shabbat and festivals together, as well as helping each other through difficult times. Many lasting friendships formed, and the Wexner Foundation also likes to keep in touch with its graduates, old and new.

Of course, I missed Varda and the children, but at the same time, it gave me the opportunity to make two trips to the United States in that year and visit friends and relatives. On the first visit, I took the opportunity of going to Florida via Pittsburgh, where I was happy to meet again with Kitty Ruttenberg. She and her husband, Harold, had kept an apartment in Jerusalem and had visited often over many years. We were on very friendly terms. Her husband had also passed away recently and she was finding life difficult. From Pittsburgh, I flew to Miami to visit Alex's cousins, Murra and Abrasha Udem, their daughter Edith Osman and her two children, Jackie and Daniel. While there, I received news that our friend and partner, Harold Hassenfeld of Palm Beach, had passed away after a very long and difficult illness. The funeral was to be held in Nashville, Tennessee, where they had lived with their three children since their marriage. After these had all married, the parents, Rita and Harold, decided to move to Palm Beach, but kept up the house for occasional visits.

All arrangements were made for friends to fly to Nashville, including accommodation. I telephoned to Varda in Boston and told her what had happened, and she said at once that she would come and join me in Nashville in time for the funeral. When I got to the Miami airport, I saw Rita, who was to travel on the same flight, but she was in no state to talk to anybody. Within a day or two, Lonny, who also happened to be traveling in the States at that time, joined us, and he was soon followed by Asi, who came in from Jerusalem. I was pleased that most of the family had managed to be with our friends at this sad time. Only Karni had been unable to get away on such short notice.

We had first met the Hassenfelds in Tel Aviv in 1950, when they were introduced as perspective investors wanting to open a pencil factory. The father, Henry, married to Marion, had started a pencil factory years before in a small town called Shelbyville, near Nashville, which came to be known as Pencil City because of the number of factories there. His sons Harold and Merrill developed the business greatly, but Merrill later left pencils to concentrate on toys, which also became a very successful venture. The idea to open a pencil factory eventually came to fruition and Jerusalem Pencils Ltd. was officially opened in 1952. Over the years we had met often and became very friendly. They visited Israel often with their wives, Rita and Sylvia, and took an active interest in the development of other projects.

We returned to Boston with Lonny and enjoyed being together with Varda's family for Rosh ha-Shannah. I also made use of the time to visit a variety of synagogues and seeing another aspect of Jewish life in America. Before I left Boston to return home, Varda told me that I should order accommodation for Graduation Day in June. I thought that was way ahead in the future but she assured me that if I didn't reserve, I would not be able to find accommodation later, because the graduation ceremony was the main annual event of the university and always well attended. So I followed her instructions, especially as the bed and breakfast, actually named Bed and Bagel, where I stayed, was very convenient to where she lived.

I returned the following June, feeling a little more at home than on the first trip. The "Wexners" were very excited. They had finished their year successfully, in spite of occasional difficulties, and were already in the midst of preparations for their return. The heavy luggage had to be ready for shipment by a set date, the apartment was full of cartons and suitcases and with all this, many of the parents had come to enjoy the spectacle. I didn't have time to fly to Miami, and had to make do with phone calls to the Udems.

There was fine weather on the great day, and the spectacle was colorful and cheerful. There was music, flags and banners and the students of each department were differentiated by gowns of various colors. Since Varda had ordered a seat for me for the Grand Parade of the graduates, I was very comfortable, as well as happy that Varda had insisted that I come. Lunch was provided for this vast crowd, and generally the event was well organized. In addition, the "Wexners" enjoyed a special farewell dinner in one of the college dining halls, with speeches and goodbyes and much emotion.

Varda had decided to celebrate the occasion by taking her children on a cross-country trip to Alaska in a motorized caravan. She wanted to get in as much sightseeing as possible that year, so in the autumn, they had traveled in New England, enjoying the Indian summer, and celebrated Thanksgiving in New York. During the winter break, they left the cold of Boston to go south and visit Disney World in Orlando. They met the Udems in Miami, drove through the Everglades National Park and joined a Caribbean cruise. In the spring, they traveled to Nova Scotia in Canada. One of their favorite souvenirs is a photo taken in front of the Twin Towers in New York before the 9/11 attack.

Altogether, it had been a great year. Varda enjoyed her studies immensely and the children had a taste of normal American school and life. They became accustomed to mixing with adults, and their knowledge of English was vastly improved. They learned to ski and had a chance to travel to new places and meet our American friends and relatives.

Itamar, the oldest, surprised us by picking up Russian from Russian Jewish immigrants in his high school, and sought every opportunity to talk, even with my Russian friends when he returned to Jerusalem. They assured me that he spoke well, without any trace of a foreign accent. We all enjoyed hearing him chatter away, and I only regretted that Alex did not have the pleasure of hearing how one of his grandsons had absorbed the language so effortlessly, never having heard it at home. They could have had nice conversations together.

I think this Harvard year was an "education for life." Indeed, Varda's investment in herself and her career, not to mention the unique experience she gave her children, will go down in their memories as an unforgettable adventure.

Varda graduates from Harvard, 2001.

Packing Up

April 2005

ONCE I HAD MADE THE DECISION TO GIVE UP THE APARTMENT, I had to consider the formidable task of how to reduce the mass of my possessions and move to a new home. We had lived in this apartment for some fifty years without ever doing a thorough appraisal of what there actually was in those cupboards and wardrobes. Here and there, I had made sporadic attempts to do so.

As the children grew to adulthood and moved out, they took some bits and pieces with them, but most of their "stuff" remained at home. This had become a source of argument and aggravation. "Yes, yes," they always promised, "one day when we have time and space, we'll do it," but the schoolbooks, photo albums, bar mitzvah and birthday presents and the old clothes remained where they were and took root undisturbed. When the children eventually married, the situation improved only slightly. Sometimes, I envied friends who had moved house every few years, discarding their unwanted belongings along the way.

I made myself a tentative plan of action. First, to start looking for an apartment, which took about six months. Then I told the children to earmark any items they would like to have, and began to get rid of things which I knew I wouldn't need, specially the white baby grand piano. Despite parental hopes, it transpired that none of our children was musical. Though I continued to play when and if the mood struck, the piano was only used occasionally for musical evenings or by the grandchildren while they were in their explorative stage. But it provided a useful space for family photos and flowers.

The next major problem was the books. From experience, when we had tried to trim our collection, I knew that this would be surprisingly difficult. Libraries and collectors were only interested in rare or specialized titles, and certainly not in any fond memories or history attached to this book or that.

The children did find books that interested them, mainly those with dedications from friends and family, or art books, but certainly not those in Russian or German. It had not occurred to me before that the books were a real mirror of our lives and personalities.

Alex's mother tongue had been Russian, so there were classics and poetry in this language. He had been interested in Jewish history and contemporary politics from an early age, so there were books by Jabotinsky and other Zionist thinkers, and twentieth-century Hebrew poetry on Zionism. His mother had insisted he learn German and at twelve, he was sent from Riga to Germany for a year, returning home in time for his *bar mitzvah*. This became a factor in his decision to study at Heidelberg University. There he became fluent in the language and continued to write and speak German with family and friends of this period. He studied sociology with eminent teachers and kept many of their textbooks.

After coming to Palestine in 1933 and becoming involved in local politics, his grasp of Hebrew improved and he could read and write on economic and political subjects, and read the new literature of the times. During the years spent in America (to which he had escaped from Europe in May 1940) and in the American army (1940–1949 all told), he learned to speak, read and write English, and enjoyed American literature and poetry. All this he brought with him to our marriage, plus a collection of African masks.

My contribution was less impressive but well beloved. Starting with *Uncle Tom's Cabin*, which I had received for my eleventh birthday, I slowly worked my way through the popular English classics. During my high school years, I spent many hours on my way home browsing through the book sections of department stores and building up my little library, mainly Jane Austen and the Brontë sisters. In those days the publishers put out neat little series of books in uniform format, such as World Classics and Everyman. They were not expensive and looked good on the shelves. I felt very proud when I wrote my name and the date in my new books, and today the inscription makes me smile and remember "the good old days." The earliest date of any was a small Bible with olivewood covers, which I received as a prize from the Zionist Organization in 1933/4 for a story I wrote about Pesach. No memory of this. In 1935 I won second prize from the Jewish Education Board in their annual exams: *The Laws and Customs of Israel* – hardly interesting reading for a nine-year-old, but in fact I did sometimes refer to it in later years. A souvenir of my Australian period is an anthology of the works of Australian poets.

My university studies in English language and literature brought the more serious *Complete Works of* – the great poets, modern poetry, classic novels, drama and literary criticism. Fortunately, my daughter Varda has a friend who specialized in English poetry and I was able to pass many of my books on to her.

Widening interests after marriage gradually brought in books on archeology, art, new novels, history, biographies, Judaism and Jewish humor. Later there came memoirs and autobiographies from our circle of friends. Only a fraction went with me to my new home and I was happy to find a bookseller who took away the remainder for a very nominal fee.

The toy cupboard was also a source of nostalgia and recollection. The little compact folding stroller my mother had brought from Australia in the early 1950s … a wonderful new invention for transporting toddlers, which faithfully served all my children and grandchildren for more than fifty years and is now a cast-off relic in Karni's garden in Ra'anana. The little pink plastic bath which I had to buy for my youngest because the previous year, after a miscarriage, I had given away all the baby equipment, thinking that there would be no more babies. And the stuffed animals and teddy bears! Each revealed the depth of the owners' affection and dependence, or lack of it. One of my periodic jobs of that time was to "operate" on Varda's blue bear, repairing a variety of fractures and ailments. He was blessed with a long life and was finally "retired" before being done to death by Varda's daughter, Inbar, who insisted on keeping the bits of "comfort" scraps for years till she agreed to replace him with a stuffed puppy, which ultimately suffered the same fate.[1] My younger daughter Karni inherited all the dolls that had belonged to her sister and received many more, of all types and sizes. A very pretty brunette one was named Bella, but I liked a pert blonde charmer with a modern face and clothes, whom we called Maggie. In those days, dolls and tea sets were the ideal gifts for little girls, but my kindergarten-age granddaughters today show no interest in dolls at all. I filled a big carton with the dolls and their clothes and sent it to a children's cancer centre.

The wardrobe with my old clothes also evoked many memories of past fashions, and special events in my life. They had been "too good" to give away, but of course that's exactly what I eventually did with most of them. I kept the a black and pink evening dress from my student days – evening wear was always formal in Melbourne for twenty-first birthday celebrations, Purim balls or dance dates in nightclubs. I kept the black two-piece Christian Dior "New Look" outfit, which I bought for my first trip to the States in 1952 – a little fitted jacket and very full flared skirt, a delightful fashion which came in as a reaction to the austerity during and after World War II. Perhaps my favorite was a soft grey tweed suit I bought in Switzerland during an intermediate stop of the cable car while going up the Matterhorn. I had never made such a quick decision about clothes, and I don't think I ever did again.

I found a couple of summery "maxis" made by the fabulous Gypsy studio of the 1970s, and a very elegant black dress of my mother's with black beading down the back, which I sometimes wore for costume parties. I even

---

1 Inbar insisted on keeping the "comfort" scraps for years. The blue bear was restored to supremacy after being rescued from the cupboard. Much in need of plastic surgery, it now lives on one of the armchairs in Varda's apartment.

remember going to this dressmaker with my mother in the early 1930s and hoping that one day she would make a dress for me, but that wish was never fulfilled. Among some sundry children's clothes, I unearthed three little blue blazers, which the children wore on our trip to the Olympic Games in Rome in 1960. My husband, ever the patriot, wanted the emblem of Jerusalem sewn on their top pockets. When I showed these to the kids, they couldn't believe that we had ever had such an idea.

The last cupboard held the biggest surprise of all. There, among some old shirts and sports pants, were two of Alex's U.S. military jackets, which he had worn during the years 1942–1945. The trousers had long been discarded. What to do with the jackets? They were too historic to throw away, so I decided I would give them to the two families who had boys so that they would have a souvenir of their grandfather in their wardrobes. After checking the pockets of the first, I folded it neatly and put it aside.

I picked up the second to check the pockets and suddenly felt a pinprick. I examined the collar, then the lapels – and there, under the left lapel, was a red rosebud! I looked at it in amazement. Maastricht, it fairly shouted at me, the liberation of Maastricht in 1944! Alex had participated in this campaign and sometimes told us about the tumultuous welcome they had received from the inhabitants. We had even attended the fiftieth anniversary of the liberation of the city, as recounted in Chapter 18 above. Of course, on second thought, there could have been other end-of-war parties as well, celebrating the end of the horrible six-year war and of the Shoah, but my first reaction seemed the correct one. Now here in Jerusalem was the rosebud, a footprint of history, dried out but intact. If only Alex could have seen it and told us the circumstances in which he had received it.

I gave this jacket to my second grandson and showed him the rosebud, telling him never to throw it away. He would have a historic reminder of a difficult period in world history and in his grandfather's life.

The day came to leave the apartment and move to my new home. I turned the key on fifty years of intense living, with no regrets.

The whole family celebrating my 80th birthday, 2006.

Alex Rafaeli: A Eulogy

SOME YEARS AGO, AN UNUSUAL AND UNEXPECTED EVENT HAP-pened in our family and I said to my daughters, Karni and Varda, "You see – if you live long enough, you see everything." This saying has become part of our family folklore, used on various appropriate occasions. Today is one of those occasions. Did I ever imagine that I would one day make a special trip to New York, with members of my family, and stand before a distinguished audience to talk about my late husband, Alexander Rafaeli? Yet here I am, a bit of an authority on Sasha-Alexander Rafaeli after fifty years of marriage, trying to convey to you the essence of this unusual man.

Our story begins after I arrived in Tel Aviv with my brother Alec in February 1949, and found work at the WIZO Head Office as a writer for their international magazine. The Women's International Zionist Organization is the parallel of Hadassah in England and Europe. One day in November, an extremely attractive gentleman came to the office to visit a staff member, Dr. Vera Lewin, with whom he had studied at Heidelberg University. I thought regretfully that some women have all the luck. We were introduced and talked about how to entertain his Uncle Isaac, a WIZO donor from Sydney who was coming to visit. This pretext wasn't really a lie because Isaac did come at the end of 1950. The truth was that Vera had told him about the "new girl" from Australia and he decided to have a look. I was very surprised when Alex phoned me and invited me to see the Ingrid

Bergman film, *The Arch of Triumph*. I said I had already seen it (that's how naïve I was), but Alex was very gallant and soon invited me to a concert, the first of many dates.

A few weeks later, he asked me if I was free on January 20th. I said primly that I didn't make arrangements so far ahead. He said it was his late mother's birthday and he would like us to marry on that day. I had already told my brother that if Alex should propose, I would accept. And so it was. I informed my parents in Melbourne and the family in Israel and we quickly began to get organized. We wanted to marry in Jerusalem and came up to register with the rabbinate. We were told we would have to bring two witnesses to vouch that we were both single. I could supply one but where would we find another at such short notice? We walked out of the rabbinate on to Jaffa Road, and the first person we met was Dr. Haim Shalom Halevi, the husband of Hillel Kook's sister Cilla. He and Alex knew each other from the early days of the Etzel and were happy to meet again, especially on such an occasion. We returned to the rabbinate and completed our registration.

Unexpected guests at the small noontime wedding on January 20th were Mike ben Ami and his first wife, Marcia. They happened to be in Tel Aviv and heard that Alex was to be married. "This I have to see," he said, which sounded a bit ominous to me. Later, I heard that some guests were sure that I was not Jewish, and that bets were made about how long Alex could survive marriage. It is very fitting that Mike's son, Jeremy, is here with us today. I first met him when he was four or five years old.

Alex grew up in turbulent and bewildering times. He was born in 1910 in Russia (Latvia was not independent at this time) to Rosa and Boris Dov Ber Rafaelowitch, whose family had lived in Drissa for several generations, dealing in the production and sale of flax. As a child, Alex felt the effects of food shortages caused by World War I, and witnessed the Russian Revolution and Civil War first-hand. His background and Russian education endowed Alex with a Slavic soul. He was a romantic who loved poetry and was intellectually adventurous; he was generous and loved the grand gesture, but could also be a formidable opponent. He was known as Sasha until he came to the States in 1940, and is still called so by relatives and friends who knew him during those years.

His mother, Rosa Kahn, came from the German-speaking province of Kurland and believed in the superiority of German education. At the age of twelve, Sasha was sent for a year to Memel to learn German, returning to Riga for his *bar mitzvah*.

There he learned to be punctual, to behave correctly, to plan meticulously, and to be orderly and responsible. He became a Yekke as well as a Russian.

Alex's family was not Zionist but *he* understood the need for Jewish nationhood at an early age. In 1924, at the age of fourteen, he heard Jabotinsky speak in Riga. He was captured for life by his personality and by his ideas and became a founding member of Betar. Now he was a Yekke, and a Russian and an enthusiastic Zionist. So enthusiastic that for a whole year he attended the Hebrew Gymnasia (high school) in Riga without telling his parents. As you can imagine, the family was not at all pleased with this deceit.

His mother was a campaigning Socialist and two of her sisters were communists and went to live in Moscow and St. Petersburg. "Why do you bother with the problems of such a small people as the Jews?" they asked him. "When Communism will be established their problems will also be solved. You should be helping us."

However, two of Rosa's brothers, Isaac and Louis Kahn and her sister Ella, came to Palestine in the 1920s. We later discovered that my father, then a laborer in the building trade, actually worked on the house Louis and Hannah were building on Rambam Street in Tel Aviv. This became a home away from home for Alex when he came to the country in the 1930s. I am happy to say that Louis's American grandson, Michael Klausner, is here today with his wife, Allison, and their children.

Rosa visited Israel in 1928 and saw the country and the efforts being made to develop it. In spite of their differing ideologies, her attitude softened and she began to encourage Alex in his political work even though it took him away from his family.

His knowledge of German became an important factor in his life. It led him to choose Heidelberg University over Oxford, where he found busy Jewish fraternities and an active group of intellectuals and devoted Zionists. Many lifelong friendships were made, and in the 1930s quite a number of the graduates made *aliyah*, contributing greatly to the economic and intellectual life of Palestine. A representative of this period is Rabbi Sara Paasche-Orlow, a granddaughter of one of Alex's Heidelberg friends, who is here today from Boston with her husband, Dr. Michael Orlow. Alex was the last Jew to graduate from Heidelberg before the Nazis took over.

Alex joined the American army in 1943, and after participating in the Normandy landings, he was transferred from the infantry to the Counter-Intelligence Corps because of his command of German and Russian. In this unit, which was searching for Nazi leaders in hiding, he was responsible for the arrest of Alfred Krupp of the munitions family, and interrogated him in preparation for his indictment. He felt a measure of revenge for the murder of his mother and brother.

Unlike Alex's family, my parents were religious and Zionist. They made *aliyah* from Poland in 1922 with my brother, and I was eventually the first baby girl born in Herzliya, so I was always told. Conditions were very difficult then and after an attempt to settle in Jerusalem, my parents decided to go to Australia with the big emigration of the late 1920s. In Melbourne we were foreigners. The people we mixed with were foreigners; we spoke Yiddish at home, and the focal points of our lives were our families in Poland and Palestine, and Zionism. There were always foreign letters in the mail box. Europe was a living entity for me, and I felt more European than Australian.

When I came into Alex's life, I could relate to the stories of his past. In addition, my father was a great admirer of Jabotinsky and was a member of his party, the New Zionist Organization. We followed the activities of the Etzel underground insofar as they were reported in the Jewish press. Alex did not have to make any explanations or educate me.

In the early 1950s, all the members of the Bergson Group, except Mike ben Ami, lived in and around Tel Aviv. Although Alex's political work was over, the camaraderie of this group continued. I remember cheerful parties where Russian and Hebrew songs were sung, and wine glasses occasionally smashed in true Russian tradition. There was a constant stream of supporters and activists coming to inspect the new Israel. At long last, the entire group of bachelors was married, and the second generation was in the making. Betty Kook and I were pregnant at the same time, my Asi being born at the end of November 1950 and Asti a month later. I remember that Hillel came to the hospital to wait out the hours with Alex and my mother, who had come from Melbourne for the birth of her first grandchild. In his excitement, Alex celebrated by walking on his hands.

I was fascinated by the group and their stories. I was impressed that six young men of the Etzel Movement, who did not all know each other, could band together and "advance" on the U.S. to fight the battle for public opinion. Without knowing English, they quickly learned the psychology and techniques of public relations. They learned how to work "the system," and succeeded in making a tremendous impact on public opinion nationwide. The dedication to their ideals and concern for the Jewish people, their intelligence, their enthusiasm and engaging personalities were the tools at their disposal. They were a great team.

Alex and I made Jerusalem our home in 1954 and raised our four children there. He loved Jerusalem from the moment he first set foot there in 1933, and he took great satisfaction in the fact that he could contribute to its industrial development by opening several factories. He gave much time to public matters. He had time to develop his interest in art and to expand our collection of paintings and African masks. Our home became a meeting place for friends we had made at various times and in various countries. They constituted "Our Crowd."

The Russian aliyah, which began after 1967, rejuvenated Alex's neglected Slavic soul. Many of his school friends from Riga arrived, and their stories about Jewish life behind the Iron Curtain were fascinating and incredible. Alex's command of Russian recovered its fluency and he was asked by government departments to lecture to the newcomers about the economic conditions in Israel, work possibilities, politics, etc. He was also extremely helpful to many *olim* in their trials of absorption.

Alex had a deep historical consciousness and saw great importance in "telling the story." After Jabotinsky was reburied in Jerusalem in 1965, a process of legitimization of the Etzel underground soldiers began, which was accelerated after Menchem Begin came to power. A renewed interest in the Bergson Group brought many students to Alex seeking primary source material for their doctoral theses. Later, he wrote his memoirs and published some of the letters his family in Riga had written to him in the early years. These letters were his most treasured possession, the only tangible evidence of his loved ones and of his destroyed world. Even I had not known about them previously.

Besides his intellectual attributes, Sasha was also an athlete, a runner. In his youth he belonged to Jewish sports clubs and ran in national competitions. All his life he maintained a great interest in athletics. At first I went with him very unwillingly to international sports competitions, but I began to enjoy the excitement of the games and the beauty of the athletes in action. In 1958 Alex insisted that we absolutely must go to the Rome Olympics in 1960 and began in good time to get tickets, no easy matter then for Israelis. He bothered his friends in the States who thought he was crazy, but in the end it was a wonderful family excursion. Later in life, Alex took up walking and became a familiar figure on the Jerusalem scene as he took his twelve-kilometre walk every Saturday morning, measured of course by stopwatch. He participated in many of the four-day marches, which were then an annual national sport, and our sons Asi and Lonny joined him when old enough.

A few words about names: Sasha arrived in New York in 1940 and was taken directly to a press conference with Jabotinsky. He had to adopt a pseudonym immediately and chose the name "Hadani," which he used professionally for many years, but in the very early Etzel years in Palestine, he had used the name Nahshon. As you know, Nahshon, of the tribe of Judah, was the first to plunge into the Red Sea when he saw that everyone else was hesitating, and so he has come to symbolize courage and initiative.

Through his PR work for the Committee, which took him all over the States, Sasha gradually metamorphosed into Alex and his three-year stint in the U.S. Army helped him acquire an American patina.

The multiplicity of his names has led to an interesting development. When Alex first came to New York, he found a cousin from Riga, Judith, and her husband, Abrasha Udem, who had left Riga at the very last moment, shortly after their marriage. They kept up a close relationship since neither had any other relatives in the States. The Udems had two children, Dr. Steven and Edith, both present today, and Edith in turn had two children, Jackie and Daniel. A few weeks ago, Jackie gave birth to her second daughter and decided to call her after Sasha, because of the great affection they all had for him, and Judith, after her grandmother who was killed in a car accident just a year ago. So now there is a little girl Sasha in Miami, and a little Alexander in Ra'anana who are both named after the same person. Edith has come from Miami with her son Daniel to be with us today.

During the last years of his life, Alex felt the need to tidy up loose ends. In 1991, after an absence of almost sixty years, he decided he must return to Riga and revisit his childhood. But mainly he wanted to say *Kaddish* at his father's grave (he had died in June 1940 before the Germans came) and to visit the mass grave in the forest of Rumboli, where his mother had perished in the winter of 1941. His brother Asya died in a skirmish between partisans and Latvians in the forests, and his burial place is unknown. It was a very emotional journey, and suddenly a neglected factor in my own background emerged into my consciousness.

I, too, had a real connection to Riga. My great-uncle, R. Moshe Shapiro, second son of R. Aisel Harif of Slonim, had been Chief Rabbi of Riga from 1882 to 1909. We looked up population directories and found the site where he and his family had lived for some forty to fifty years, within the compound of what was then the Jewish school. My shares went up tremendously, and if only I could have spoken Russian, I would have been accepted as an honorary citizen of Riga.

In 1995, we made another trip to the States as Alex wanted to see his good friends one last time. These visits were an important "closure" in his emotional life.

The last years of Alex's life were not easy. He had endless trouble with his eyes and his sight was failing. It was a great effort to maintain his usual, cheerful self and his favorite Russian proverb at this time was *Staress ni radiss* (old age is no joke). One morning in February 1999, he fell in the bedroom and broke his hip. To our amazement, when he woke after the operation, he reverted to speaking Russian and to reliving childhood experiences. We had to have Russian-speaking help so we could understand what was happening to him. He passed away on the 28th of February 1999 after a massive heart attack.

Yet there was still a surprise in store. When I eventually got around to sorting his papers, I found poems written in his dashing handwriting, which gave expression to his feelings in times of stress or intense emotion. There was a poem he had written to Asya, our first-born, soon after his birth, and I quote:

> Above all, have no illusions, Asya,
> And look this world straight in its crude face,
> Taking note of its tough and cruel manners
> And its tricks, treason and deceit;
> But remember it's your world too,
> And behind the curtain of blood and dirt
> There is hidden beauty and goodness
> And myriads of sparkles and warmth.
> Some day this beauty will be strong
> Enough to break through
> And make the bad disappear.

Alex was always aware of the fact that he lived in momentous times. He saw himself as a soldier in the service of the Jewish people. His multicultural background and many talents enabled him to make his contribution in various ways. He survived the terrible years with courage and determination, but they left their mark. He was a dreamer and a doer. His time and his energy were dedicated to the Jewish people and to the State of Israel. That was the essence of his life.

Although Alex loved to quote Russian proverbs, I will quote a traditional Hebrew one, from the book of Proverbs, chapter 17: עטרת זקנים בני בנים, ותפארת בנים אבותם. That is, "Grandchildren are the crown of the aged, and the glory of sons is their fathers."

Perhaps at this moment, you will allow me to fantasize in Hollywood style, and think of our happy band of warriors observing us from some corner in Paradise. "Look at them," they are saying, "our friends, our children and grandchildren – they are talking about *us*, they haven't forgotten *us*" . . . and we never will.

I want to thank the Wyman Institute for all its outstanding work to ensure that the Bergson Group will indeed not be forgotten. Special thanks to Dr. Rafael Medoff, the director, for his ongoing work, and for his tireless and devoted efforts to bring this special event to life today. I wish to thank the speakers who are participating and the relatives and friends from Israel and the States who made the effort to be here with us today. I take it as an affectionate tribute to Alex, and my family and I appreciate it very much.

Thank you.

Appendix: Hello, Earth!

A Poem by Alex Rafaeli
ca. mid-1940s

I. Love

I am a man:
a son of people
who search for sunshine,
who search for smiles.
I look for love:
my eyes are thirsty
for eyes
which sparkle,
for skin
which trembles
when fingers touch.

I like to hold
in hungry arms
a body,
tense and laughing;
to speak to her
with my shouting skin,
and meet in her
talking forests,
dancing rivers,
racing subways and planes,
smoking chimneys of busy factories.

I like to lie on quiet grass
between trees,

which run into the sky –
on my back,
calling the sun
by its first name,
challenging the stars to appear
in bright daylight,
and to imagine,
that the slums of Chicago or
　　Bucharest
are only a crazy dream
and that all the wars
and the wholesale slaughter
are only a great
silly
mystery
story
with a big publicity campaign!

I like to climb
the grey rocks of the Pacific
and look with the birds down to the
　　sea,
greeting every tired green wave,
asking about her great journey,
and then
wail and die with her
fading among sand and stones.

My Blue Kitchen

Then,
with every new wave,
to be born and reborn,
laden with joy
and the will to embrace oceans
to my narrow chest.

I like to rise
with fiery birds
and veil myself
with pink clouds;
to look down at earth
and pity the mankind
which marches over fields.
Then, to stop on remote quiet isles
and listen to their stories
of countries under the sea.

I like to walk on the highway of stars,
which is red as lust
but is called the Milky Way
and meet there ages
which have passed
and ages
which will come,

and laugh at their jokes
about OUR strange times.

I like to sit
on grey and cluttered wharves
among quiet fishermen,
who breathe the strong air of sea and
    fish
around them,
tending their small boats
and wondering about tomorrow's
    wind.
Then to push my way to market
among hundreds of men and women,
smelling oil and food and dirty
    washing,
the odors of busy humanity.

I like to listen
to boys who shine for a nickel,
to blaring headlines:
"Ten killed in crash;"
to voices shouting:
"Old clothes to sell?
Old clothes!"
to placards calling
"Gouldsteen for judge."
Listen, listen,
to the noise of motors, to suffering
    women,
to striking workers,
to unfinished symphonies,
to people dying under trains
and under the rain of bombs;
from pain of loneliness,
from hate and love and hunger,
shrieking, crying, shouting
their last farewell.

Listen
to tongues,
to accents
to dialects.

Listen
to birds
to flowers and waves,
to war machines of future struggles
and whining engines of diving planes,
to the roar of rebellious masses.

I like to listen
to all this thunder,
to know I hold
the body of a woman
in my searching arms.
A body full of lust
and desire,
of wisdom
and unspoken teachings,
of songs unsung

and music unheard,
and dance revealing secrets of the
    soul.
A body laden with strength
and might,
full of goodness
and tense readiness
to give itself away.

Away
to the first who will come,
the poorest of paupers
the meanest of men,
who will discover in her
the great joy
of being a man.

II. CHALLENGE

I came to a morgue
in a dusty building
and saw there people
with eyes sadly pale
and long thin faces.
The air around
was a grey poison
and grey became words
leaving the lips.
But the corpses were fresh,
their flesh full of color
as if Tintoretto had painted them.

On one table lay the body
of a smiling girl,
with big black eyes
and fair wavy hair.
Her slender figure
looked like a palm,
but it had a long purple cut.
Her heart and her stomach
were on the same table,
a big red spot blinding the eyes.
Nobody had remembered
to put them back in the body.

Her neighbor was an old man
with a tiny violet beard,
who had jumped from a bridge
having lost faith in life.
Many days he lay in the water
and became a big balloon,
like those which fly
over besieged London,
only he was green,
and his mouth firmly shut.

I left the morgue
full of desire for people,
for people good and bad,
but laughing
struggling
cursing,
fighting every hardship,
knocking down every tyrant,
robbing each other
and then sharing generously
the loot with poorer brothers.
Looking for beauty,
but not knowing it,
lacking the name for it,
but nevertheless searching;
feeling its attraction as the blind
    know
on foggy days
where the sun is.

Shame on you earth!
Thou art too quiet,
Thy mountains too low,
Thy valleys too narrow.
Thy oceans are too flat,
Thy earthquakes are tame,
Thy fires are cold,
Thy rains are feeble,

Look at me, earth,
look at the man;
look at the tornados of my soul,
at the volcanos of my mind,

at the storms of my loves,
at the depth of my devotion,
at the poison of my treason,
at the barbarity of my heart,
at the blindness of my lust,
at the winds of my desires,
at the insatiable hunger
to be one
with this
crazy
topsy-turvy world.

Look at me!
I search for God,
I search for love,
I look for eyes
which mirror the souls
of people,
millions like me
hungry and dirty and crazy.

Look at me!
I speak
I shout
I pray,
I talk to God
and to animals.
I pray, for
I lack happiness.
But I am happy
knowing that I
fight for it.
I see colors
and feel movement,
I hear sounds,
millions of sounds.
I am strong.

Hello, earth!
Let's be pals!

Dear children – Presumably, this poem was written in the 1940s after World War II, when Daddy was very depressed. I found it after he passed away, and only recently felt I should bring it to your attention. I have made some small corrections to improve the English and the style.

– E.R., February 2005